P9-CLC-967

MARK HOPKINS

BOOKS BY J. H. DENISON

MARK HOPKINS

EMOTIONAL CURRENTS IN AMERICAN HISTORY

THE ENLARGEMENT OF PERSONALITY

EMOTION AS THE BASIS OF CIVILIZATION

CHARLES SCRIBNER'S SONS

MARK HOPKINS

MARK HOPKINS

A BIOGRAPHY

By

J. H. DENISON

NEW YORK
CHARLES SCRIBNER'S SONS
1935

Printed in the United States of America

A

PREFACE

Now that fifty years have elapsed since the death of Mark Hopkins, I am continually meeting with inquiries as to who was the man of whom President Garfield said that the ideal university consisted of a log with Mark Hopkins on one end and himself on the other. Although his bust is in the Hall of Fame, it nevertheless seems fitting that for the benefit of this generation some statement should be made to make it clear that the aforesaid Mark Hopkins was not the builder of the Union Pacific who is so well known in California; and that there should be some account given of those ideas and characteristics which made our former President regard him as the equivalent of a university. The ideas of Mark Hopkins as to education were so surprisingly in advance of his age that they repay careful study even today.

As a philosopher his great work lay in stimulating thought rather than in contributing it. But his great achievement lay in bridging the gulf between the old system of thought which formed the basis of the character and social order of past centuries and the modern thought which has undermined the groundwork of all the old beliefs. In order to show what he accomplished, and make vivid his achievement, there seems

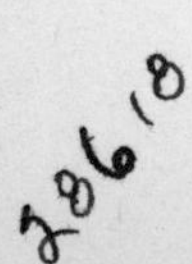

to be no better way than to picture the life from which he sprang and all its conditions of thought and environment.

The recent discovery of a number of old letters and documents, some of which have been published by Miss Susan Hopkins, his daughter, has made it possible to reconstruct the early life in Stockbridge, and to picture his immediate ancestors with a certain amount of vividness. It was these persons who founded the institution to which he gave his life, and which served as the battleground of the old ideas and the new—the field where ultimately his genius trained men to select from the confusing welter of conflicting thought, those ideas which are of permanent value and upon which the life and character of the new age could be built. In picturing those early days I have drawn upon family letters, the history of Berkshire County and of the Stockbridge Mission to the Indians, the journals of Catherine Sedgwick, Esther Burr, President Griffin, and President Dwight, Professor Perry's books, *Origins in Williamstown* and *Williamstown and Williams College*, the life of Mark Hopkins by Doctor Carter, the histories of Williams College by Doctor Durfee and Professor Spring, and many other minor sources. To add to the vividness of the picture I have at times filled in conversations of which only the substance was given in the sources, but in many cases the exact words are reported.

The amazing changes in thought and manner of

life that are covered by the lifetime of Doctor Mark Hopkins are as surprising as are the extraordinary repetitions in feeling and circumstance shown by such letters as that of the students to President Adams.

Any one who is interested in the progress of education and in the development of thought, should find suggestive material in these old letters and documents, which is my excuse for resuscitating them in this busy age, which is prone to regard with indifference, if not contempt, the ideas of an earlier generation.

In a separate volume the life of the ancestors of Mark Hopkins in early Stockbridge has been described. His grandmother, Electa Sergeant, was the first white child born in that frontier town, the daughter of John Sergeant, missionary to the Indians, and Abigail Williams, the sister of Colonel Ephraim Williams, whose bequest resulted in the foundation of Williams College. Electa married Colonel Mark Hopkins, a promising and wealthy lawyer of Great Barrington, who lost his life at the battle of White Plains, and who sacrificed his possessions in the cause of the new republic. Upon Electa devolved a desperate struggle to maintain her four children. She moved to the Cherry Cottage in Stockbridge and there her eldest son, Archibald, gave all his energies to developing the farm and earning enough money to enable his brothers to receive a "liberal education." Sewall took up the study of medicine and Henry of the law, while Archibald remained tied to the farm, giving all his strength to the support of his mother and sister.

The Cherry Cottage was located in the south end of the town on what was known in recent years as the McBurney estate, and efforts are being made by the present owners to restore it as far as possible to its condition at the time of the birth of Mark Hopkins. It is here in the Cherry Cottage that our story must begin, one hundred and forty years ago, in the year of our Lord 1795, and in the first decade of the American Republic.

CONTENTS

ILLUSTRATIONS

CHAPTER I

THE BEGINNINGS OF WILLIAMS AND POLITICAL CONFLICTS

Archibald Hopkins had just finished unloading a wagon load of corn, fresh from the field on the hillside, at the wide sheds that stretched back from the Cherry Cottage and had stopped for a moment to look up with pride at the fine lines of the house his hands had helped to rear for his mother and sister. With its wide-spreading mansard roof and many well-glazed windows it seemed to him a very beautiful and dignified residence for Stockbridge in that year of our Lord 1795. It was a beautiful day in early September and beneath the arch of the great elms he could look off across the lush green fields of the valley to the great crags of Monument Mountain, whose densely wooded slopes rose just opposite. A shout called his attention to the road in front, and he turned to see his young friend Jared Curtis in the old Curtis buckboard with the gray flea-bitten family horse. Jared was arrayed in his best suit of black broadcloth with a stock so high it threatened to choke him. "Wish me luck!" he shouted. "I'm off to the Williams commencement to try the exams!"

By his side, with her billowy silk skirts neatly

tucked in beneath a dust robe, sat a young girl whose piquant face was rendered more charmingly elusive by the huge calash that concealed her dainty head. Her dark eyes flashed mischievously as she called out: "I'm going too. I'm sure I'll get in before either of you two."

A slow flush crept over Archibald's sun-tanned face as he came forward. He stammered an awkward greeting and could not help showing how he envied his friend the opportunity of a college education. Jared caught up the reins and flicked the old horse. As they drove off he spoke of the cruel fate that had condemned Archibald, whose great desire had been for education, to toil ceaselessly on the old farm. He had fulfilled his father's charge. He had cared for his mother and provided the means to give his three brothers the education that was denied to him. There was no hope for him to be anything but a hard-working farmer. Henry, who had studied law, had died just as he became self-supporting. Sewall had had his training as a doctor and gone West to seek his fortune. His youngest brother, John Sergeant, had married and was established in a store in Stockbridge. But there still remained his mother and sister Louisa, and it was only by ceaseless toil that the old farm could be made to pay and provide them with the comforts they needed.

The Curtis boys had been Archie's chief companions of late. The family had been among his mother's best friends. Colonel Elnathan Curtis had distinguished himself in the war. Abel had disgraced himself in the Shays rebellion, but had been reinstated in favor. A third brother, Isaac, enlisted for the war, but had been sent back with a commission to provide flour and provisions for the army. He had married and settled down and had assisted the development of Berkshire County by producing a family of fourteen children. Although they did not belong to the same circle with the Sedgwicks and Dwights and Wests, they were in the main better educated and more entertaining companions than many who claimed a more aristocratic position. Old Isaac was a great bee hunter, and the children loved to go off into the forest with him after the wild bees. He knew how to track and capture them and secure their honey, and he took them into the most enchanting spots, and wild mountain glens. The three boys, Jared, David, and Alvah, were Archibald's special friends.

Fond as Archibald was of the boys the chief attraction of the family lay elsewhere. Their sister Mary was one of the brightest girls in Stockbridge. Her mind was quick as a flash, and she had a keen sense of humor that led her into many a mischievous prank. To Archibald, as he plodded along the dull road of duty and drudgery, her daring sallies and swift retorts were a constant amazement. She seemed as elusive, as fascinating, as a flitting fairy. Her mind seemed to dance all around him while he stared bewildered. Her piquant face and laughing eyes seemed constantly to haunt him, but today as usual when he met her he found himself tongue-tied and helpless in her presence.

The graduating class at Williams were all Stockbridge boys and they had invited Mary up to see them graduate. College commencements were something new, and it was an honor to be asked to the first commencement of the new college. Mary's eyes were dancing with anticipation and her delicate cheek flushed as she waved her farewell to Archibald. She knew how hard it was for him to see them drive away to enter upon that life that fate had denied to him. Fate had blocked him at every turn. He had accepted his responsibility as head of the house, and he could not set up a home of his own while his mother and sister were dependent on him. And he might lose Mary.

There was a fairly good road to Pittsfield and five miles beyond, along the beautiful shore of Lake Pontoosac to Lanesboro, which then, with a population of 2142, was larger than either Pittsfield, with 1992, or Stockbridge, with but 1336 inhabitants.

From thence they climbed up a narrow mountain road, steep and muddy in places, over a shoulder of the Greylock Range to New Ashford. This had been quite a prosperous settlement and a rival of Pittsfield and Lanesboro, but its population was beginning to fall off. They followed the narrow road along the sparkling mountain brook that led them down to the valley beyond. They stopped a few moments at the

Inn at South Williamstown, which was kept by Colonel Rossiter, who commanded the Berkshire company at the battle of Bennington. He was said to have a carefully traced pedigree through which he could claim descent direct from Charlemagne. His daughter had just married a young man named Hubbell, who had built a worthy mansion for her on the hill dominating the valley. We mention them, for they will later bear an important part in this narrative.

It was late when they reached Williamstown, and Mary was glad to get to her room in the inn on the corner of the square just across from the old church.

Doctor West, who was vice-president of the college, had also come up from Stockbridge and greeted Mary on her arrival. He was boiling with indignation because he had been outvoted by the trustees. He was now the champion of the old theology and wished it to dominate the new institution. He and Doctor Fitch, the president, and Doctor Seth Swift, the minister of the town church and a trustee, had introduced into the curriculum the study of the Hopkintonian System of Theology, which he considered an essential of Christian education. The old theological battle was still on and feeling ran as high as ever. The lay members of the board of trustees, and especially Abigail's brother, Elijah Williams, at their meeting that afternoon, had decided that it was not in accord with modern educational ideas and had voted nine to seven to remove it from the curriculum. She had never seen the little doctor so excited. He was stamping up and down in his black small clothes and powdered wig, declaring that the Devil was triumphing over the righteous. He showed Mary a letter to President Dwight that he was just writing. It ended: "Though the world seems to be made for Cæsar we know that Zion's God reigns. The time is not yet come for the Truth to prevail. The Evil one intends to hold the college, but the Lord will support His own cause." He regarded the three great volumes of Doctor Samuel Hopkins' system as a second Bible and gave it to all candidates for admission to the church to study until they were convinced of the vileness of their sinful nature and of the infinite mercy of God in saving the elect from the burning. He always hoped to bring them to the point where they would be glad to be damned for the glory of God. He was anxious because Mary had not reached that point and insisted that she must study the Hopkintonian Plan as she hoped for salvation. He was more disturbed over this vote of the trustees than over the virulent personal attack that had been made on him by a colleague in Stockbridge, who had slandered him in the most unscrupulous fashion and accused him of drunkenness and immorality. To such a point of scandal and defamation of character had men been brought by their theological differences. Never had the doughty little man shown his Christian character more truly than during these trying weeks, when he was actually brought up for trial. In some ways it is less trying to be damned for the glory of God than to be condemned for the glory of a disagreeable colleague. But he stood the test, and was gentle and kindly to all and spoke no word of bitterness. His people believed in his character even when they questioned his doctrine and were overjoyed at his complete vindication. Now, however, that men were no longer questioning his own morality but casting aspersions on the total depravity of all mankind, he was deeply stirred, and especially against the Williams family, who had always been leaders of the opposition to the sovereignty of God and Jonathan Edwards.

The examinations for entrance were held the day before commencement, which fell on the 8th day of September. In the morning Mary walked down to the college with her brother and he left her in a state of great trepidation to meet the examining board. He had to pass in geography, arithmetic, algebra, English, Latin, with Virgil, Cicero, and Cæsar, and New Testament Greek. In the hall he found a row of stately examiners in tie wigs and small clothes seated on the platform and looking most omniscient. His heart sank into his boots when they summoned him and began to fire question after question at him on one subject after another. They nodded their heads ponderously when he answered and looked dubiously at one another. His spirits sank lower and lower and by the time he came out had taken permanent residence in his boots. He was sure that college was not for him.

In the meantime Mary's friends in the graduating class undertook to show her the town. The town lay on three hills between the Green River and Hemlock Brook, and the main street climbed the three heights in succession and after crossing the Brook ascended the steep acclivity of Buxton Hill. On the summit of the Western Hill was the old Block House which had been the town fortress against the attacks of prowling Indians. In front of it the street broadened to a wide common and in the center of the common and of the street, looking eastward from the hill's summit, was the village church, a focal point visible the whole length of the street. At one side was the inn where Mary stayed. The street was lined by neat white houses and bordered by young elms recently set out. On the central hill was the college building erected in the center of the wide street with an archway passing through it for pedestrians. Thus long before Smith and Vassar the young ladies of Williamstown who had passed through the arch would boast that they had been through college. Mary walked through and saw the chapel and recitation rooms, and was told there were some sixty boys in the bedrooms upstairs. Opposite was the beautiful old colonial house of Major Sloane, the handsomest in the town. Mary and her companions walked over to the East Hill, where foundations were laid for another building which was to provide quarters and recitation rooms for the seniors and juniors. They passed but one house between the two colleges—a small brown one, but there was a brickyard in the valley between where 300,000 bricks were being made for the college.

In the evening, to Mary's delight and astonishment, Jared was told that he had safely passed the examination and was enrolled in the class of 1800. He could now go home for four weeks' vacation before the term began. In jubilant mood Jared took Mary to the Prize Speaking or Moonlights, where three members of each class competed, and she was pleased to see the prize taken by one of her Stockbridge friends. She was quite the belle of the ball at the dance that followed, for many of the young men were old friends from the neighborhood of Stockbridge, and her quick wit made her a favorite with all.

The next morning she attended the commencement exercises in the village church. It was a lovely day and as Mary stood at the summit of the hill and watched the procession marching up the street from the college building, between the white houses with their green lawns and shadowing trees, with old Greylock towering in the background and the mountains, forest clad, all round about, there was a solemn beauty in the scene that almost brought the tears to her eyes. Here in this valley girt on all sides by mountains and forests Old Ephraim had surveyed the village that was to be, and young Ephraim had defended the valley through the anxious years, when French and Indians were descending upon its settlements to slaughter and burn, and now the little town of which he had dreamed lay there at peace still guarded by its barriers of mountain and forest, its white houses lining the long shaded street, with the steepled meeting house at its head, and up the street came the lines of young men to whose education he had devoted his fortune, the first class to complete their studies on the foundation he had laid.

First came the students of the academy, younger boys, trying to look as dignified as the reverend seniors, then the students of the college, then the sheriff of the county "acting as Bedellus" with his wand of office, then "the Reverend President and Vice President and other members of the Corporation: the Tutors the Reverend clergy and other respectable gentlemen," according to the Stockbridge paper of September 8, 1795.

When Mary entered the church she was surprised to find it in very wretched tumble-down condition. The president, Doctor Fitch, seemed out of place in the dilapidated pulpit. Indeed, his first effort, after opening the exercises, was to start a subscription to rebuild the church and put it in condition so that the college might have a proper place for their exercises. He had come from Yale to be head of the school when it opened and had brought with him a college friend named Charles Denison, to assist him. John Lester and Noah Linsley also acted as tutors for the school, which increased rapidly. Doctor Fitch was ambitious and felt that there was room for a real college here in the western counties. He applied for a charter from the state, but apparently he was opposed by Harvard, which had already squashed one such attempt in 1762 by insisting that a "seminary" in Hampshire County "would hurt Harvard and make learning contemptible." After a year's delay the fears of Harvard were overcome and in 1793 the school became a college. It had prospered and the lower classes were crowded. They had as tutors Jeremiah Day, later president of Yale, and Henry Davis, who became president of Hamilton. In this period when the French Revolution was the chief subject of interest to the youth of that day, Williams was up to date in that her only professor, MacKay, covered the department of French language and literature. He was married to the daughter of the Marquis de Lotbinière and therefore had some understanding of the French, though he is said to have been an ensign in the British army. Theodore Sedgwick had been appointed professor of civil law and polity, and occasionally gave lectures when his public duties permitted it. Mary saw all these notables on the platform, along with the trustees. President Fitch was a tall man of distinguished appearance. The requirements for a college president were somewhat different then than now. The committee of trustees had been instructed to find a man "of good moral character of the Protestant type, skill in teaching, polished manners and a mild disposition"—and they felt they had discovered what they wanted in Mr. Fitch.

Those who are bored by the brief exercises of the modern commencement should have had the opportunity to attend this first commencement of Williams College, which lasted from morning till night and covered every possible field of human interest and discussed questions which are still of vital importance to us today. Fortunately we have quite full accounts of the day. The president opened the exercises with prayer, and then several of the young ladies of the town joined the students in singing an anthem. Mary listened with admiration to the salutatory oration in Latin by her friend Mr. Lusk, and Mr. Bishop, another Stockbridge boy, then delivered an oration on the French Revolution. An anthropological discussion followed in the form of a disputation between Messrs. Lusk and Stone on the question: "Can the differences in the complexion and features of the human race be accounted for by natural causes?" Jared had remarked that no other college was so modernistic in its scientific outlook and this discussion seemed to prove his statement. There followed an oration on the Government of the United States by her friend Collins, and this was followed by a dispute between Collins and Bishop on the question "whether a Republican government was as well adapted as Monarchy to promote the security and happiness of a numerous people." It was evidently felt that America like many other subsequent democracies would have to adopt a dictatorship to succeed, just as today some clamor for an American Mussolini.

Another modernistic feature was an oration on female education by Mr. Stone, for certain passages in which Mary felt responsible. At this point all retired and partook of lunch, and Mary had a chance to congratulate the participants. They reassembled in the afternoon and listened to an ode, a French oration, an oration on the iniquity of the slave trade, a humorous dialogue on the folly of frivolous conversation, and a serious conference on religion and marriage by Bishop, Collins, and Stone. It is not stated whether birth control was advocated or denounced. The exercises ended with a "pathetic and excellent valedictory address" from the president, who then conferred the degree of Bachelor of Arts on the four graduates, each of whom had earned his degree by speaking four times.

It was a memorable day for Mary, and later when her son became president of the college she would often recall her visit to its first commencement.

Life in Stockbridge went on its even way. Jared Curtis, now in college, kept Mary informed of college events. Archibald, working hard on his farm, had given up all hope of a liberal education. It was a stern battle to conquer the rugged soil of New England and wring from it the comforts so necessary to his mother and sister. Sewall had built for his bride a fine new house in Clinton, clapboarded and panelled and shingled and with glass in the windows, and he begged his mother to venture out and visit him. And in the fall of 1797 she set forth. There was no Empire State Express. It was nearly a week's journey, a trip that only a mother's devotion would lead a lone woman to undertake. Archibald drove her to Albany and thence she had to take the old four-horse stage, and sit all day jammed in with a dozen other passengers, with children climbing in her lap and babies squalling. She spent the nights at roadside inns, where she sat up, terrified by the shouts of drunken teamsters at the bar. She was quite exhausted when Sewall met her at Utica and drove her to his home. But the climate did not agree with her. There was trouble with the water in Clinton, many were taken ill, and thyroid symptoms appeared. She returned to Stockbridge feeling weak and wretched and soon took to her bed. Her brother, Doctor Erastus Sergeant, tended her with utmost care, but in spite of the tenderest ministrations of Louisa and Archibald, Electa, the first child born in Stockbridge, died in the old Cherry Cottage on July 11, 1798.

Archibald was now thirty-two and he and Louisa kept on the old home until the season of mourning was over. In the meantime, Mary Curtis was advancing in years and had passed the point where New England girls were supposed to marry. She had persistently refused the young men who paid her their addresses. She had even taken to wearing "a pinnacled cap and spectacles," and her brothers amused themselves by jeering at her as a confirmed old maid. Her brother Jared had rashly married, though he was still at Williams College in the class of 1800, and on April 14, 1799, she replied to his jeers in a witty letter in which she defended the celibate state. "Why are ladies of the single life more to be despised than those of the matrimonial, if she can marry and will not, is she not the more to be admired; if she would marry and can not, why is she to be despised, is a Pearl the less valuable because it is disregarded by SWINE?"

Archibald was still devoted to her, and seeking some gift that would express his affection had presented her with the three volumes of his uncle's System of Theology which Doctor West had recommended to her. The worthy doctor had long sought to bring her into the fold of the church, and failing to imagine that there could be any romantic associations with so ponderous a tome, when he saw her poring over its pages, he thought that at last her heart was touched. But, alas! it was not he who touched it and she remained obdurate to his suggestions that she should publicly accept the Truth and enable him to receive her among the saved. On March 3, 1800, she wrote her brother, who was now a senior and had also been studying the Hopkintonian principles at Williams: "I have often been told that the Hopkintonian principles were always by the natural heart rejected, and you know well that I have a stubborn, rebellious heart, ever unwilling to comply with anything of that nature. Although I have been told by our best Christians that they are the best principles in the world, and although I am myself in conscience convinced that they truly are so, yet I have no heart to embrace them. Sad situation—but to make the sinner's plea, how can I help it. I did not make my own heart, nor have I the power of changing it. You will learn from the above that in Mr. H. I have not found a Valancourt though I will tell you that in every respect he is a Dupont."

It was a strange doctrine for a sprightly girl with a sense of humor and fund of common sense to accept as her philosophy of life, and like Abigail and Electa she found the God of Jonathan Edwards one to whom she could not surrender her heart even though she was forced to admit His existence. Even then girls had cryptic methods of announcing their engagements and the last mysterious sentence in her letter indicates that Archibald at last had risen to the occasion. Poor man, he had waited long enough! But now in 1800 his sister Louisa took her flight and was duly married to Joseph Woodbridge. Archibald's last responsibility had fallen from his shoulders, and he was free at last to think of himself, and to make an assault upon Mary's "stubborn heart." She evidently anticipated the attack and sought secretly to fit herself for future responsibilities for she wrote to her brother Jared, in whose discretion she confided: "Do not fail of sending to York by your Williamstown merchants for a book which I have never heard called anything but a cook book, but it doubtless has some other title. It is about as large as a testament and contains all the rules of cookery. If you have not money to spare I will send it to you when you return. Tell the merchant it is for your wife that you would purchase the book, and there will be no need of further questions."

And so after a few months' diligent study of the cook book, to the neglect of the "Hopkintonian Principles," Archibald Hopkins and Mary Curtis were married on October 22, 1800. Jared, who had just graduated, came to the wedding, which was an occasion of great festivity.

The next two years were for Archibald and Mary a period of comparative freedom from anxiety and responsibility, a honeymoon of peace and happiness.

When reports began to arrive of the progress of Napoleon's armies and the conquest of nation after nation until only England remained free, and that was threatened by an expedition designed to conquer and humble proud Albion, the alarm began to spread across the sea. Friends in England begged for aid, appeals were sent from the State and National Government.

On December 5, 1804, Archibald was commissioned lieutenant of a cavalry squadron in the First Brigade and Ninth Division of the Militia of the Commonwealth by Governor Caleb Strong. He showed such energy and capability in drilling and maintaining the standard of the company that four years later he received the following commission placing him in command of the company:

His Honor

LEVI LINCOLN, ESQUIRE

Lieutenant-Governor and Commander in Chief
of the
Commonwealth of Massachusetts.

TO Archibald Hopkins Gentleman GREETING

You being elected on the twenty third day of December A.D. one thousand eight hundred and eight to be Captain of a Company in the squadron of Cavalry in the First Brigade, and Ninth Division of the Militia of this Commonwealth; Reposing special trust and confidence in your ability, courage, and good conduct, I do, by these presents, Commission you accordingly. You are therefore, carefully and diligently to discharge the duties of said Office, according to the Laws of this Commonwealth, and to Military Rule and Discipline. And all Inferior Officers and Soldiers are hereby commanded to obey you in your said capacity; and you are yourself to observe and follow such Orders and Instructions as you shall, from time to time, receive from me, or others, your superior Officers.

Given under my Hand, and the Seal of the Commonwealth, the twenty seventh day of April in the year of our Lord, one thousand eight hundred and nine—and in the 33 year of the Independence of the United State of America.

By His Honor the Lieutenant-Governor.

(signed) Levi Lincoln

Wm Tudor Secretary of the Commonwealth.

He insisted that his men should appear well equipped and maintain a soldierly demeanor, and he secured a prompt discharge from his company for all who failed to do so.

Now at last the time of testing had come. Those of us who can remember the excitement in this country when the great war broke out, and the demand for "preparedness" lest the resistless army that was overrunning Europe should cross the seas and crush America also, will be interested to read the Brigade Orders which Archibald received on August 27, 1810, and which he read aloud to the men of his company on the green in front of the Stockbridge Church. The language was so appropriate to the crisis in 1917 that these orders were read a second time on July 4, 1917, to the company assembled in Williamstown by Colonel Archibald Hopkins, grandson of the original Captain Archibald.

COMMONWEALTH OF MASSACHUSETTS.

First Brigade, Ninth Division.

New-Marlborough, Aug. 27th, 1810.

BRIGADE ORDERS

The Brigadier General, having received a Division

order of the 10th of August current, directing the review and inspection of the several Corps of Militia in said Division, enjoins it upon the Commanding Officers of Regiments, Battalions and Squadrons, and all concerned in the first Brigade, suitably to notice the aforesaid Division order and to govern themselves accordingly.

The Commandants of the several Regiments in said Brigade, will, forthwith, issue their orders, directing their respective Regiments to meet on the days and for the purposes specified in the aforesaid Division Order.

The Band of Music will accompany the Brigadier-General in the review and inspection of the several Regiments in the Brigade.

The Commanding Officers of Regiments, Battalions and Squadrons will see that the troops, under their command, are furnished, on the days of Review, with a sufficiency of cartridges, without Ball, to perform the usual firings on said days. They will also see that their troops are on the ground, and paraded, precisely at Nine o'clock in the morning, as specified in the Division Order aforesaid.

The Brigadier General cannot, on the present occasion, forbear suggesting to the Officers and Soldiers of his Brigade, the very great importance and responsibility of the stations which they hold in community. In a free government like ours, when every Soldier is a Citizen, and the defence and salvation of the country rest upon the exertions and patriotism of the Militia, it becomes every Officer and Soldier to acquit himself worthily of the rank and title of free-men.—A spirit of the strictest subordination, a cheerfulness and alacrity in the performance of every duty, a patriotic ambition to become thoroughly versed in the system of military discipline of the country, and a pride, not only to appear like Soldiers, but in reality to deserve the name, ought to characterize all those who claim the privileges and protection of a free government.

It ought to be a prime object with every soldier to meet the laws of his government, in every article of equipment, be it ever so small. It is not, however, sufficient that he furnish himself with the number merely—they must be good, suited to actual, efficient service and corresponding with the strictest requisitions of Law.

The present situation of the country renders the duties of every soldier imperious. We live at a most interesting and alarming crisis. While the whole of the eastern world is convulsed to its centre, and the nations of the earth are dashing one against another; while every civilized nation on the globe is threatened with universal domination and the rights of neutrals find no protection in the laws of nations, or the sanctity of treaties; and while ours is the only Republic on the globe which is left amidst the wreck; where is the man who needs the aid of flattery or persuasion to urge him to the performance of duty.

A Roman could weep that he had but one life to

sacrifice for his country, and cannot an American exhibit a soul as patriotic, as godlike as a citizen of Rome? Let it then be the ambition of every man to be so equipped and so versed in duty, as to be ready, at a moment's warning, to face, in the field of battle, the enemies of his country.

The Brigadier General would, for a moment, address himself to the military pride and ambition of the soldiers which he has the honor to command. It has, with him, been long a subject of regret, that so few of the troops on the days of review and inspection appear with a military uniform. It is true that the laws of the State do not oblige the soldier to procure a uniform; still the General would conceive, that every soldier would find in his breast a law of patriotism urging him to the performance of that, which would redound so much to his own honor, to that of the State and of his Country. The General would be far from recommending any thing needlessly expensive. But a neat, handsome uniform coat may be procured by every soldier at a very trifling expense.

Whereas Captain Archibald Hopkins of the Cavalry, has made a return to the Brigadier General of a number of men belonging to his company, who have neglected to equip themselves according to law, viz. Billy Mesenger jr. and Isaac Childs of Becket, and Brainard Spencer of West-Stockbridge, it is hereby ordered that they be discharged from said company, and they are hereby discharged; and the said Messenger, Childs and Spencer will hereafter be enrolled and do military duty in the several companies within whose limits they reside, and in which they originally belonged.

The Brigade staff officers will accompany the Brigadier General in the review of the several Regiments in the Brigade.

David Tracy, Brigadier General.
Jared Curtis, Brigade Major.

A true Copy.
Attest Elisha Foot Adjutant.
True Copy

With the aid of Jared Curtis, his brother-in-law, who was now Brigade Major, Archibald got his company into exemplary form, discharged the delinquents and enlisted others to replace them and marched his men over to the Brigade inspection on September 20, each man being provided with six blank cartridges "to perform the usual firings," as his squadron orders demanded. Thereafter the company was drilled diligently each week, until the men of the Housatonic Valley began to feel safe from Napoleonic inroads.

The attention of Archibald had not been entirely absorbed by military matters. Home obligations were again accumulating.

In February, 1802, a son had been born to Archibald and Mary and named Mark in memory of his grandfather who had died in the Revolutionary War. Two other sons were born to them, Henry in 1804 and Albert in 1806. Mary gave all her spare time to the education of her family of toddlers. She would start Mark spelling out his letters, while she worked away making a tiny pair of trousers for his approaching birthday. The boy had an amazingly quick mind and when he was four, at the time of Albert's birth, he could already spell out short stories and read them to himself. Then she started him on *Pilgrim's Progress* and the Bible, and by the time he was five she could give him a passage anywhere and he would read it off, though it is doubtful if he understood all the long words. Then she thought the time had come to send him to school. The village school was a mile and half from Cherry Cottage and was kept by Mr. Danforth. The little boy appeared before him on the opening day of school. Mr. Danforth got out the school reader and looked with some amusement at the miniature figure before him and asked: "Well, my little man, where can you read?" The little boy looked up at him with dignified courtesy and said: "Anywhere you please, sir." Danforth looked serious. This seemed like foolish braggadocio. He gave the boy a hard passage, and was completely astonished when the child read the words without the least difficulty. Thereafter the little fellow walked the three miles to and from school every day, and even when the snow was deepest and the storm fiercest Mark would manage to wallow through the drifts to his accustomed seat. Harry learned his letters with equal facility and two years later when Mark was seven, he proudly escorted his little brother to school and established him in a seat of his own. Thereafter the two youngsters had companionship in fighting their way through the drifts on the long road to school.

The years went by quietly in Stockbridge.

One day in 1812 school had just been let out and Mark, then about ten years old, after bowing politely to his Uncle David, who had been teaching him his arithmetic lesson, started home with his brother Harry who was two years younger, and little Albert who was then only six. With him was a group of his cousins. Huldah, Electa, and Lucinda were the daughters of his Uncle John Sergeant Hopkins, who kept a store on the main street, and Callista and Pamela were the children of his Uncle Alvah Curtis, who had started the great industry of the Housatonic Valley by building a paper mill. With them were some of the Dwight children, and little Robert Sedgwick. Robert was lamenting the cruel treatment of their aunt. His mother Pamela had died in 1807 after months of suffering, and as Doctor Erastus Sergeant had also died and left very little property, Theodore Sedgwick had asked his wife, the step-aunt of the children, to come and act as his housekeeper. Brought up to stern frugality she kept the children down to rigid economies, and when Robert had visited his brother Henry in New York she had sent him down in a suit woven from wool from his father's sheep and dyed with butternut, to his intense humiliation. Now he had been sent to school in a pair of trousers that once belonged to his brother, so tight that he feared they would burst every minute. He had asked if he might walk to school with a charming young lady whom he adored from afar, and she had declined with a conscious blush, and he knew it was because she feared his trousers would burst on the way.

As they came opposite the Sedgwick house an old moth-eaten horse appeared driven by a rabble of ragged boys and covered with abusive placards denouncing the Federalists. Theodore Sedgwick was just coming out of the house. He was the most distinguished man in the town, if not in the state. He had been speaker of the House, and prominent in all public affairs. He regarded the old horse with indignation, shook his cane at the rabble and they dispersed rapidly. "Those wretched Democrats downtown!" he said. "Don't you children ever have anything to do with them! The miscreants are Jacobins, French revolutionaries, who think they can turn the men of intelligence and culture out of office and put ignorant atheists in their place." He went on his way still fuming. "He is angry," said Robert "because the Democrat who lives next door boarded up all his windows on this side and said he would not receive air and light from a Federalist." Huldah asked if all the French were wicked. The boys pictured Napoleon as an arch demon, and the British as the armies of the Lord who were preventing him from subduing the earth.

The Sedgwick house was the handsomest in town and its yard was a fine place to play. Miss Catherine, then a little over twenty, and a very brilliant charming girl, invited them in to play, and there they found Charles Sedgwick, a handsome young fellow back on vacation from Williams College. Stockbridge, doomed by fate to be a center of battles theological and political, was now torn in twain betwixt Federalist and Democrat. The children as ardent little Federalists inquired of the young collegian if he thought the Democrats were all wicked. He had no doubts on the subject and proceeded to explain how Williams College had been nearly wrecked by their machinations. General Skinner who was an arch Democrat and treasurer of the college, had been elected by the Democrats to be treasurer of the commonwealth. He had made way with some $70,000 of the state funds and defaulted. This had ruined all the trustees of the college who had gone on his bond, and brought the institution into disrepute.

According to Charles the college was in bad way, apparently as a result of these Democratic influences. Professor Olds who taught the sciences, was a great man and had made the college famous as a leader in scientific thought, but he had been forced to resign by the president's folly and indecision. The president was a pompous dictator, with a stentorian voice and a gelatinous backbone. A crisis arrived when the students discovered the two tutors peeping through their shutters to spy out delinquents, and sent in a request that the tutors should be discharged. Professor Olds regarded this as an insult to the faculty and told them they must apologize. The president upheld him with a pompous declaration of the dignity of the faculty. When the students refused to apologize and threatened to leave, the president backed down. Professor Olds was left standing alone, indignant and disgusted. He promptly resigned and departed, taking with him the prestige of Williams as leader in the sciences. He was to be replaced by a young tutor named Chester Dewey. All the students were discontented. Charles said his room-mate was a young man named Bryant who was very bright and amusing. He had written some very clever verses about the College, which all the boys were repeating. Charles had copied some of them and when Catherine asked to hear them he read a few lines:

Why should I sing its turbid springs
That trickle through its rocks of lime,
And why those domes where science flings
Her far diffusing ray sublime,
Where through the horror breathing hall,
The pale-faced moping students crawl,
Like spectral monuments of woe,
Or studious seek the unwholesome cell,
Where dust and gloom and cobwebs dwell,
Dark, dirty, dank and low.
Yet on the picture dark with shade
Let not the eye forever gaze
Where Lawless Power his nest has laid
And Stern Suspicion treads her maze.
The storm that o'er the wintry waste
Rides howling on the northern blast,

In time will curb its furious way;
But that o'er Hoosac's vale which lowers
Will never know serener hours
Or open to the day.

He explained that in this allegory in lofty Spenserian style, "Lawless Power" represented President Fitch, and "Stern Suspicion" was really the two tutors. "Treading her maze" meant poking around in the students' rooms. Bryant certainly lacked appreciation of those charms of the Hoosick valley which had delighted Ephraim Williams. He spoke of the "Slimy Street," "a frozen desert now it lies, and now a sea of mud," and gave a picture of repellent rusticity that would hardly draw the elegant youth of New York to Williams. He was evidently in a dark mood and it is said to have been the scenery of Williamstown that stimulated him to write *Thanatopsis*. They were still talking when Theodore Sedgwick returned from the post office evidently in great excitement. "These wretched Jacobins have forced the President to declare war on England," he cried. "England is our only friend and the hope of the world, the only power that can check that demon Napoleon."

Soon the bells were ringing and all the town was in a turmoil. Nothing could have served better to split old Stockbridge down the middle. The Democrats were strong for the French and wanted to start at once to fight the British. The Federalists hated the French and said they would never bear arms against the British. Archibald was a strong Federalist, but he was captain of the militia and under orders to fight. He thought it wicked to fight the British, and so did his friends the Sedgwicks and Williamses and Curtises. He consulted Doctor West who suggested they should hold a prayer meeting and ask for divine guidance. The Democrats suspected treachery. It was a conspiracy to win the Lord over to the side of the British by Doctor West's eloquent prayers and they swore they would break up the meeting and beat up any one who was found diverting the blessings of heaven from them to their political opponents. The meeting was held, however, at Doctor West's house in the greatest secrecy. Mark never forgot how silently and in complete darkness, without lanterns, they crept through the streets and all met at Doctor West's—the Sedgwicks, Dwights, Curtises, Williamses, and many others, and the impassioned prayer of the little doctor made a deep impression on all. They decided to keep the militia under arms and await developments.

The Democrats outnumbered them in all the towns, and a cantonment was formed at Pittsfield where all who were willing to go to the war gathered under the inspiring direction of Parson Allen, one of the few clergymen who was a Democrat. Feeling grew stronger than ever against the Democrats. A visiting minister proclaimed that although he did not know that all Democrats were horse thieves he did know that all horse thieves were Democrats.

It was a sparkling winter's day in February, 1812, when the firing of a gun called the boys out to the street. Sleigh bells were jingling and their runners crunching the crisply packed snow. And then at a gallop came sleigh after sleigh loaded with soldiers in gay uniforms of blue and buff and beyond more sleighs with boys in sailor caps and baggy blue trousers. As the flags went fluttering by the boys raised a cheer. An old Federalist gentleman shook his stick at them. "Hush! they are going to the lakes to fight the British," he said.

It was annoying that boys couldn't cheer their own soldiers. Sedgwick and the Federalists decided that if they must cheer they should be given a proper object. Who better than George Washington? Swiftly sprang into life a Washingtonian Association to maintain the old ideals of America. On Washington's Birthday the street echoed to the martial music of a brass band, and all the stately Federalists paraded, decorated with blue and gold badges, and escorted by the militia in their gay continental uniforms, with Captain Archibald, sword in hand, at their head. Then was the time for cheers. The boys were even allowed to wear blue and gold badges and to march at the tail of the procession.

All through the state feeling was bitter. In Boston, where the Federalists were dominant, there was a movement to secede from the United States and support the British.

It was a time of want and humiliation. In the West

the war went badly. From Clinton Uncle Sewall wrote:

"The war is quite unpopular and, I am informed, more so to the Westward. Numbers of our young men about here have been three months and have returned with joy as soon as their time was out. You have seen by the papers that Gov. Hull and his army were taken by the British. I am informed they have released all the militia and sent them home, but Hull and the regular troops they are going on with to Quebec—the accounts here are that Hull gave up with little or no fighting and that the British had cut off his supplies so that the army was almost in a state of starvation.

Believe me, Yours Sincerely,

S. Hopkins."

This was one of the disgraceful episodes of the war and it was near enough to Sewall to make Archibald anxious.

News came of the attack of the British on Washington and the burning of the Capitol. Supplies were cut off, and prices mounted rapidly. Stockbridge began to feel the general distress and as usual at such a time the clergy began to thunder from the pulpits that the Lord was angry with His people because they had forsaken the old faith, and terrible punishment would fall unless they repented. Prayer meetings were held all over town and some of the most hardened sinners were moved to confess their sins and repent. The little doctor was in his glory and under his denunciations a revival was soon in progress that equalled the old days of Jonathan Edwards. Under the influence of French thought men had turned from the old beliefs, but now, in the distress and dangers of the war, the old theology was triumphant. Archibald and Mary kept on their serene way, attending church regularly, but making no public professions. Mark was a thoughtful boy and kept inquiring with some anxiety if God was going to punish them all. Even the children discussed religion. Huldah was anxious about her father, John S. Hopkins. Her mother feared he would be eternally lost. She had heard her husband blasphemously attack the solemn utterances of Doctor West. In his sermon on Moral Inability the pugnacious little doctor had proclaimed that no man was capable of himself of doing any good thing and that no amount of virtue would avail to save him from the condemnation of God. Huldah's father had been heard to say to Doctor Jones that this was preposterous and that he had little use for a God who would condemn to eternal torment men who were trying their best to do right. Lucinda, his wife, listened in terror, expecting him to be struck dead for his blasphemy. Mrs. Jones was equally disturbed and they met to pray for their husbands. The children waited with terrified curiosity to see what would happen. Then Huldah appeared in great excitement and announced a miracle. Her father was transformed!

Alone in his room a bright light suddenly shone around him; a voice spoke. He sank to his knees, confessed his sin and surrendered to the heavenly vision. But that was only the half of it. Lucinda running out joyously to tell the good news met Mrs. Jones coming to announce a miracle of her own. Her husband had seen a similar vision at the same time, had been converted and promised to join the church.

The children were greatly impressed by these extraordinary experiences. Huldah and Electa called them miracles. Mark could not understand it. His father and mother did not have any of these experiences and he was sure they were as good as his uncle and aunt. But the rest of the town was swayed by the revival. Over a hundred members were added to the church. Even Theodore Sedgwick was moved. He could not accept the old theology, but he went to consult Channing in Boston and finally joined the Unitarian Church just before his death in 1813.

As the months went by sentiment gradually changed. The burning of the Capitol caused bitterness, and the old Federalist prejudice began to weaken. When in 1814 the news came that the British were sending a fleet to destroy Boston and an army to descend from the lakes and attack from the North, the town was roused. Even the Federalists agreed that the time had come to fight. Boston sent an appeal for help and Mark went out to see his father drill the militia and get them in readiness to march. Two of his Curtis uncles went with them. General

Whiton commanded the Berkshire troops, and Henry Dwight, Archibald's step uncle, went with him as aide. Archibald was to stay at home to organize another company. Women who remembered the old war, were weeping at the thought that they might never see their men folk again, and the band was playing and flags flying as the men marched off. Mark, then 12, followed along and wished he was old enough to go.

Some days later when the children returned from school they found the town all agog. A squad of red-coated soldiers were being marched through the streets by a troop of Americans, and they were told that these were English prisoners who had just been captured on the lakes. The children stared at them as at some strange monster. They were to be quartered in town and Mark wanted to take one home with him to work on the farm.

In October the militia came marching home, rather crestfallen, for they had seen no British, though they had had a pleasant time in camp at Boston.

A few months later in February, 1815, the old Indian conch was blown and the children all ran to the Square and heard the news proclaimed that the Treaty of Ghent had been signed and the war was at an end. The Sedgwicks gave a great party and Mark and Harry and Huldah and Electa, and the Curtis children and all the cousins had a grand celebration with nuts and cakes and fireworks.

It was all very well to celebrate but the war had

left them in trying circumstances; every penny counted, and even a cent was hard to get. It was a problem to Archibald to get clothes for the children.

At school Mark was told that the Reverend Timothy Woodbridge, a minister in a neighboring town, and a relative of his aunt Louisa's husband, had been stricken with blindness and wanted a bright boy to come and read to him every day from his books on Theology. He promised to pay a small sum. Mark was eager to go, and proud of the chance to actually earn money. Satisfactory arrangements were finally made and Mark began his career as reader of Theology. He was bright and quick and read well, without stumbling over the long words, and Doctor Woodbridge gave him high commendation and was anxious to see him acquire an education and fit himself for the ministry.

Day after day one might have seen the boy sitting up very straight in the big armchair in Timothy Woodbridge's study, with the great folio of the Hopkintonian Principles in his lap, and the blind doctor sitting opposite listening intent while the boy with careful precision read off the long-syllabled words and sonorous arguments to prove the depravity of man and the Infinite Mercy of God.

CHAPTER II

MOVING WESTWARD

The lure of the Wild Unknown—the unfathomed forest, the savage and wild beast—how it has called to the heart of man wherever he has settled down in comfort and luxury until, filled with restless discontent, he has risen up from his comfortable seat by the fire, and plunged away into the unknown, leaving home and wife and child and all the certainties of life behind. There are always the stodgy conservatives to leave behind—those who fear change and shudder at the thought of adventure. They breed rapidly even in pioneer stock. Stockbridge had been founded by the adventurous spirit, by men who went forth from comfort and luxury to live among savages in the untamed forest. And now that their energy had tamed and subdued it and comfort and luxury had followed after them and civilization with all its train, they grew restless again. The call of the wild unknown stirred in their hearts. They could not settle down to seed and plough, to toil and spin in the old weary routine. They must fare forth to the front of the battle with fierce old Nature, red of tooth and claw. Stockbridge was no longer the home of savage Indians with their bark houses built around the Council fire. It was a neat, respectable village with white farmhouses, clustered around the tall spire of the church; with its stores where the housewives went shopping for their groceries and garments. The free air of the forests was polluted by the smoke of mills and factories. What wonder that the Indians had left to join their relatives in the forests and lakes of Central New York! Young John Sergeant with the spirit of his father and mother had gone with them. So had the Kirklands. Sewall Hopkins, the young doctor, stirred by the same adventurous spirit, had gone forth to carve out a place for himself in the wilderness, to tame the forest as his forebears had done. And under the stroke of his axe the forest fell away, log cabins appeared, the steepled church, the schoolhouse, the white houses of a village. The great miracle went forward—the mind of man shaping the wilderness to his ideals, subjecting Nature to his institutions—law, religion, education—civilization sweeping forward on its westward way. Already Clinton, where Sewall was, had become too tame. The adventurous souls of Stockbridge were fixing their eyes on a goal farther west.

Sewall had carried the old traditions with him. Not only had he carved out his farm from the forest, and built his house and barns, and ministered to the sick. He had found time to help rear the church, and as his children grew up, like all New Englanders he had given his first attention to education. The school had grown under energetic leadership. These men were ambitious that their community should fall behind in nothing. They could build colleges as well as Massachusetts! And so the foundations of Hamilton College were laid and Sewall was soon boasting of its preëminence to Archibald and advising him to send his sons thither. His great cross was that he had no sons to help him plough the fields and tend the cattle. To hire labor was extravagance and all alone he wrestled with old Mother Nature. He brought up his three girls with a reverent regard for old Stockbridge and for the older brother whose self-sacrifice had given him his start in life. Every two or three years he got out the old wagon and drove the long three days' journey back to the old home and renewed the bonds with his brothers, Archibald and John, and his sister Louisa Woodbridge. He did not want his children to grow away from the old home connections. When his oldest daughter Cornelia was fourteen he yielded to Mary's urgent plea and sent her to visit her uncle and aunt in Stockbridge. A bright pretty girl in the family of boys was a novel experience and they reconnoitred one another shyly at first but she was soon adopted into the home life. Happy times they had; Harry and Mark, sturdy little farmers of ten and twelve, worked with their father on the place. Work over, off they would go, a gay crowd of cousins, Cornelia, with Huldah and Electa Hopkins and Pamela and Calista Curtis, to fish for pickerel in the river or up into the woods after chestnuts or to hunt for squirrels. Harry was a good shot with the old family gun, but every time he brought down a squirrel there were remonstrant shrieks from the girls.

Cornelia soon fathomed Mark's great longing for a liberal education and his fears that his hope would never be realized, for in these years after the war, he knew it was a terrible struggle merely to gain the necessities of life. Prices had risen so that they could no longer afford the comforts to which they were accustomed. How could they eat bread with flour at the preposterous price of fifteen dollars a barrel? The cost of everything had quadrupled. How could they have a comfortable afternoon cup of tea—that most essential luxury, when tea was eighteen dollars a pound? Archibald could not afford to hire help—the boys were put on their mettle to help their father and make the most of their crops and cattle and sheep. For a time cattle were used as currency. Not that they complained. Mary would joke about their riches and Archibald was always cheery. Cornelia was not deceived. She knew they could not afford to send Mark to a fitting school or to spare him from the farm, and that Mark would never mention to them his great ambition. His readings in Theology with old Timothy Woodbridge, however they might equip him for the world to come, scarcely served to fit him for a college in this mundane sphere. Moreover they were dull, and the pay barely covered the shoeleather he expended in walking thither.

Cornelia had the wit and resourcefulness of a frontier girl and proceeded to put two and two together. Her father had no boys. He needed muscle to work on his farm. He had brains and a good education.

Why not exchange Mark's muscle against her father's brains? Supplemented by the school at Clinton, which was excellent, her father could put into Mark's brain the equivalent of his expenditure in muscle and fit him properly for college. Incidentally she would secure Mark's companionship for herself for two or more years, an item on the frontier where eligible escorts were scarce. She wrote her father outlining her clever scheme to secure him cheap farm labor. The two conspirators approached Archibald with some trepidation and asked if he would allow Mark to go to Clinton if his uncle would engage him as a farm hand, and provide board, keep and education. Archibald looked at the thirteen-year-old lad and laughed. The idea of the youngster earning his keep as a farm laborer was absurd. Sewall needed a full-grown man. And when eleven-year-old Harry stood forth and announced that he would run the home farm with his father if Mark were allowed to go, Archibald smothered his smiles, and thinking himself quite safe, agreed solemnly with the excited three that if Sewall would engage the little farmer he should go. The conspirators awaited a letter from Sewall for nearly a month with despairing anxiety. When it arrived they brought it to Archibald and stood with a tremor of excitement while he put on his spectacles and read it aloud:

Cornelia wrote me that you wish to know what I thought of Mark's coming. The case with me is this:

I have sometimes a man six or eight months and sometimes I am destitute—I have no boy at present. If you think of giving Mark a liberal education, he would be young enough to enter college at the commencement of his 17th year; if I mistake not he must be about 13 now. We have a grammar school, and the scholars board around in different families. They pay two dollars and twenty-five cents per week for their diet, inclusive of their washing, lodging, wood and candles, and some contingent charges. . . . If Mark should come and board with me I think I could board him and fit him to enter college at 17 for the assistance he might render me and not interfere with his studies, provided you clothe him. After he enters college his time must be almost wholly devoted to his studies except vacations. I should be pleased to have him come as soon as is convenient and I hope you will write me your mind upon the subject as soon as is convenient. Our family are well. My health is better than it was several years after I had the typhoid fever.

Yours affectionately,

Sewall Hopkins.

Archibald, thoroughly astonished, pushed his spectacles up on his forehead and said: "Well, well. I suppose you can go if he really wants you!" and the boys rushed out and executed a wild dance with Cornelia. Archibald sighed. He would miss Mark who had just begun to be a real help not only with the chores, but with the hoe and plough, for he was a sturdy chap, tall for his age and unusually broad-shouldered. The work was becoming almost too much for Archibald and he wondered if he could swing it without Mark. But he said nothing to spoil Mark's delight. To fare forth into that wild country in the West where Indians lived, and where wars were fought, was in truth a romantic adventure, and his brothers looked at him with awe and some envy as his mother packed up his scanty wardrobe and equipped him for the long journey by wagon and stage.

It was a solemn and exciting moment when the boy climbed into the wagon that was to take him away from home and friends into the unknown West, and he waved his hand in a last farewell to the two brothers whom he was not to see for many months. It was a four days' journey to Clinton, a tremendous undertaking for a small boy who had never been away from home. It was a lonely and anxious boy that arrived at Albany the first night and asked for a room at the Inn. But when a friend from Stockbridge who kept the bar invited him in, he felt quite a man of the world. The next night was a real adventure. Darkness overtook him on the road and he had to seek shelter in a dirty tumble-down hostelry, where he lay awake expecting to be robbed and murdered. Fortunately the next day he found a friend at Herkimer and was invited in to breakfast. He had hardly set forth when the gates of heaven were opened and torrents of rain nearly drowned him, and turned the road to a morass in which he floundered all day, failing to reach his goal. He stopped at New Hartford and found a Curtis cousin who took him in and dried him out and kept him over Sunday, for no one could travel on the Sabbath without permission. Curtis drove him out to Clinton in the morning. He pulled up in front of Sewall's house with a shout and the girls came running out. "Here I've brought you a passenger," he cried. Sewall appeared in the door. "Bless us if it isn't young Mark!" he cried. "Didn't you expect me?" the boy asked with his heart in his boots. "We hadn't heard a word. We only get mail about once in two weeks, and I thought your father wouldn't let you come. Well, that's fine. Come right in and I'll show you where you can hang up your hat. The girls will double up and you can have a little room to yourself. You're just in time. I've no one to help me with the chores and the farm and you're a good husky lad for thirteen years. School is just beginning and we'll start you right in with geography and parsing, and I'll help you to begin your Latin."

So the young boy of thirteen took his share in pushing forward the chariot of civilization, and joined in the hard battle with the stubborn soil, making the crooked straight and the rough places plain and preparing in the wilderness a highway for progress and culture, for the railways and automobiles, the industries and institutions that were to come. It was hard toil and a strange reward.

The Yankee is famous as a Jack of all trades and

we might add a few professions. Mark's uncle was a doctor, but in the intervals of bleeding his patients or pulling their teeth, he had hewn himself a farm out of the forest and built himself a house and now there were fields to be planted, corn to be hoed, sheep to be sheared, cows to be milked, in addition to such chores as carrying up the water and chopping wood for the fire, all hard back-breaking work. And upon the young lad of thirteen now fell the burden of this work under a contract that the modern boy would scarcely view with enthusiasm, for his pay was in terms of Latin verbs and algebraic formulæ and English grammar slid into his brain in the interstices of labor.

In the autumn the balance was certainly against him as the work piled up. But his letters chronicle no complaint as he registers one week planting, one week hoeing, enough to crack the vertebræ of the usual high-school boy—seven weeks haying, swinging the scythe and sickle with no McCormick reaper to help. Coming home in the evening after that, with aching muscles and eyes drooping with sleep and numb brain, one wonders how he could absorb the equivalent of his work in Latin grammar and mathematics. These boys of 9 to 13 had stood up to take on their shoulders the burden of family responsibility, and when Mark's schoolwork required a Latin dictionary priced at four dollars the boy was overwhelmed with the thought of the sacrifice at home involved in that four dollars. And then his shoes gave out and he was in despair at having to ask his father for four dollars and twelve cents to replace them and three dollars and a half for a new hat. As for clothing, his mother had woven a fine piece of homespun for him and when it arrived Cornelia got a friend of the family to cut out and sew together a suit for him at a cost of only two dollars and a half. He was conscience-stricken to take even that from the family income.

Hospitality was a necessity as well as a virtue in those pioneer sections where there was no inn. Mark would often come in from the fields, exhausted by toil, and planning an evening's work by candlelight in his little room, to find his bed occupied by some belated traveller. Cornelia would get out a blanket and help him find a soft spot in the hay in the barn, and he would go to sleep listening to the champing of the horses in their stalls.

One day he was given a holiday and told he could take the horse and ride over to the settlement and see the Indians. This brought great excitement and even more than he anticipated, for the horse was not accustomed to Indians and bolted, with Mark's arms and legs flying wildly. Somehow he managed to stick on and reached home breathless but triumphant.

In 1886 Mark Hopkins received a letter from Myron Adams asking if he remembered a tragic event of his schooldays. He and six other boys in Clinton went to a school kept by William Groves on the road leading south to Hamilton College. Myron lived with a minister, Reverend Oliver Ayer, and he and

Robert Norton, the son of the minister of the Clinton Church, and a friend named Elihu Norton, stopped for Mark on the way to school, and led him by a short cut through the fields to a spot where it was necessary to cross the Oriskany Creek. A fallen elm formed a bridge some sixty feet in length across the muddy torrent. The boys led the way over, but when Mark attempted to cross, they shook the branches so violently that he lost his footing and fell with a splash into the stream. He does not state what Uncle Sewall said when Mark appeared in his dampened condition. Thereafter there was daily competition among the minister's sons as to which should shake the others off. The letter comments on the fact that boys of that age are prone to strangely reprehensible behavior, which they consider humorous.

In spite of the company of his cousins Mark had his homesick moments, and he felt qualms of conscience at the thought of his father and little Harry toiling away on the home farm without his aid. No New England farmer could make ends meet without his sons' help. Mark was tall, heavily built and strong for his age, though a bit slow and awkward from his rapid growth. Harry was only eleven—dark, slender, lithe and graceful. He had been a brilliant scholar, but had given up school on account of his eyes. He had promised to take Mark's place on the farm, but Mark worried continually for fear he would not have the strength, that his father would never be able to get the work done, that the crops would fail, and then where would they all be? He wrote anxious letters home to Harry, asking if they could manage to get on without him. Harry, then only eleven, would never confess how blue he was at Mark's absence, or how wearisome he found the work, but answered with gay braggadocio in one of the most astonishing letters ever penned by a child of eleven: "I shall begin abruptly by answering your request which was that I would inform you how business goes on at home, which gives me the happy opportunity of telling you that your absence renders it necessary that much of the management of business should fall to the hands of one particularly capable, and although my health has been much impaired, yet I rejoice that my uncommon abilities quite makes up the deficiency of health so far as respects business. For a good calculator will really perform more with little labor than one who labors hard without calculation; do not think I am boasting for you know that one of my good sense would disdain everything of that nature. I know too it is an old proverb that a wise head keeps a close mouth, but I see no reason why a boy of my understanding may not write the truth and the whole truth. I shall therefore tell you that I think business is much more forward than I have hitherto known it at this season; my crops upon the ground more forward than usual, and the business so far finished as renders it hard to know what to do first. There is no spring grain within my view that appears as well as mine, wheat, barley, oats, peas, flax, all flourishing, and my corn of a beautiful color somewhat resembling that which the ancient poets called cowslips. The orchard is walled and adjoining the wall thereof Southward, round about the garden to the great gate Eastward, is a stately fence. The garden flourishes and sends forth a delicious flavor; the timber drawn home for the cider mill, a hundred dollars subscribed to the college, etc., etc., and if you can tell more that you have done I shall be very glad to hear it. No more about Pickerel. The coves are dry and they have fled to deep water. I wish I could have seen you riding to Brothertown. I shall be ever happy to receive a letter from you. Your affectionate brother, Harry Hopkins."

Education had certainly advanced since old Colonel Ephraim struggled with his pen sixty years earlier. Even in this age few lads of eleven could turn out such a letter. The old New England discipline had done a good job to produce a child who could tackle such a load of work and responsibility and chaff his brother about it. How much of the planting of those great and various fields of grain that he alludes to as "mine" was actually done by Harry may be open to conjecture; but even allowing that his father was not idle, Harry's achievement seems almost incredible. Without the pickerel in the background it would seem inhuman.

Archibald could ill afford to subscribe $100 to colleges, but there had been a proposition to move Williams College from the Hoosick Valley where they claimed it was shut off from the world, to a more favorable environment, and several towns were competing by offering subscriptions to be paid if the college were located in their environs. Stockbridge raised $13,000, and Archibald felt that he would save his $100 in the education of his sons, if the college were located there. It is surprising that the college was not originally placed in Stockbridge, and it probably would have been but for Colonel Ephraim's eye for the beauty of the Hoosick Valley and his devotion to the men who helped him defend it. In the end it was decided to respect his wishes, and Archibald kept his $100.

Politics and religion were the chief emotional outlets for the New England village, and the feeling between the Democrats and the Federalists was kept at white heat. The Federalists still held the dominant position and all the men of wealth and position belonged to their ranks. The Democrats made a determined effort to oust them. Archibald's brother, John Sergeant Hopkins, by working hard had saved enough money to buy up the most popular store in town, which belonged to a man named Plumbs. He had every reason to expect success when the Democrats clubbed together and opened up a rival store next door to his and began to sell everything at cut rates, hoping to drive him out of business. The Federalists were indignant and Mark's Uncle David wrote him a letter excoriating a political party that was mean enough to sacrifice the wealth of its adherents to wreck the prosperity of its opponents. They openly avowed that they sought not only a public victory but to bring to ruin the private fortunes of their enemies, and David felt they would bring unhappiness on the town, and especially on John Hopkins, though he had no doubt of the ultimate victory of the great Federalist cause.

But Mark was not the only one in Stockbridge who was moving westward. The front line of the great battle with the wilderness was moving further and further west. New lands had just been opened in New Connecticut, now the state of Ohio, and the men of Stockbridge were eager now as ever to be in the thick of it and in the front line trenches of the great fight with primitive nature—the battle with wild beast and savage, the struggle to transform the primeval forest into cultivated fields.

Uncle Alva, whose daughters, Pamela and Calista, had been Mark's playfellows, wearied of his paper mill, and sold it out, receiving one-fifth of the price in cash and the rest in New Connecticut land valued at $3.50 an acre. He then set out with two of his neighbors on the long journey of several hundred miles to view his purchase, in the neighborhood of the present city of Cleveland. Clinton had seemed far enough but this was a plunge into unknown wilds.

In the meantime John Hopkins and his wife Lucinda had been struggling to make their new store go, against the machinations of the Democrats. No matter how hard they worked it seemed impossible to make ends meet. They had now six children; beside Huldah and Electa there were two girls named Lucinda and Mary and two boys, William and John. Archibald saw that his brother looked pale and anxious, and Mary told him that she thought Lucinda was wretched and ill. After her great happiness in her husband's conversion, and her high expectations from this new business venture, it seemed cruel to have everything wrecked by mean political enemies who bore them all a grudge. And then one day Huldah ran into Cherry Cottage in tears to say her mother was ill and out of her head with a high fever. Mary went over at once to help nurse her and found John in despair. He was thin and wasted and seemed to have a temperature himself. The doctors seemed powerless. It was only a question of hours and Lucinda passed away. The shock completely prostrated John. The same fever evidently had attacked him and in spite of all that Archibald and Mary could do, in two days he was dead, leaving six children and a bankrupt business. The Democrats had made a clean sweep and eliminated all competition.

The blow fell like a thunderbolt upon Archibald. All his plans had been laid to send his boys to college and by careful thought it had all been worked out. It could be done but with hardly a penny to spare. And now here were these six helpless children! If he adopted them how could he provide for their six extra mouths, to say nothing of clothing? It meant good bye to all hopes of college for his boys. Archibald and Mary sat late into the night and discussed it after they had put the tear-stained little girls to bed. There could be no question as to what they would do. Archibald who had always carried all the family burdens bravely and uncomplainingly had now this heaviest burden of all dumped upon him.

But he could not bear to tell Mark that he must give up his great ambition. He wrote Sewall of the calamity and Sewall replied with suitable reflections that "Man is born to trouble" and "We are but pilgrims here," rejoicing that at least "our departed friends left this world clothed in the wedding garment of Christ's righteousness." He added that Mark had been doing well in his studies and would be ready for college at seventeen.

The new brood were all installed in Cherry Cottage with some crowding.

Henry and Albert greeted their cousins with sympathy and joy. It was fun to have such a fine crowd of young people in the house, and they knew little of the cost. The months dragged by and still Archibald could not bear to write to Mark, knowing how the boy's heart was set on his college course.

In April, 1816, six months later, he and his uncle were still planning on his college career and arranging to save toward it the twenty dollars that a visit home would cost. Albert, who was now nine, wrote: "Dear Brother: I now go to school, am placed in the first class and stand at the head at least half the time . . . I am now dressed in my new suit trimmed with uniform buttons. On my coat I have thirty or forty buttons which make a brilliant appearance so that I am daily strutting about in great style." Alas, pride came before a dangerous fall in which he dislocated his elbow and was badly hurt. Mark writes, "I hope you will bear it like a man."

He was to have his own dislocation to bear, for his father could no longer defer the blow and with a sad heart wrote that with these added expenses it would be impossible for Mark to go to college. Mark was broken hearted. All the year he had toiled in the fields with all the strength of his young body to gain his goal. And it was all for nought. His uncle, too, was bitterly disappointed and wrote on April 29, 1816:

"Dear Brother: I received your letter last evening of April 4th. I am glad to hear that Albert has nearly recovered his health and limb again. The intelligence Mark has received by your letter seems rather to cast a gloom upon his countenance—he has doubtless flattered himself that he should receive a liberal education—and indeed I think that such geniuses as Mark should have their minds cultivated and I can not but think it wise for you to reconsider your former determination. If I judge right respecting him he would from his present habits and genius leave college with the first honors of the class and the expansion that science gives to the mind of industrious young men places them in a situation not only to be more useful to mankind but to go through life with far more intellectual enjoyment." He goes on to suggest ways and means and says that if Mark goes to Clinton he could board him and, with what the boy could earn, $120 a year should see him through.

"If you find yourself straitened for money after he enters college had you not better part with some of your landed property and charge Mark with the expense of his education as so much toward his portion. It would be better for him to make his way in the world than so much cash."

Poor Mark, in his bitter disappointment, made a last plea and wrote: "I had rather have a liberal education and nothing else than to have considerable more money than to carry me through—but if you want my help I know that I owe a very great debt and am willing to pay what I can. I wish that you, sir, would send me your determination, and whatever it is I shall be content. Your affectionate son, Mark Hopkins."

His father, deeply moved by the boy's suffering, wrote that he saw no way out. It could not be done. He could stay another year with his uncle and learn what he could, but beyond that they could not spare him. He must bear his share in the sacrifice and help to maintain his orphaned cousins. In these hard times they could hardly pull through even with his help.

He was received with joy when he returned to Stockbridge in 1816; back to the old Cherry Cottage which was now overflowing with young people. His brothers pitched upon him promptly, and his new sisters stood waiting shyly to welcome him. He did his share of the farm work, for a time. Then he found that he could get a job teaching in the school which would enable him to advance in his studies and at the same time to earn enough to enable his father to hire a man to take his place. And finally in 1818 he got a position as teacher of the school in Richmond near by, and saved enough to enable him to attend an advanced school in Lenox the following year, where he completed his preparation for college in all except Greek. In vacations and spare time he helped on the farm. In spite of the hard work it was a jolly group of young people that made the farm go, and many a happy time the boys and girls had gathering nuts, or squirrel hunting, or husking corn, along with their cousins Calista and Pamela. Times improved gradually but still there seemed no possibility that Mark could acquire the five or six hundred dollars necessary to take him through college, even if he were fully prepared to enter.

Although Mark had returned from his Western venture, the lure of the Western wilderness was still felt in Stockbridge and it was to break in once again upon the happy group of cousins. In all that we say of the heroism of the pioneer we sometimes forget the women and children who accompanied them when they plunged into the unknown wilds, away from all the comforts and safeguards of home, to endure hunger and exposure and face sickness and death in the desolate forest. Mark's cousins, the two girls with whom he had played so often in childhood, were to bear their share in the great conquest of the continent, to suffer even to the utmost limit before the wilderness could be conquered and the way prepared for the many thousands who were to come and build the great city of Cleveland on the foundations they had laid. In 1818 Mark's uncle Alva Curtis returned from the West and said that he had marked out the land he had purchased, and asked his wife and his two girls to go out with him and help him build his log cabin and clear the forest and plant his crops. So Mark and Harry bade good bye to their little cousins Pamela and Calista and saw them ride away with tearful faces, on their creaking oxcarts loaded with all the family furniture. Little did they realize what trouble and danger lay before them.

It was two months later that Mary received a tragic letter from her sister-in-law Chloe (Mrs. Curtis), telling of their terrible journey by wagon through the trackless wilderness. The last day their teams were worn out and through the dense woods they only made nine miles all day. No house was near. It was pitch dark; they were nearly frozen and had no food. Fearing they would perish of cold and hunger, Alva told his wife to get out and walk as far as she could along the trail in search of shelter. She and the girls waded on through the mud, feeling their way by the bushes at the side. They kept on all through the night and it was not until seven in the morning that they arrived at a wretched log hut where the poor people took them in. Calista was taken ill from the exposure. Alva in desperation tried to find some more decent place to stay instead of being herded in one room with this poverty-stricken family of strangers. After two days' search he found a little empty hut and they all moved in. Alva cut poles and made beds, for there was no furniture, and they fixed up a board for a table and found an old chair.

They could find no doctor for Calista who had a high fever, but they got an old deacon to come and pray for her, which gave her great comfort. At last they found a doctor, but it was too late. He could only sit by her and close her eyes when death came. As the Hopkins family read Chloe's pathetic account of their last parting and their efforts to bury their beloved child in that wilderness they could not restrain the tears, and even today it is hard to read that letter, stained with tears and age, without emotion. After Calista's death they went on to their own land on the Vermillion River and put up a log cabin which, with its wide chinks, was a poor shelter from the winter storms.

Just after receiving this letter the Hopkins family had their own tragedy. The boys were fishing on the bridge over the river when William, one of the adopted brothers, slipped and fell into the swift current. He was carried under and before they could reach him he was dead. It was a terrible shock to the little family group.

In October Pamela wrote:

"Oh my dear aunt, I cannot forget how many pleasant visits Calista and I have had together at your house, how we us'd to love to come and see you and have some good plays with our cousins and pretty rambles around your garden. I think that Cousin Harry if he was here would have a little sport with his gun for here are a great many pigeons. Last Saturday just at night I see thousands and thousands and ten times thousands flying across our fields and lighting on the oak trees but if Cousin was here I don't know that I should like him to disturb them they seem to take such pleasure in flying together. I am sure they are not as lonesome as I am. I have no little girls to visit nearer than two miles. This last summer I was ten years old, and if aunt and I should live ten years longer I shall see her. We have heard how little William Hopkins fell off the bridge and was drowned, so we see that little children die in Stockbridge as well as in Ohio. Please to give my love to Uncle Hop and to my cousins, from your affectionate niece, Pamela W. Curtis."

Mark's uncle Sewall kept writing to urge him to go to college at Clinton but the pull of the family was toward the college founded by his great uncle. His cousins Henry and Robert Sedgwick had graduated from Williams in 1804 and were quite enthusiastic. Then while Charles Sedgwick was in college had come the period of dissatisfaction to which allusion has been made. When Charles graduated in 1813 affairs were in better shape and there were rumors that Fitch was about to resign. This he finally did in 1815, and Doctor Zephaniah Swift Moore of Dartmouth was chosen to take his place. His advent soon made a marked change. He was a stately, dignified man with the typical corpulent build of the college president, a man of great decision and force. Mark's cousin Henry Hopkins Woodbridge, the son of his aunt Louisa, who had been greatly dissatisfied, now wrote that things were going well and that he enjoyed his course.

In 1820 Mark was eighteen and still as far from college as ever. Though he had prepared himself in everything but Greek the family funds were still too low to give him any hope of support through his college course. It was at this time that a friend, a Mr. Sherrill, returned from Virginia. He had been teaching school there and had married a young Southern girl. He thought he might get for Mark the position he had held. Two men who had large plantations in the back country were anxious to secure some education for their children and clubbed together to start a school. They seemed to think all wisdom was in the North and Sherrill thought they would accept any man whom he recommended. He was taking Mrs. Sherrill down for a visit to her relatives and Mark could go with him. They promised to pay $640 a year, which seemed a small fortune to Mark. There were long discussions with his father who decided finally that now that the other boys were grown he could get on without Mark's help.

It was a hard decision for Mark. To teach school at home was one thing but to go to a strange country with different customs and adapt himself to their requirements was another matter. He felt much as did John Sergeant when he set forth to teach the Indians, for his work was to be in South Western Virginia near the Carolina line, a country then as wild and unknown as the farthest West. Mark started off with Mr. Sherrill after many tearful goodbyes from his mother and cousins. They heard nothing for more than a month. He seemed to have dropped into the void. Then came a letter and they gathered about the tallow candle in the kitchen to hear Mary read it.

On April 30, 1820, Mark found himself in a situation that seemed almost incredible to him. He was on the deck of a schooner sailing out from New York harbor. The tall lanky somewhat ungainly country lad in his best homespuns sat there on a bench as the schooner with all sails set went plunging out into a northwest gale and the wide unfathomed sea. He had had no experience with boats nor had he ever seen the ocean.

"It is a noble sight. It is grand," he said to Mrs. Sherrill, who with her daughter was seated beside him. But she was still upset, for her husband had nearly missed the boat and she thought she had lost him forever. Mark was lost in meditation. His mind was not that of an observer, but one which translates outward events into the realm of thought and ideas. "It is like a glimpse into eternity," he continued, turning to Mrs. Sherrill for sympathy. But she was in no mood to contemplate eternity. A sudden lurch of the ship sent her in a dash for the rail, and she retired gasping to her cabin along with her daughter. Mark had much to think about—his two-day trip down the Hudson in a sloop, his first sight of New York, which overwhelmed him with its great buildings and thronged streets and the clatter of the hacks. He smiled as he thought what his father would say of the rows of them drawn up in City Hall Square—how he would wonder that they could afford to keep so much horse flesh inactive. He had been especially impressed by the chiming and ringing of the bells on the Sabbath, and he remembered with gratitude the kindness of the Sedgwick cousins, in taking him in, shy and bewildered as he was, and making him at home in their spacious house. And then the ship gave such a violent leap that he was thrown from his seat. The waves rolled up in terrifying masses that threatened to overwhelm the little boat. The sailors could only cross the deck by clutching at the rail. To Mark they seemed terrible beyond description, "mountain high," but he corrects himself, they are really only "as high as a house." Feeling very unhappy he sought his cabin. He tried to go out for supper, but he was no sooner seated than a violent roll threw all the crockery off the table, and he rushed back to his cabin heedless of food, to pass a troubled night.

It was a week later that he was driving over a rough road through the back woods of Virginia in a ramshackle old vehicle with a man whom he had never seen before. The frightful two days' storm at sea was only a memory and he preferred to think of the peaceful two-day sail from Norfolk up the James and Appomattox to Petersburg with the Sherrills. He felt alone and helpless without the Sherrills. Sherrill had hired a hack the day before and driven with him thirty-six miles from Petersburg to the house of a friend, a Mr. Smith, with whom he and his wife were to stay. In the morning he had left his friends and ridden off on horseback with Smith's son fourteen miles through the forest to the plantation of Major Nelson, a wealthy relative of the Nelson who had started the school. The Major had received him with Southern courtesy and given him a fine dinner, and his son-in-law then took him the last six miles on his long journey. They came to a river, and Mark held on anxiously while the rig was driven onto a flat-bottomed boat and poled across the river. Another mile or two and they reached another river, and the perilous process was repeated, which these Southerners took as a matter of course. And then they came to Nelson's plantation, open fields in the midst of the forest. He inquired of his guide and found that Nelson had some fifty cattle and ninety hogs and many sheep and innumerable slaves to aid him in raising his wheat and corn. They met wagons loaded with tobacco, but he was told that Nelson would not raise that weed.

He was expecting a palatial manor house and was somewhat disappointed when they drove into a wide yard in front of a little house surrounded by outbuildings. His guide threw down the reins and gave a shout, and soon a dried-up little man appeared who might be anywhere from twenty-five to sixty. He looked Mark up and down and in rather a surly fashion inquired who he might be. Now that he was actually at his destination, Mark felt decidedly out of his element and uncomfortable and wished himself back at Stockbridge. But he pulled out Sherrill's letter and said that he was the teacher from the North. Nelson looked him over again in his surly fashion and then read the letter. Finally he was invited to enter and Mrs. Nelson received him with hearty cordiality, set before him a fine Virginia ham and a delicious meal. There were two boys and a girl at the family table. Mr. Nelson told him that he would send for Mr. Speed in the morning and they would decide his fate. After the children were sent to bed the white servants were called in and Mr. Nelson read a chapter from the Bible and a prayer, and then read out two lines of a psalm which they all sang, one man starting the tune and the rest joining in with the chords. Then Nelson read out two lines more which were duly sung and so on through the psalm. There was no extra room in the little house and Mark was given a shake-down in the kitchen and at last got to sleep after wondering what his fate would be, for the surly Nelson gave him no encouragement.

Next Monday, however, saw him in happier mood though still somewhat anxious, walking along the path through the forest to the deserted old meeting house where the school was to be held. Mr. Speed came the morning after his arrival and after long consultation, Mr. Nelson told him they had decided to engage him at the salary mentioned by Sherrill. Nelson had said that he would board him, but that he had no room for him in the house. They had looked over the outbuildings and Nelson found one, a mere shell, that he said he would knock into shape for him so that he could have a house to himself. He had been as good as his word, had floored and ceiled it, and Mrs. Nelson had found a spare bed, but instead of having it to himself the two boys were put in a little bed at his feet to sleep with him. Nelson could spare no time to introduce him to the school, so here he was, tramping along through the woods all alone to face his new charge.

Soon the meeting house came in sight. It was dilapidated enough, roughly boarded inside, and nothing to suggest a school about it. There was no one there, but by searching around Mark discovered a pile of old school books. He wondered what his scholars would be like. He had heard of rough bullies who loved to do up a new teacher, and he feared a youth from the North would not be acceptable here. He had put on his best clothes to make a good impression the first day, his blue broadcloth suit with its slim-waisted, long-tailed coat, and slender trousers, a high collar and new cravat. He was over six feet and broad shouldered with a chest of nearly forty inches, but his waist was slim. His legs seemed unduly long and he had not yet learned to manage his height. The door opened and a boy entered who was as tall as he and heavier in build. He was sandy-haired and freckle-faced and barefoot and dressed in the roughest homespuns. Mark looked him over with some trepidation and wondered what would happen if this youth defied him. He approached shyly and in response to Mark's questions said he was fifteen. When Mark asked how far he had ciphered, he responded, "Right fur." In the meantime two girls had entered, barefoot also, and dressed in the plainest calico, but neat and clean. Their faces seemed strangely pale to him, after the rosy-cheeked New Englanders. Others entered now until he had a school of fifteen. Eight of these were Mr. Speed's children and three Mr. Nelson's.

Mark busied himself in finding out where they were in their various studies, and found that they were in nearly every grade. He finally succeeded in assigning a lesson to each one. He then asked them to take their seats and formally opened school. At home school was always opened by prayer, and this troubled him. He was not a professing Christian and was not certain if it was right or sincere for him to make a prayer in public. On the other hand he was responsible for the teaching of these children, and to start with no recognition of God seemed heathenish. He believed in an all-guiding, all-mastering Power, but toward such a God he could feel no such passionate devotion as characterized Jonathan Edwards or Mr. Coan, a revivalist who had spoken in Stockbridge and who now by some strange chance was touring Virginia. He decided, however, that not to make the prayer would show that he was ashamed to recognize his creator and that it would be more insincere than to pray. So he called the children to order and made the opening prayer and then told them to study their lessons.

On Sunday he hesitated whether he should go with Mr. Nelson to the Episcopal Church and finally decided it would be no sin. The church was fifteen miles away and they had to start on Saturday. This involved another strain of the conscience, for Mark had been used on Saturday to watch the sun's shadow on Monument Mountain and as soon as it reached the top to lay aside tools or playthings and to keep the evening as the Sabbath, for did not the Sacred book say "and there was evening and morning the seventh day"? But here Saturday evening was spent in jollification and it was hard to be serious when every one around was in sportive mood. He finally decided it was better to follow the custom of the country and keep Sunday eve with them. Accordingly they all set off in the family wagon on Saturday afternoon and crossed the two rivers on the perilous flat boats and reached Major Nelson's in time for supper. After a jolly evening the Major put them up in his large Manor House. On Sunday morning they all drove on to the church, a fine old building, and Mark listened to the Episcopal service and a sermon from an old bishop of rotund figure. Mark wrote "He made me think of the words of the Poet, not goosey goosey, but 'plump as stalled theology.'" He met Mark after church and surveying the lanky lad with a humorous eye he said genially: "Depend upon it, go where I will, I find these Yankees. I came from New York myself," he added, with a twinkle in his eye. The afternoon troubled Mark's conscience a little. Instead of quiet reading at home there were gay visitors and calls to make, and the young people even engaged in a contest with the cross bow and started playing games. He did not quite know what to do. To stand aloof seemed priggish and to join in games on the Sabbath was a strain on the conscience even of an unconverted New Englander. To balance off, Mr. Nelson was regular as the sun himself at morning prayers, which was more than can be said for the most pious professor of religion in New England. They got up at dawn on Monday in order to get back to school on time and Mark was in his seat at the appointed hour.

One evening Mark was passing through the slaves' quarters when the strains of that weird minor music, so characteristic of the negro, came to his ears. He turned aside to one of the huts. The door was open and a crowd of the slaves was packed into its narrow space, all singing, as they swayed from side to side, one of the haunting old spirituals. They made room for him on an old box and he entered. After the song ended a white-haired old negro, in a threadbare long-tailed black coat, arose and made a prayer, so moving in its simple devotion, that Mark was touched. When the prayer was over he asked why they did not read some selection from the Bible and learned that not one of these slaves could read. It seemed to him unspeakably pathetic that they should be struggling to maintain their religion against such odds and he asked if they would like him to read them a chapter. They assented eagerly and thanked him most earnestly when he finished. He was so moved that he promised to come whenever they had a meeting and read to them some appropriate selection from the Bible.

He had been thinking much about these slaves. All were ignorant but all were not religious; many were dirty and drunken and vicious. When he returned, he asked Mr. Nelson what he thought of slavery, and was surprised at the emphatic way in which he condemned it. This Southerner felt more strongly against it than the New Englanders whose comments Mark had heard. He said that although it was a source of wealth to them, it was a curse to the community. All his friends condemned it and wished they were free from it. But they had inherited the system and they could see no way out. He said to Mark, "You see what they are like. There are more of them than of us; what do you think they would do—or what wouldn't they do if they were set free and let loose on society?" Mark shook his head. After a moment's thought he said: "You would have to give them the vote." "Yes, if we didn't someone would stir up the ignorant and violent to rebellion and massacre. If we did, they would elect niggers to Congress! Imagine what a state of things that would be, for us to be ruled by ignorant niggers. No; there seems no way out." Mark said, "Up North they all criticize you but they have no idea what you have to deal with. Some of them seem to be good Christians," he continued. "If you could convert them all that might help. If they believe in Christianity they would either struggle toward its ideals, or be kept from evil by its awful threatenings." And so, not knowing what else he could do to heal the sore he continued his ministrations to the group of slaves.

His little house was finished now and a chimney and fireplace built on to it and in the evenings he would often sit in front of the fire and dream of Stockbridge and of his plans for the future. Some nights the future seemed golden—he was sure of his education and of a path to fame. He would make his name known in scholarship, he would acquire wealth and fame like his Uncle Sedgwick and restore the family fortunes. And then again after an annoying day at school and after struggling alone over his Greek grammar he would sink into the depths. He would never be able to do what his uncle and his family expected of him. He was doomed to failure and ruin. The ancient system of thought with its inexorable logic rose up against him.

Mary Hopkins had never joined the church, and yet nothing could exceed the tenderness with which she brought home the truths of religion to her children. Mark's religious life began one day when as a little boy she called him into the north room alone, and said she did not want him "to make religion a strange or distant thing," but that he should think and talk freely about it. She saw that Mark was to be reached by the reason rather than the emotions and told him that it was reasonable, perfectly reasonable, we should ask of God those blessings we daily needed at His hand.

He never forgot that simple talk. It was the beginning of prayer for him. It was her manner more than anything she said that moved him. She was so sprightly, so full of fun and good humor, so practical and courageous in the way she attacked the problems and faced the trials and discouragements of daily life, that he never forgot this little glimpse into her inner life—this vision of the mainspring of her strength.

As the end of the school year approached gloom descended upon Mark. Scrape as he would there was certainly not enough cash to take him through college. He was now a year past the age when he hoped to enter. Nelson, with a kindly gleam on his thin surly face begged him to stay another year. At first he could not face another summer away from those who loved him, but finally he girded up his soul, and decided to remain until he had enough to make college sure.

In the meantime while Mark was getting ready to move toward Williams College it began to look as if Williams College was going to take wings and flit away from him, clean out of Berkshire County. President Moore had never, like Ephraim Williams, appreciated the beauties of the lovely valley at the foot of Greylock. To him it was a forsaken spot, shut off from civilization, where it was impossible to gather and train cultured youth, and after much bickering and dickering, and in spite of the protests of the trustees and the clearly expressed will of Ephraim Williams, he accepted the invitation of the people of the Connecticut valley to move the institution to Amherst, and picked up the college, students and all, and carried them off over the mountain barrier to that new site, leaving a wrathful and empty town, a board of angry trustees and a few disgruntled students behind. It looked as if that was the end of Williams College and the ambition of Colonel Ephraim Williams. Mark had no wish to go to Amherst. He much preferred a well established college like Yale to one which was flitting around over the mountains.

Moreover Yale was easier to reach than Amherst. Mark planned to do enough work that year to enter Yale as a sophomore, and hoped even to make the junior class. He had a despairing feeling that he was being left behind in these southern backwaters. His Aunt Louisa's son, Henry Woodbridge, just his age, was graduating and here was Mark, nearly nineteen and not yet started.

He had a tragic feeling that he was blocking the way for his brother Harry, who had made so many sacrifices for him, "that dear old Yake" as he called him, whose gayety and versatility won all hearts, and he implored Harry to take the money he had earned in Virginia and forsake the toil of the farm and go forward on the path to a liberal education in his place. Harry, moved almost to tears, laughed it off in one of his inimitable letters, which more than anything else kept alive Mark's sense of humor and his touch on home with their vivid descriptions. Old Grandpa Curtis, though he had a stern and gnarled physiognomy, was a jovial old soul at heart, and Harry loved nothing more than to go off with him on a bee hunt. He would gather a jolly crowd of young people and they would have a grand lark off in the woods together and come back with a fine load of honey and perhaps a sting or two. Grandpa had been having bad faint turns and said he must give up bee hunting, but he kept his boxes and hatchet ready in the wagon and whenever Harry found a tree, off they would go. The forest was rough and the old gentleman found it quite exhausting to keep up with the boys. Harry writes:

"The other day after being almost gone with fatigue and hard labor, coming home he said if he only had about a qt. of spirit he would have one scrape getting drunk and stay out all night. After coming a little farther I being some distance behind, looked and he was getting over a fence, when all at once he fell like a log, flat into a ditch. I laughed until I could hardly stand: at last I saw him peeking through the fence to see if I saw him: I soon came up with him and he said he had a fall almost equal to Adam's."

Grandpa certainly demonstrated his genial nature by rising above his bruises to cap his grandson's ribald laughter with a joke.

Mark naturally wished his school children to show off the learning he had injected into them. So a grand examination was arranged in the old meeting house, and all the folk of distinction were invited. There was not a large crowd, but several prominent ladies attended in addition to the parents. Mark had taught each of the boys a "piece" to speak, and listened in strained anxiety as each one mounted the platform with the usual combination of shyness and pride, and spouted forth his declamation. Fortunately all got through without a slip. The parents seemed greatly pleased at the amount of knowledge their children had accumulated, and Mark felt that his dignity was established when they all inquired from what college he had graduated, and refused to believe that one so learned was not an alumnus of some university.

Then came a letter from Mark's mother that turned his face back toward Williams: "Your friend Kup is going to Williams College this faul, and as I told you in my other letter that they had lost their President, so I will now tell you that they have chosen a Dr. Griffin of Connecticut who they expect will accept their invitation."

There had been an acrimonious dispute over Doctor Moore's departure. The trustees had appealed and the courts, moved by an eloquent speech by Josiah Quincy, decided that Colonel Ephraim's funds could not be carried away from the spot he had chosen. Half the students finally decided to remain, and now with the advent of Doctor Griffin the prospects of Williams were booming once more. The family were strongly in favor of Williams. Mark would be much nearer home, and then expenses were much less. Three years at Williams would cost little more than two at Yale.

CHAPTER III

LIFE ON THE FARM IN 1822

At last Mark is on his way back to the beloved old Cherry Cottage of which he had dreamed so often in his two years' exile in the South. His cousin, one of the Curtis boys, gives us a picture of him as he tramped out from the village to the farm on the day of his arrival. The boy heard a loud raucous skwawk and looked up to see Mark striding along the road, tall and lanky as ever, blowing on a blade of grass between his thumbs "a la grandpa," to express his joy at the sight of the old chimney top. Mark, overflowing with delight in the old surroundings and expecting an enthusiastic welcome shouted out a greeting. But the boy, who really worshipped him as a sort of hero, hung his head, and said nothing. "Don't you know me?" asked Mark. The boy overcome with shyness, shook his head, and left Mark to stride on ungreeted. Such was old New England—not unfeeling, but tonguetied—feeling too much for casual expression.

The picture of the family life in the old Cherry Cottage that we find in the boys' letters is a charming one—all the more so that it has faded away into the forgotten past, never again to be reproduced. In this day of Harvesters it is hard to picture the life of the old New England farmer. Perhaps never elsewhere save in Scotland, has there been such a combination of hard toil and intellectual life, of stern manual labor and the highest refinement. In few places can one find a family so intensely devoted, so loyal to one another, so mutually helpful, so happy in spite of cruel hardship, and where each is so proud of the achievements of the others.

In this mechanical age when we have plants which manufacture every sort of article we may forget that old original plant the home, where character is manufactured by the machinery of family life. The old New England home was not a place where parents and children idly sought to relieve the boredom of their leisure hours, lolling in armchairs and divans, or where they sat down to many courses of rich food cooked and served by a corps of domestics. It was a place of manifold interrelated activities, where each worked for all, where the hands and brains of each were constantly working in co-operation with others, where daily sacrifices of time and comfort and cherished desires were offered freely to one another, and where, under the stimulus of love as well as of necessity, the full strength and ability of each individual was called upon to serve and help the common cause. And thus from all this interrelated mechanism of family life there was turned out a product which combined the strength of iron with a beauty and delicacy of finish that can only be produced where stern toil is shaped by loving sacrifice. Most interesting is the fact that in the midst of the struggle for existence that seemed to absorb every energy, means were in some way found for intellectual development that fitted these boys to become leaders in the thought of their day. The life on the New England farm may well claim our attention.

Today we seek to produce character without the old manufacturing plant. Such homes seem to have sunk out of sight in the mists of the past along with the hand-hewn panelling and gambrel roofs and huge stone fireplaces that housed them. It is for that reason that we turn to the stained pages of old letters which by some mysterious process of television give us glimpses here and there into such a home and enable us to trace in its interrelated activities that wonderful process by which men strong and true and great of soul, and women unselfish, loyal and brave were shaped and sent forth into the world. The hand that penned these letters is long since turned to dust, but the pictures stand forth vivid and fresh as if we saw them today and through them all runs that undercurrent of devotion to the home.

They loved the old farm with its fields where the yellow wheat rippled in the breeze, and the tall corn stood with its golden tasselled ears, and the oats and clover showed their luscious green in contrast with the deep red of the buckwheat. And the wide pasture with its spreading elms beneath which some two dozen cows chewed the cud, and "four cherry-red

THE CHERRY COTTAGE

April fool calves" gambolled. Out beyond were the sheep, some seventy head, and beyond them the marsh, full of alders, bordering on the woodland, as glorious in its splendor of autumnal coloring as in the early Indian days. There was the orchard, its trees heavy with ruddy fruit, and nearby the cider mill, over whose construction the boys had spent many a weary day. Such was the estate that Archibald had developed by hard unremitting toil from boyhood to manhood, a great transformation from the wild hunting ground of the Indians that his grandfather had found here seventy-five years ago.

Archibald was beginning to show his years, but was still proud of his great strength and endurance—a man outwardly stern and severe, shaped by hard work and the cruel battle with poverty and adversity, but beneath the rough surface was the tenderest devotion to his three boys and his adopted brood. His life had been one long sacrifice—stern, bitter toil, in behalf of his mother and brothers, and later for his own boys and his brother's family of six. In desperate want and cruel disaster his courage had never failed; he had toiled on uncomplaining, unembittered, wresting year by year a blessing from the reluctant hands of old Mother Earth. The winter was supposed to be a time of respite but even when the crops were harvested there was still hard work.

Every day there were the twenty cows to be milked and the pigs to be fed. And when the shearing season approached, the seventy sheep must be washed and sheared without any of the modern machine shears. Then all hands would set off for the woodland, axe on shoulder, and cut and blast out the winter's supply of wood—enough to last out the bitter storms with the thermometer ten or twenty below zero. And the old ox team must haul it all down to the yard where it must be stacked. In winter they are up at dawn and trudge over the snow and watch the sun come up with a "faint cold light" and chop away until they can swallow with eager appetite their lunch of frozen potatoes, and frozen bread, and suck away at a lump of frozen cider. Even gathering apples is no soft job. Harry says: "My fingers were actually in more pain this morning picking up apples in the frost than if frozen and stiff with numbness, when Pa declared his were perfectly warm. All I get is he calls me a gosling and tells the story of Hans Berket making all blue in telling how cold it was and what he suffered. Ah if he had not had pluck in him he should have died on the road."

Pa did not encourage the boys to complain of the cold, and evidently believed that a large part of suffering was due to talking about it.

Mother and Electa and Lucinda and Huldah had their job too. In addition to the spinning there was the churning to be done—and the boys sometimes helped at that. Then there were luscious preserves to be put up—from the fruit in the garden—currant, quince, peach, and grape—enough to last the winter through. And, of course, the cooking and washing and mending and cleaning—enough to keep the girls busy through the day.

But what they enjoyed most was to gather in the kitchen of a winter's evening around the huge fireplace.

They sit around the fire with a bucket of apples and a pitcher of cider, and walnuts and chestnuts, and perhaps some doughnuts, too, and Pa tells hunting yarns of the old days, and the young folks gossip, or Mother reads aloud from one of Scott's novels while Pa protests against wasting their time on fiction and busies himself in the encyclopedia, until mother, with some malice, stops in the most exciting part, and Pa exclaims "Well! what happened then?"

Even on those evenings which they enjoyed most the work went on—transformed indeed to a pleasure by their mutual participation. Today we have but little idea of that relentless struggle for existence by which the pioneer farmer won a livelihood for himself and his children, toil so severe that it left him at night with every muscle aching. Harry writes: "I am tired to the backbone! Let a man hoe corn from 6 A.M. to 7 P.M. thermometer at 92, and unless his stuff is better than mine, his temper will be started, he will be pretty well annealed. If I make out to borrow a book it falls from my swollen hands before I can half read the title page. Last night I was worse off than I am now. I hobbled away to my room with my candle, took up Ben (Franklin) on Electricity and read one sentence over six or seven times without getting a sign of an idea—dropped my book and went to bed. It is not difficult for me to account for the stupidity of Farmers."

Few boys today would get far in their studies of science and literature after such days as these. Perhaps it was the stern discipline to which they were subjected that enabled these boys to go forward with their intellectual interests after a day of grilling work at the farm. In some way that New England home wakened in them the most consuming thirst for knowledge, and stimulated them not only to study but to experiment and explore in all directions. Their minds were keen to observe nature and sensitive to beauty, and they continually sought to express their ideas in mechanical inventions or in the forms of art and literature. The reaction of one keen mind upon another gave them an education far ahead of that of the schools.

Franklin had just opened up the wonders of electricity, and chemistry and physics were like a magic land of enchantment to the quick minds of the three boys, who were reading and experimenting with some quaint machine or invention every spare minute. Harry and Albert are at work on a steam motor car that they call the "kicker." They make a boiler of tin and a firebox, and the steam is driven through hollow axles that they manage somehow to forge. Harry tries compressed air as a motive force, when steam proves difficult to manage. Then he concentrates on a flying machine, and finally constructs a glider in which he makes quite a flight before he crashes to earth to the delight of his brothers.

But his chief interest is in drawing and painting. Up in his room he is always sketching, and on the wall is still to be seen the sketch he made of the view from the window. He is very clever at getting a likeness and draws portraits of his brothers which are quite remarkable and which are still preserved.

Then he gets old Grandpa Curtis to sit to him and the old gentleman is marvellously pleased when he sees his gnarled and wrinkled features looking down at him as large as life from the frame of an oil painting. Grandma Curtis too, grim and austere as a downright Roman grandmother looks out as natural as life. All this was without instruction, the product of keen minds in constant interaction and mutual stimulus. Those who see Harry's work say that he has genius and must go to the city and study. He prepared to go when he met with a bitter disappointment. His eyes gave out, and he was told that he must give up all hope of a higher education and live an outdoor life on the farm if he is to save them at all. It was a cruel blow, but Harry took it gallantly; cut off thus from his chief desire it seemed that his inner life and character grew to heights he might otherwise have failed to attain.

One might expect genius in one line, but it is surprising that the same New England home should have developed intellectual life of such different types and all so remarkable. Mark, tall, serious, dignified, even at twenty was the recognized genius of the family, with a penetrating mind of the philosopher. He was always thinking out some problem, and is constantly joked for his absentmindedness, but none can equal him in scholarship and they are all delighted with his poems and essays. As Harry took to art and Mark to philosophy, Albert had a natural bent to science. When still a mere boy he had a versatile mind, full of queer conceits and quaint fancies. He knew all the flowers and birds and was constantly working at some experiment. Their mutual helpfulness and interaction was a large factor in their development. Each was devoted to the others and continually seeking by some sacrifice to gain for the other some pleasure or profit.

John Henry, their little cousin, grew up to be a stalwart lad and helped with the work some years before he went South as an engineer. It was not long before Huldah was married to Theodore Pomeroy and left the old nest. Electa too took her flight to Boston with Lieutenant Webster, and wrote gay letters of her adventures in the social whirl with the young naval officers, her husband's friends. Mary and Lucinda remained and helped mother with the churning and housework, save when David Field dropped in and took Lucinda off to some entertainment.

Devoted to one another as were the boys, they were strangely different. Even at twenty-five Mark had a certain dignity and austerity of bearing, derived perhaps from much teaching of school, which overawed the "hité tité" young ladies of Stockbridge. Harry writes that Miss P. and Mrs. S. asked to see his portrait of Mark. "Mrs. S. said she had seen a great many heads intended to represent Study but had never seen one which indicated such thought and entire abstraction—in fact she said that it was one of the most apostolic faces she ever saw. Miss P. said Mrs. S. made Mark an apostle and she would make him a saint next. Mrs. S. said there was no need of that; he was a saint already!" A strange opinion for a girl to give of a young fellow of Mark's age! but indicative of thc casual impression he made. Harry and Albert certainly made no such impression!—Harry in the midst of all the sports, the life of all the parties and dances, beloved of all the girls—and Albert full of mischief, with his quaint phrases, and rather sardonic humor.

In accordance with the old New England idea his "will had been broken" at the age of four. His mother long remembered the struggle, when he refused to obey and was whipped, and refused again, and was whipped again more severely and again refused, and the punishments went on until his mother was frightened and feared some injury. Then after the most severe punishment of all he ran to her, threw his arms around her neck and sobbed: "I'll be good. I'll be good." Sooner or later every man must learn that he cannot have everything he wants and that he must adjust himself to the laws of the universe and of society. The New Englander believed in training him thus as a child, instead of trying to preserve as long as possible the illusion that he is to have what he wants. Cruel though the method seems it probably saved much suffering, for the only road to happiness is through the acceptance of law and the sooner the adjustment is made the nearer is the man to happiness.

Such a method might easily have embittered, had not the children been conscious of the greatness of the mother's love. A wonderful woman was the mother of the boys—erect and sprightly even to the age of ninety-six, with a quick well-trained mind a keen sense of humor, great joy of life, which irradiated her home, so that the boys all felt, in spite of their stern toil, that it was the happiest spot on earth. They loved to see her sitting erect in her chimney corner in her white frilled cap, busy at her knitting, or peeking out from beneath her great green calash to see how Pa would take some sly shaft she had let fly at him. Sitting there in her corner in the background she was nevertheless in some mysterious way the mainspring of that surprising intellectual life that sprang from Cherry Cottage.

CHAPTER IV

LIFE AT COLLEGE IN 1823

The time had come at last when the happy family life was to be broken up. Mark had won out in his battle for a liberal education, and had returned from the South with $540 in his pocket. In 1822 he was able to start in on his course at Williams College in the sophomore class, two years later than he had hoped, but perhaps all the better able to appreciate what the college had to give him, and certainly far better able to produce upon the college the impression which was to result in his permanent connection with it. Little did he realize when he entered that, save for a brief period from 1827–31, his whole life would be centered in that college, first as undergraduate from 1822–24, then as tutor from 1825–27, and finally as professor in 1831. The case of Albert was no less remarkable. Entering in 1824, two years later than Mark, he was at loose ends for one year after he graduated in 1826, a mere boy of nineteen, and then was called back to be a tutor at Williams where he remained the rest of his life. During their lifetime these two men poured into the college all that they had of knowledge and inspiration, Albert on the line of science, and Mark in philosophy. Thus for sixty-five years, from 1822 to 1887, either one or the other of the Hopkins brothers was connected with the college. The picture of the college, given in the letters of the boys when they entered, is a strange and amazing one, when we compare it with the college as we know it today.

The American college had advanced somewhat from the day when old Ephraim had exhorted his son at Princeton to learn to spell correctly and put his capitals in the right place. There were now two buildings at Williams, the old West College containing the chapel and the lower classes on the central hill, and East College where dwelt the seniors and juniors, on the eastern hill. This had been built in part from the proceeds of a lottery, and in part from a grant of land in Maine, given by the state, from which the college derived $9500.

A dormitory was a poor place for a chapel, and the benches in the chapel were so impossible that the students sought for comfort by sprawling with their feet extended on the seats during prayers, to the disgust of the president, who wished all things done decently and reverently. He protested in vain and finally decided that a chapel must be built where they could worship reverently. Doctor Edward Dorr Griffin, the president, was one of the most eloquent pulpit orators in New England, of commanding presence, six feet three inches in height; and of 240 pounds' weight. Doctor Moore had tipped the scales at the same amount, with the result that when Mark was later proposed for the presidency one critic remarked

WEST COLLEGE, ORIGINAL BUILDING OF WILLIAMS COLLEGE

that he lacked "abdominal dignity." Doctor Griffin was well proportioned, however; his hair was white, and he had an aspect of "venerableness and of brooding benignity" that created a great impression on every one. He had a small nose and small eyes which yet kindled to brilliancy as he spoke. His voice had extraordinary compass and melody. Like Whitefield he could so pronounce the word "Mesopotamia" as to bring tears to the eyes, and on occasion he could "bellow like a bull of Bashan" to quote Professor Perry. Perhaps none but he could have raised by their eloquence $10,000 to build a chapel for a little unknown college in the remote hills. After demonstrating that he could only afford to give $100 himself, he finally started the subscription list with a contribution of $1000 and his appeals did the rest. He supervised all the construction, with the result that Griffin Hall with its tall cupola and great fan windows remains one of the most beautiful colonial buildings in New England. As president of Andover Seminary he had built on Andover Hill a house that still commands the admiration of the critics, but had so overrun his budget in making the building beautiful that he received severe criticism. He had learned by experience and kept within his budget at Williams. He was graduated from Yale in 1790 and had been minister of the Park St. Church in Boston and a pillar of orthodoxy. He was a stickler for decorum. He always addressed the students as "Young Gentlemen," and was so exaggeratedly polite that many considered him pompous and affected. He was very particular, however, never to "Mister" an undergraduate.

He came to the college in 1821, the year before Mark entered. Mark was much impressed by his dignity and eloquence, but thought that he emphasized form above substance. He was particularly annoyed when during church service the good doctor stopped in the midst of an eloquent period and requested Mark to face him and keep his eyes attentively fixed upon the preacher, which Mark thought unwarranted interference with his personal liberty. When Doctor Griffin preached in the chapel or schoolhouse it would be so crowded that the candles went out for lack of oxygen. Once a week the college was assembled in the chapel, and each in turn declaimed a "piece." The president then criticized his effort. Mark states that the doctor spent more time in training them to bow correctly than on the speech itself.

There were but two professors so that the underclassmen had to gather what learning they could from young tutors, usually recent graduates.

Professor P. K. Kellog held the class of languages from his advent in 1815 for some thirty years. He was a dry-as-dust drillmaster, of the old schoolmaster type. He lived in West College and every night he prowled around peering into the students' rooms on the lookout for any misbehavior, so that they made use of his initials P. K. to call him "Peek." Professor Chester Dewey taught the sciences and was fortunately a very inspiring teacher. He had studied theology with our old friend Doctor West of Stockbridge, but had been lured away by the charm of science. Williams was quite unique in that day in the attention paid to the sciences. As already noted the world was just awakening to the great discoveries in chemistry, electricity, and physics generally. Williams had been fortunate in having eminent scientists such as Professor Olds and Professor Amos Eaton as teachers from the start, and Dewey and Emmons proved worthy successors.

The original law of the college provided a definite curriculum. For the first year, English, Latin, Greek, and French. For the second, the languages, and also arithmetic, geography, algebra, geometry, conic sections, rhetoric, and logic. For the third, trigonometry, navigation, surveying, natural philosophy, astronomy, and chemistry, and for the last year metaphysics, ethics, history, national law, civil polity. The president taught the senior class and covered nearly all their subjects.

Professor Dewey taught the juniors and held them all thrilled by the new world of mystery and miracle to which he introduced them. To Mark and Albert the recitations were as fascinating as a séance of Houdini, or the performance of an Indian juggler. Albert tells how the professor enjoyed adding to the thrill by pretending that his experiment would not work, and then setting it off with a terrific bang. He would call up a boy and pour alcohol into his hand,

and then touch it off with an electric spark, causing the youth to leap in terror, to the great joy of the class. Or he would pass an electric current through the class and give them a sudden terrifying shock. One day he covered their faces with phosphorus, so that, in the darkened room they shone like ghosts. Mark's letters are full of these amazing miracles, performed before his eyes, which seemed to open a new world to his thought and turned him temporarily away from philosophy to science. The magic lantern filled him with astonishment and admiration hard to conceive in this age of the cinema.

There was a dearth of materials. In the freshman recitation room in 1822 there was only one bench with no back. The students assessed themselves six cents apiece to buy another. Blackboards were unknown. The students drew diagrams on paper and slates, and Professor Dewey drew his illustrations and worked out his problems with chalk on the floor of the recitation room; Professor Kellogg was the only one to boast the luxury of a carpet in his room.

Education depended entirely on the contact of student and teacher in those days. There were no material aids. Personal influence and intimate relationship counted for much more than today. It was really a case of the oft-quoted log and the teacher. The tutors received $400, the two professors $800, and the president $1200, not a tremendous budget. Each boy was supposed to get through his education for $400—Mark had earned a little extra.

The students roomed in the college buildings and boarded in various places in town. Mark at first was very elegant and boarded with fifteen others at the hotel kept by Mrs. Hawkes, for the sum of a dollar a week. Albert, when he came, boarded at Noyes's. It was then fashionable for the boys to board themselves in college. A group of nineteen succeeded in feeding themselves for sixty cents or seventy cents a week apiece, and Albert tells us that one group got by at the rate of ten cents a week per person, which in this age seems utterly preposterous. One only regrets that Albert did not give the bill of fare.

In addition to the West and East Colleges the college owned but two houses: the president's house, a small building on the north side of the street, that was later removed to the site of the present library and occupied for many years by Professor Safford, and a small house that stood on the hill near the spot occupied by the present art building. The college owned no land, save three acres around the president's house. There were no collections of minerals or flora and fauna. Chemical apparatus consisted of a blow pipe and a few retorts. The complete outfit for physics and astronomy was contained in a small room in East College, and the library was in another small room in West College. The college buildings were surrounded by woodpiles, for each student had to buy his own wood and saw and split it himself, and one of Mark's first jobs was to bargain with an old farmer for a couple of cords which he suspected were short measure. To provide himself with water he had to take his pail to the spring at the foot of the East College hill, and carry it back laboriously up the West College hill, a tedious and difficult performance which did not encourage frequent bathing. A gymnasium had never been heard of, and it was not until Mark was a tutor that he was sent to Northampton to investigate this new idea. As a result of his expedition a swing and some parallel bars were erected in the open air near East College. Later Albert was made gymnasium director and erected a small building where the students who still felt the need of exercise after sawing their wood and carrying their water, could be supplied.

Mark Hopkins went up to take his examinations for entrance at commencement in September, 1822. The commencement was now a little later than formerly. It was a grand festal occasion for the folk of Northern Berkshire. The farmers came from far around to listen to the speeches which supplied mental pabulum for the year, and their wives all appeared in their choicest garments, for it was their greatest opportunity to reveal their charms and their finery. When Mark went up to secure a seat in the church, he found the fence which was the general hitching post, lined with buckboards, buggies, farm wagons, barouches, and one or two elegant chaises. It seemed as if all the peddlers in the state had collected, for standing near the door were gingerbread sellers, booths selling candy, cakes, and peanuts; vendors of pins, lead pencils, shaving soap, bracelets, and jewelry; all crying their wares with Yankee impudence and humor which kept the crowd in a roar. Here and there a wrestling match was in progress, between rival farm hands. Barrels of cider were being broached and even stronger drink was at hand. Mark heard the band strike up and saw the procession starting from the hill in front of East College. Down the street it came beneath the arching elms; alumni of twenty years' standing, the distinguished body of trustees, followed by the majestic and portly president, then the seniors followed by the student body, the men decorated with the pink and blue ribbons of the rival debating societies. On they came through the great archway of West College and up the wide village street to the white steepled church, a building much larger and more commodious than that which Mary had seen twenty eight years before. It was only with difficulty that Mark could get a seat when they had once poured into the church. It was a sudden change from the rough jokes of the uncouth crowd without, to the solemn atmosphere and classic diction within. Mark listened, wondering how long it would be before he had a share in this scene.

The day before he had tried the examinations for the sophomore class. In addition to the subjects given Jared, he had to pass in Euclid, Latin composition, the Iliad, and higher algebra. He then worked on the farm for four weeks and returned to enter on his studies. He paid down the sixteen dollars for his tuition for the term, one dollar for rent, and seventeen cents for use of the library and was assigned a room in the college with a classmate named Mooar, a tall cadaverous chap who died of consumption just after graduation. He learned that the term would end the third Wednesday in December, when the students had their long vacation of six weeks to enable them to teach school in the winter term, for many paid their tuition in this manner. He would return in February for the second term which lasted until the first Wednesday in May, when he would have threc weeks vacation for work on the farm. He would return again at the end of the month for the summer term which lasted until the commencement in August.

We wonder sometimes why college vacations are so much longer than those in the business world, and this is the reason. The vacations were not for recreation but for work, and were planned to enable the boys to do the necessary farm work at home and also to earn the money for their tuition by teaching school. Mark found himself well isolated in the lonely little valley in the mountains. Once a week a solitary messenger on horseback came over Hoosac Mountain with the Boston mail and papers, and once a week a man named Green drove a one-horse wagon up from Stockbridge with the mail from home.

Mark was given a small volume of college laws and told that in the middle of the second term he would come up for the ceremony of matriculation, in which he was to sign a solemn agreement to obey the college laws, and was then received as a member of the college. The laws provided that each morning and evening the president should pray in the chapel and that any student who was absent should be fined four cents. The tardy paid two cents, seemingly a small price for ten minutes more in bed. At sunset in the evening preceding the Lord's Day, students must abstain from diversions of all kinds and retire to their chambers. "Whoever shall profane the Lord's Day by visiting or walking in the streets or fields, or using any diversion, shall be fined not above one dollar, or make a public confession, or be rusticated, according to the gravity of the offence." "Any student absent from Public Worship shall be fined fifty cents. Those who arrive after the first singing shall be fined ten cents."

"If any student admits a barber to his rooms on the Lord's Day he shall be fined fifty cents, and one dollar for repeating the offence."

"If a scholar shall associate with a person of dissolute morals he shall be fined thirty-four cents," which seems a surprisingly exact estimate to put upon corrupt influences.

"If he shall wear woman's apparel he shall be liable to suspension or rustication."

"If any student shall for the purpose of tippling frequent any tavern or house of ill fame he shall be fined no more than one dollar."

"If he shall be guilty of profane oaths or singing

obscene songs he shall be fined not more than one dollar and a half."

"If he shall play at cards, dice, billiards, or backgammon he shall be publicly fined five dollars." This seems to have been the climax of criminal behavior.

"If he shall be guilty of making tumultuous or indecent noises he shall be fined one dollar or make public confession."

"If a student shall be actor or spectator at any stage plays or theatrical entertainments he shall be punished by a fine of one dollar and on repetition shall be liable to rustication."

"He shall not be permitted to attend more than three balls annually."

These rules gave Mark a theme for meditation for the next three months until he signed them.

Nothing is more interesting than the varying scale of moral values as mankind develops. Each community and age has its own tabus, and we cannot help wondering why at Williams the extreme obliquity should have been wearing women's clothes and playing backgammon, and why walking in the fields on the Lord's Day should have been a more serious offense than immorality, intoxication, and singing obscene songs.

The bell rang for prayers before sunrise and the boys had to rise in the dark and run through the snow, some of them half a mile—to arrive in chapel on time. The chapel had a stove but there was no fire in it in the morning, and the scripture was read by candle light.

When Mark entered college he had three recitations each day; one before breakfast, one before dinner and one before supper, and there were six hours a day set apart for study, in the fashion of a boys' school. He found no difficulty in preparing his lessons in this period and got to bed by 9:30. He notes with surprise that many stayed up until 12 or 1! This was apparently due to that strange desire of youth to do something wild and desperate, like the theological student, determined on wickedness, who sat up till midnight, smoked a cigarette, said damn! and went to bed with his boots on. In addition to the cultural subjects and the sciences, chemistry, and physics, he took mineralogy, botany, and French—quite a comprehensive curriculum for 1822. There were fourteen in his class and the whole college numbered less than one hundred.

He was somewhat appalled at the prospect of an examination at the end of each term on all the studies he had taken since entering college, an accumulating affair that was truly terrifying at the end of his college course. The examination was oral, before an examining board of venerable gentlemen who sat up in a solemn row. But when it came to the point it proved not so terrible as he had anticipated. Every one passed and he says "the Reverend and Honorable Examiners nodded and slept half the time, though in their declaration they say 'after diligent examination, etc.' "

Wednesday and Saturday afternoons were free;

Mark would read, and Albert, when he was in college, would get into a game of ball, twenty on a side which would last about two hours, played with great enthusiasm and excitement, for "we had three or four bottles on the carpet, and some of the fellows got pretty well on toward the West Indies before we got through."

We have already noted that intoxication was a minor offence compared with playing backgammon.

The students sometimes petitioned the faculty for a day off to climb the mountains and the privilege was granted to six from each class, a rule having been passed to allow no more than that number to be absent at a time. This custom has developed into the holiday now known as Mountain Day. As the students chopped their wood in the college yard, by the end of winter the campus was littered with chips, and a special holiday, known as Chip Day, was granted, in which the whole college turned out to clean up the grounds. Another somewhat unique holiday was granted in the autumn to enable the whole college to go out and gather chestnuts.

Mark was a successful speaker and was one of the prize declaimers or Moonlight speakers chosen to speak the night before commencement. According to custom this entailed the privilege of treating the class. This custom had proved dangerous and had been forbidden by the faculty. The orators determined to treat none the less, and the two lower classes took their share of the liquor and marched off a mile from the college to enjoy their potations in peace without any disagreeable interruptions. Mark says "they returned through the street with considerable irregularity and noise, and the footing of several as they stepped, seemed rather precarious. However, they did return; most of them attended recitation and all was quiet till perhaps half after eleven." The liquor seems to have had a dangerous afterkick for at that hour "one of them set on fire a certain small college outbuilding —as soon as it began to go, they rang the bell and cried Fire! They rousted several townspeople and all college and after seeing it burn," says Mark, "they were still." A wise attitude on their part one would suppose. The faculty did not act until the next week when they began an exhaustive investigation. Mark notes the strange fact that although many knew who started the fire the faculty was unable to find the culprit. They had to rest content with imposing a fine varying from one dollar to five dollars on those who had joined the party in the fields. This greatly annoyed the celebrants and they drew up a petition and list of grievances which was duly presented. Mark thinks that the end will be that some who are dissatisfied will leave college. He states that he himself treated "in a regular manner and without any great outrages and was suffered to go clear." It is not surprising that when Harry received this report he should have written: "I suspect you have not told the whole of your own story of which everything seems to be so calm, for I cannot see why you have not infringed the injunctions of the faculty as much as any one."

In those days it was quite a favorite little escapade to set the college on fire. Later when Albert was tutor in March, 1829, the students started by burning down the "town house." He writes: "Pa says you know that one thing follows another—and so it is. About three this afternoon there was a cry of fire in the hall—Going out—'Run with your pails upstairs!' The South End of the College roof was on fire. About a dozen of us manned the roof, of both Colleges and the town rallied—and we had it! The wind blew brisk out of the North and for some time I assure you I stood ' in suspen.' At length, however, we conquered it. There will be more." He evidently feels that the students had not yet finished with their little joke. Two weeks later he writes: "A week since I wrote Harry telling him that the College roof took fire and concluded by saying as Pa always does 'there will be more fires.' " About a week later the alarm was given: "The College was afire in the garret. It was evidently the work of an incendiary. After a tedious examination we expelled two and sent one away. It was perhaps nothing more than a boyish freak!" Evidently quite the thing to be expected from college men of that day, but it seemed necessary to treat it with severity or there would soon be no college left.

Later in 1832 when Mark was professor he writes casually of the celebration on the Fourth of July. "The boys here have thrown fireballs for several years contrary to law, and having thrown them into the College last year and set it on fire, we determined to stop them this, and we did it, but we were obliged to be up until near two and to be constantly in motion." A strange occupation this would be for college professors today to patrol all night to keep students from burning down the college—but accepted then as quite in the natural routine. "In order to make a diversion while we were at the West College, they fired the outbuilding over here, but some clever fellows put it out before we got here, so they were disappointed all round. That was a little too much so they tried it again Friday night, when they were as completely put down as before. Only one student threw a ball, and him the C. (Albert) took after and tore his coat off. Then the fellow took to his heels again and the C. after him till he came to a kind of a ditch, where he tumbled and the C. on top of him. Some fellow was so much piqued that on Saturday he set the West College on fire, but it was put out without doing much damage." This was pushing the matter a little bit too far and action was taken as follows: "Having sent off three fellows we shall probably send another, besides various fines and warnings." In the main, however, there seems to have been a spirit of kindly tolerance toward such boyish pranks.

At times they seem to have been unduly severe, so that rebellion resulted among the students. While Mark was a senior, our friend Kup, who had distinguished himself as the impersonator of Holy

Daniel, and who was now a student, applied for leave to walk to Lebanon Springs and take the baths for his health, and also to see about a position in a school. When his request was denied, he went without leave, and received a public reprimand and suspension, which automatically deprived him of a scholarship fund upon which he was relying to finish his course. The students felt this to be a great injustice. They gathered a group and fastened Professor Kellogg and the two tutors in their rooms and barricaded the doors and covered them with tar. Then they broke into the bellroom at midnight and rang the bell, "set up a tremendous yell all over college," and tore down the professor's woodhouse. To show their sympathy with Kup they gave him a letter of recommendation and raised fifteen dollars to help him out. He left college the next morning. When Doctor Griffin tried to address them on the subject they "made such a scraping" that he could not be heard. The faculty discovered who rang the bell. Mark was not in that, but he suspected that they had Albert's name. Several of Mark's class were in it and he feared they would get into trouble.

In certain ways the collegian of those days was surprisingly immature if not childish, while in other respects he seems far more mature than the boys of today. When it came to self-reliance and ability to earn a living and make a way in the world, these young men seem far ahead of the college boy of today. Their pranks and amusements, however, would be regarded as childish by young men accustomed to spend their holidays in the night clubs of Broadway.

Psychologists tell us that to destroy and to make a loud noise are the activities that appeal most to the mind of a boy, as they demonstrate his growing sense of his own powers. The students of that day gave abundant evidence of these characteristics. One favorite pursuit was to take a huge back log that some unfortunate underclassman had laboriously lugged up the long flights of West College, and roll it all the way downstairs, with a noise like thunder and the threat of tearing the building to pieces. When Albert was tutor in November, 1827, he writes: "I had got myself gathered up to write when suddenly I heard a log rolled down stairs. The noise did not arouse me." Evidently it was a customary experience of trifling significance. "In about five minutes another started and, as I judged, lodged. Having learned therefore from rolling rocks down Monument Mountain what the result would be—to wit—that the fool would go and start it again—I hied me out and caught a glimpse of a man's back just as the door shut. I immediately entered and found four very deaconly looking young men sitting around a fire. They all rose with great respect and with a look as much as to say 'What would the Tutor wish?' I clapped my hat down on the table—says I 'My business here is to find out who rolled down that log: Did you do it?' 'No, Sir.' Thus it went round, no one did it or knew who did. Turning then to the first—'I suppose it's allowed on all hands that one of you four did it—you'll allow that, do you?' Unfortunately he didn't know whether he did or not. Having therefore cross-questioned sufficiently, I turned to the fellow and says I: 'Friend if I'm not much deceived you are the man who rolled down that log. You'll own it, won't you?' I saw the flesh begin to quiver—then you see I pinched, 'Come,' says I 'I'm waiting.' Now the fellow had denied plumply and repeatedly that he did it or knew who did. The case therefore was a hard one and I saw that to compass my end I must sink down into a principle of human nature—so throwing myself right on a level with him in a sort of laughing way, 'Come! Come!' says I, 'You may as well own it.' Seeing me look rather good natured he said that as he was coming upstairs, the log lay right on a tippee; he just touched it and it rolled. Then planting myself on my heels, says I, 'Neighbor, you'll find it cheaper to tell me the truth the first time. I'm one of them sort, etc.' Thinking it best, however, not to kill a second time a man once dead, I left the room only remarking that I didn't know whether I should take the matter up or not."

One is impressed by the respectful attitude of these youths toward a tutor who was not yet twenty-one and probably younger than themselves. Albert though genial and friendly with all, was possessed of those dominating eyes that see through men and overawe them, and he had an inerrant intuition which enabled him to solve many a psychological problem. A year later he showed even more plainly his power to handle the log rollers. There had been a veritable epidemic of log rolling. He writes: "One afternoon, going to a Faculty dinner, we found College on our return an utter chaos, Logs, stones, bricks, ashes, water pails and everything nameless thrown down and dashed. 'Twas then just recitation time. They expected I would storm away some about the impropriety of each—inquire into it perhaps a little and there end it. Not so I."

One of his first principles in dealing with youth was never to do what they expected. He thus kept them in a constant state of bewilderment and anxiety. "The Recitation Room was entered that afternoon without even showing that I had noticed the scrape except in the case of one man whom I suspected—him I fastened my eye balls onto, and bored them into him like two spike gimblets." Those accusing, all-penetrating eyes were like a red hot probe and harder to endure than the most vituperative tongue lashing. "The class noticed it, and he withered like an aspen. With that I left." And he left behind him an atmosphere of suspense far more trying than accusation. "When evening came I stationed myself in one of those great two-handed chairs and whilst Caulkins sat with pen and ink ready to take down every word, proceeded to examine. The modes were different according to the human nature of each. With some after having in a very mild way asked about 20 preliminaries so fast and disconnected that they did not know what they meant (no more than two toads want a tail) I proceeded with a kind of clear headed look such as the ancient Tutor used to put on when he thought he had said something pretty keen—to say —'You either did it or you did it not, and you either know that you did it, or you know that you did not do it—and first, do you know that you did not do it?' When they did not know whether they knew whether they did it or not, then I cramped 'em right up. Another way was to keep hitching up to them, making as though you was chewing tobacco, or sometimes giving over the whole ground with a kind of sudden start—sitting down by them and saying, 'Come, neighbor, you've lied about this; now you may as well own it as to parley.' To one fellow after having denied pertinaciously, said I, 'Hamilton, how would the size of that log you rolled down compare with that chest?' 'Not so large, Sir!'—But the morning star would rise ere I told you the particulars of an examination which lasted one evening and all the next forenoon. Suffice it to say that some were scared—some scolded, some—had it told to them to their face that they were liars—some lied to the last. This is a distinct factitive view of the scrape of the fatal 28th. Ponder it well ye that effect to be elected tutors!"

Indeed it would seem clear that a tutor in those days needed to have a rare knowledge of human psychology and an eye that could probe the depths of deceit.

The honor system has done something for us and the modern student ordinarily would not lie so pertinaciously.

Such an ebullition was somewhat unusual even in those days and Albert explains that the class of which he has charge is the largest in the college, and rather an "unsteady" class even during the year before. "This year there have joined it a number of young men from Albany—determined to show the College 'what it was to have a scrape.' "

The chief amusement seems to have been horseplay of some sort. Albert tells how when he was a student his roommate started scuffling with a caller, and "betook themselves to the water pail, and discharged the contents of that onto each other alternately. When the water was spent you might see the pail, wash bowl and drinking glass sailing swiftly by each other and encountering their craniums with terrible percussion, which together with the roar of about half the College who had assembled at the field of action, and Morgan lifting up his voice like a pelican in the wilderness, with a lot of ayes and fury, made no small sport. The case was tried by a jury who sentenced each to pay a pint." Yes, those were vigorous days when men were men, and hard knocks and smashed property were the order of the day.

They were at times subject to repentance, and after an eloquent sermon by Mr. Hewitt, which resulted in a prohibition edict throughout the town, the students inserted a clause in the constitution of their society forbidding all drinking. But when the effect of the sermon wore off they decided they had acted under a "mental delusion." Unfortunately there was an article in the constitution forbidding them to rescind any vote. They got around the difficulty by rescinding the article forbidding them to rescind, and they were then free to rescind the vote that forbade the use of spirituous liquors. The which shows the value of collegiate training in parliamentary procedure.

The attitude of the faculty seems to us that of the teachers in a boys' school. Albert notes that they forbade the students to arrange a dinner on the Fourth of July. One would suppose this to be outside their jurisdiction and indeed it aroused extremely bitter feelings.

The faculty tried with a sort of elephantine condescension to get onto friendly terms with the students and their efforts greatly amused Albert, who was then a tutor. He naturally made friends with every one, and considered their voluminous discussions of methods to "come nearer" to the students ridiculous and self-stultifying. He tried to stop the discussion, but they insisted that each member of the faculty should bring in a plan of approach to the students, at the next meeting. Professor Kellog outlined a long speech, and "gave a list of questions proper to be asked—among which was this—'How long since you've heard from home?' This—take notice—and such like questions were to be asked either on the walk, or in the rooms—where we were to call in an informal manner (Professor Porter) and without seeming to come as members of the faculty." Albert says he sat by with an appearance rather "crank," and when asked for his plan, said, " 'Doctor Griffin, there are certain invariable rules I have laid down for the regulation of my conduct toward white and black, and I don't know as students will form any exception.' The doctor having looked sometime at me somewhat surprised, said, 'Are you through, Sir?' Says I. 'Yes, Sir!' Some days after the scrapes began, and I did not hear anything more about motive, making moral power bear, etc."

It was sufficiently evident to him that students should be treated as human beings and not as students. "Scrape" was then the technical word for a spree or escapade. Some regulating force was evidently needed. He says, "The general aspect of the term was boisterous. Otis had been sent away for assault and battery, Cannon rusticated—very many admonished. The West College Cop says (who by the way has had his ash pails—6 or 8—dashed to pieces, brooms stolen, etc.). 'Never was anything so bad as it is now.' There is reason to believe Satan entered College soon after the death of Ware."

On Chip Day it was customary to impose a fine of fifty cents on all who did not pick up chips. Even the faculty paid and the proceeds went to buying beer for the weary and thirsty students. The effect was sometimes a bit over-stimulating. Mark tells, when he was professor, how after imbibing, the crowd all went down to the Methodist prayer meeting and participated in such fashion that their prayers and exhortations completely upset the decorum of the meeting, and occasioned violent complaints to the faculty.

Reading these vivid pictures of college life a hundred years ago, one becomes sadly conscious that the world is growing old. All that jubilant, irrepressible youth seems to have disappeared. Many of these boys came from the hill towns and remote farms of Vermont and New Hampshire, and though outwardly uncouth, had great vigor and determination of character in spite of those boyish escapades. It is surprising to find what serious work in the world was accomplished by the perpetrators of these boyish pranks.

CHAPTER V

RELIGIOUS LIFE IN 1825

So far nothing has been said of religion, but certainly not because it bore no part in the home or the college. As we note how constantly religion was brought into every occasion, and read the continual exhortations to piety, we are prone to accuse the early New Englander of hypocrisy. It seems impossible that so much religion could have been natural. Our interests lie chiefly in other channels and we incline to think of religion as a disagreeable and uninteresting subject cultivated only by those who wanted to make their salvation sure. Those who take this point of view totally misapprehend the old New England. Religion was to them a matter of supreme interest. Three-fourths of the books in their libraries were on religious subjects. Points of doctrine were discussed with a zest that today seems incomprehensible. They would drink in sermons an hour long and talk them over for hours afterward. The reason was that God was to them a King more real than the King of England. They were on a journey to His land and there was just one way of getting there. They studied this with the same care that we would devote to the itinerary of a necessary European trip. If they disregarded the directions or disobeyed the laws they risked disastrous shipwreck and terrible suffering. The pit of Hell was close beside them, one false step and they were lost. There was only one safe path and it was of supreme importance not to miss it. There was great discussion as to what was the right way, and every one was vitally interested in finding it.

In the realm of thought a great struggle for existence was in progress. New England had been torn by the discussion between the Calvinist and Arminian theories. The Calvinist assigned to God the type of absolute sovereignty achieved by Henry VIII, who put to death without scruple every one who disagreed with him. Whether he executed apparently innocent ladies, or tortured to death men who proclaimed their loyalty—whatever he did was right. Whatever opinion he held was right, and it was right because he held it. There was a transfer to God of this fully developed idea of the sovereignty of Kings. Righteousness was what God did and said, whether it seemed so to man or not.

The Calvinist viewed man with utter pessimism. He was a worthless worm, completely impregnated with sin. How Adam could have conveyed to his descendants such a loathsome mass of guilt and sin seems mysterious, but it was there, hidden beneath an appearance of virtue in every charming lady and kindly gentleman. To think that any amount of virtuous behavior and self-sacrificing deeds would make one acceptable to God or save him from the eternal torment he deserved as the vehicle of such wickedness, was the height of presumption. His only hope was that as Christ had borne the weight of the infinite punishment due to man, God in His mercy might assign a portion of this atonement to him, and save him, not because of any deeds of his or even because of his faith, but simply because God had so willed it. Man had no choice; he was predestined to wrath or glory. This was real sovereignty of the Henry VIII type.

The Arminian took a more hopeful view of man. He was indeed in bad case, but he was free to choose good or evil, and God would reward his virtue. He was more of a constitutional monarch, willing to give his subjects a chance to assist in the progress of his kingdom.

The autocratic state church apparently felt that they could supply all the autocracy necessary and upheld the Arminian God; while Jonathan Edwards and the free churches, who rebelled against the authority of the ministers, supported the autocratic Calvinist principles. Free will was upheld by autocracy, and autocracy by those who asserted freedom—part of the general inconsistency of human nature.

Edwards's eloquence had undermined the authority of the state church and for a time Calvinism was in the ascendant. But he went too far. The reason that men hold such doctrines is that they do not fully see their implications. Edwards's logical mind pushed the old doctrine to its terrible conclusions, and the common sense of the laity rebelled against such a God as the doctrine implied. It was just at this time when Edwards's logic had undermined his own ramparts, that Mark entered the field. Stockbridge had been in the center of the battle, and between Doctor Samuel Hopkins's system and Doctor West, Mark had been well trained in the system.

Edwards made Christianity depend on conviction of sin and a miraculous conversion, with the result that the chief interest of every community was in the periods of "awakening," when they were swept by violent emotion. Men prayed and worked for their recurrence and sought to secure the conversion of their friends. The chief desire of every Christian mother and wife was to secure the conversion of her children or husband. These beliefs had a vast effect on the life and character of the day both for good and ill. The case of Mary Hopkins was a very unusual one. We have shown how she perused the Hopkintonian system, and although she admitted that it was probably correct, stated that her unregenerate heart refused to accept it. Until the day of her death she remained outside the fold of the church, a most surprising attitude in that day for a devoted Christian mother. In spite of her own stand she worked earnestly for the conversion of her sons. We gain the best idea of her real feeling about religion from a letter she wrote Mark when she discovered his discouragement and confusion of mind. She spoke of the death of a friend and added:

"To one unprepared the change of worlds must be

dreadful, but to those who are prepared, oh how joyful, freed from sin, and evermore beholding Him who is of purer eyes than to behold iniquity, and whilst unprepared let us not consider ourselves reasonable, rational creatures since no more is required of us than to love a being who is of himself infinitely lovely. I desire to be thankful that I would not ask for salvation upon more reasonable terms. How can we withhold our hearts from One who is altogether lovely, all glorious and all sufficient? Who would not wish for such a friend, is He not just such an One as we need both in time and eternity? Could we gain riches and honor, kingdoms and crowns, all earthly treasures, with the dearest of friends, still we must feel notwithstanding every effort a painful and distressing void which nothing could satisfy, short of an interest in the blessed Redeemer."

Here is real religion, something proved to have greater value than riches and honor—the friendship of God. It had kept her happy and serene through hard drudgery and pain and disappointment. The creed of the church repelled her. She could not sincerely accept that kind of religion. It is pathetic that here we find her urging Mark to accept her religion of the heart, while later it is he who urges upon her the religion she could not accept.

She is insistent and speaks of the danger that death will find him still undecided. He responds that death can make no change in character, and that Heaven would bring "no happiness to men governed by such tastes and habits as they commonly exhibit." It would be a pity to go to Heaven and not like it. Mark suggests that what is necessary is to acquire a character that would be happy there. She does not argue with him, but begs him to "supplicate the throne of Divine Mercy that he may be led into all truth."

She, herself, would never make profession of her faith. Her mind was too well balanced to be plunged into conviction of sin and she would not pretend to feelings she did not have. Perhaps her keen sense of humor made her immune to the old doctrine.

It is a strange puzzle that she should have urged her boys to a decision she would never take herself even when they insisted that without it she might be eternally lost.

Archibald is almost as much a puzzle to us today. We find no mention of religion in his letters, but apparently the boys never ventured to urge upon him the need of salvation.

Archibald seems to have been an exception to the general interest in religion. Apparently it was something he took for granted, but never mentioned. His letters are free from those pious phrases that are so common in epistles of the period. He said little and worked hard—upright in all his dealings, he performed his duty as a matter of course, and the boys would have expected water to run uphill before "Pa" would neglect an obligation or leave a duty undone.

The most surprising effect of the Calvinist system with its teaching of the vileness and guilt of man in the sight of God was its effect on the subconscious mind. It was valuable to counteract that tendency of man to think more highly of himself than he ought to think and to be discontented with his share of the world's blessings, but upon sensitive souls who were inclined to doubt themselves it had a most disastrous effect.

Mark and Albert had sufficient intelligence to think it out, but it had got so into their innermost fibers in childhood that it was bound to influence them subconsciously. In Mark it showed itself in predominant fits of melancholy which his mother called his "Highpo," a sense of unworthiness and failure that seriously affected his health for some years. He even refused to come home for his first vacation. He says: "I cannot be what my friends have a right to expect and I think the sense of this will tend to make me melancholy. I write this with tears, but I think I had better stay." His mother blew these vapors away with a wholesome blast of common sense: "I am persuaded nothing in this transitory world can ever make you happy, that you will never be satisfied with anything short of Heaven, and since that is not to be found here below upon this dirty earth I know not of a better way than to make the best of our lot and to look well to it that we are prepared for a better." And she went on to describe their need of him in Stockbridge, and said they were going to send for him anyway. Happiness is a delicate balance between what one is and what one has. If he thinks he has less than he deserves a man is unhappy. If he thinks he does not deserve what he has, he is even more unhappy. Religion should restore this balance, but in Mark's case it only exaggerated the difficulty. He was really healthy and strong, but this subconscious reaction made him wretched and ill. Later when his religious problem was settled he was able to think through to a sort of cheerfulness, but it was years before he could overcome the subconscious depression.

In 1828 he writes: "I have hardly life and spirit enough to say anything. What will be the end I do not know, but I do know that I can never be what I might have been and ought to have been. My spirits are tolerably good, that is, as much so as is consistent with their very intimate connection with the state of the body. There is a kind of animal spirit and cheerfulness depending entirely on the state of the body, which indicate themselves by vivacity of action and manner, sparkling eyes, and animated features, but besides this there is a cheerfulness which keeps the heart warm under the indications of great bodily depression and which springs from the hope of better things here or hereafter. This last seldom entirely forsakes me."

Strangely enough he thinks that his mind is affected by health rather than his health by his mind. He holds that thought cannot affect "bodily sensation and feelings," but that it can achieve a certain cheerfulness in spite of them. And yet undoubtedly it was thought that was affecting his bodily condition and causing pain and ill health. Philosophy can merely suggest "considerations to lessen sorrow," but cannot "alter the nature" of our sensations or "make pain pleasure." And yet when he had thought out his philosophy he was never seriously troubled by ill health, and seemed the epitome of vigor and good cheer to the very last. I can remember how when he was over eighty he laughed at my efforts to acquire strength in the gymnasium and had me measure his great chest of forty-two inches, and said: "Exercise! I never needed any exercise in the gymnasium. I'm stronger than most of those fellows who are always exercising and I'm always in good health."

He is very reticent about his personal feelings and beyond these general statements of depression gives no account of what the old doctrine did to him. We shall have to turn to Albert's journal to discover its effects. Before we turn to Albert's experience we must consider the attitude of the college toward religion and its effect on the boys.

Although the college was an educational institution, its primary aim at that period was religion, and the professors thought more of developing the character of the boys than of giving them knowledge. Here, too, the great aim was conversion, and the president felt it incumbent upon him to see to the religious welfare of the students and if possible to bring about their conversion. When he came to Williams, Doctor Griffin was much disturbed by the godless state of the college due to the wave of infidelity that spread from the French Revolution. He found that during the first seven years of the college, in which ninety-three were graduated, there were but five professors of religion. From 1798 until 1800 there was but one professor of religion, and in 1800, but two.

Old Doctor Swift had preached faithfully the good old doctrines and the Federalist principles for twenty-six years, always in the hope that some day he should see a great awakening and response in the people who sat under him. And in 1805 it came. Men were swept by a great wave of emotion. Fifty-four joined the church, and the effect even spread to the college. A junior named Bailey caught the fire, and his prayers for his classmates so irritated them that they laid an ambush to mob him. But in some strange fashion repentance fell upon them, and thirteen in all were converted, of whom nine later became ministers. This little group started a prayer meeting where a deep spirit of devotion was developed. One day after a lesson in geography in which they had studied of the tragic suffering and ignorance prevailing in Asia and Africa, they met as usual in the fields, and were driven by a shower to the shelter of a hay stack. Here they formed the plan of giving their lives to bring help to these foreign lands. From this little group gathered under the hay stack sprang the Foreign Missions of America.

It is strange that as Williams was first in scientific interest, so also this little remote college in the hills should have been the first to reach out in interest to great unknown worlds across the seas and initiate a movement which started colleges all through the East and Near East, where the statesmen and leaders of Turkey and the Orient were trained, and originated technical and agricultural schools in Africa and savage lands to fit the natives to meet the coming changes that were inevitable, and built hospitals all over the world where millions of sufferers were relieved or healed. The spot is still marked by a monument where that little group kindled the flame that was to sweep over the earth—the first beginning of a real international feeling—a sense of responsibility for the welfare and progress of the whole world, which in that day seemed to most men an absurdity. It originated, as most great movements must, in intense religious devotion, and it has spread now until even the irreligious feel themselves behind the times if they confine their interests to their own homes.

This little group kept alive an interest in religion which kindled again into flame in 1812 under the influence of Samuel Nott, who was about to sail for India, and twenty-four were converted. But by 1822 interest in religion had died down, and the president felt it his first duty both by his preaching and by personal interviews to see that the men in his charge developed a true Christian character and were properly instructed in the Plan of Salvation. He was a man of such eloquence and emotional power that, due to his efforts, there was a revival in college every two years until his health failed. He was in the direct apostolic line of the old Calvinist doctrine for he had received his theological training from Jonathan Edwards the younger. We may judge something of his methods from his account of his procedure with his own daughter. The first step was to convince the sinner that he deserved Hell, and if possible to cause him to be glad to be damned for the Glory of God. He says: "that evening I visited Louisa and put to her the old question, (evidently often put before): 'Do you feel that it would be just in God to cast you off?' After a considerable pause and in a low voice, she answered 'Yes, Sir.' The next day I said to Ellen, 'My daughter, where do you expect to spend your eternity?' She answered, 'Why, I have not thought about that!' 'What have you been thinking about?' 'I have been thinking how good God has been to me and how ungrateful I have been.' "

"The next day she looked more the image of misery than before. I asked her where she expected to spend her eternity. She said 'I think most likely I shall spend it in Hell.' 'Do you think you deserve Hell?' 'Oh, I know I do!' In this condition she remained two days." We have here a vivid picture of the way in which a devoted father brought his children into the fold. How a man of sensibility could perpetrate such cruelty is a mystery to parents of today. From this conversation we can gather how the president drove his stinging verbal shafts day by day into the unregenerate flesh of his pupils until at last they pierced the marrow. Perhaps no one else could have brought the cautious judicial mind of Mark to a decision at this period of his development.

The president made appointments with each boy to discuss religion and his need of salvation, and many of the boys were deeply influenced by these talks.

Soon after Mark entered college the president sent for him and spoke very "seriously and feelingly." He spoke of the tremendous "obligations that rested upon him as a rational soul who had seen the light," and then discussed Mark's chances of salvation, which he made out to be very slim. He proved conclusively that even one sin deserves eternal damnation, and left Mark "persuaded that the Drama of this world in which we are all actors will have a very serious catastrophe!"

Mark found it very difficult to decide whether he was a Christian or not. He was not conscious of the exalted emotions that seemed essential. Intellectually he accepted the main facts of Christianity. It was its reasonableness that chiefly appealed to him. He reacted against the emotional outbursts that surrounded him. In 1825, his last year before graduation, there was a revival in town which spread to the college. A friend of Mark's named Morley was deeply affected, and when Mark invited him to his room, Morley, as soon as he was seated, burst into tears and wept steadily for half an hour—saying that he was in utter despair and had no hope. We can hardly imagine a modern collegian in such a state of mind. It was a reaction from the old doctrine. Impressed in childhood with a sense of hopeless guilt before God, the youth of that day usually forgot the impression and his conscious self was absorbed with other interests. But deep underneath the old sense of guilt was gnawing away until some emotional climax set it free, and it broke loose, overwhelming the victim with its accumulated force.

The college boys held a meeting in the room of one of their number, and most of them broke down and wept. It seems a strange reaction for the type of boy who could burn down college buildings without a qualm, but such is human nature. Stored emotion ultimately explodes. A classmate of Mark's, named Hathaway, was the leader of the movement, and he spoke "with great candour and calmness." Beside all this emotion Mark was conscience stricken that he felt so little. Religion "certainly does not have the influence upon me that it ought. I am inclined to hope myself a Christian. When I think of Christ and His character I think that I love Him; when I think of His gospel, I think that I approve of it." Was there ever a more cautious expression of faith? "When I think of the gospel I think that I approve of it!" Certainly there is no enthusiasm here—no outburst of irresistible emotion—only a very cautious hesitant half step forward. Mark is of those who advance by trying to help others forward, and it is amusing to find his first efforts directed toward the mother who had been so anxious for his own conversion. "My dear mother I hope you are not at present slumbering with regard to those things to which you have been so often awake. I hope that all the family pay more careful attention to their Bibles."

It was no simple matter to know that one was saved. During another period of "Engagedness," as they termed it, Albert speaks of a young man who was genuinely converted, but says that "before conviction he exhibited as fair an example of uncorrupted youth and virtuous simplicity as I have ever seen." In other words as far as his life without and within could be judged he showed a true Christian character. "He, however, possessed that carnal heart, which in all places and at all ages is enmity against God." By this he seems to mean that the boy had never experienced this sense of conviction of sin and of complete dependence on the Divine Mercy, and therefore was defying God and a lost soul.

Whether Mark went through this experience is open to doubt. A mind such as his does not usually reach its decisions through emotional crises. It was a year later in February, 1826, during another revival in Williamstown when seventy or eighty were converted that his mother writes: "Last Sabbath Mark made a public profession of the faith he has so long manifested."

We can gather something of his own experience from his letter to his mother five years later. He is now definitely urging her as she once urged him. It seems at first strangely unfilial and yet is an indication of the close ties between them. "I often think, my dear mother, with no small anxiety of the religious aspect of your character. It is sufficient ground for this that you do not think yourself a Christian, and must therefore, instead of having the peace which religion naturally brings, be distressed with doubt or fear, for who can think of being banished forever from the presence of God. You seemed at one time, I thought, to have a strange distrust of God as if He would not receive you." He goes on to show that it would be strange if God sacrificed His Son for us and then was unwilling to save, and stranger still that there should be any sinner so sinful as "to render God bankrupt in mercy. I sometimes think there is a degree of pride in dwelling on the greatness of our sins. If the religion of the Gospel is our life, I cannot but wish you to receive it and enjoy it. The act, the voluntary act of turning to God is so simple that it is in that that its mystery lies. It is only to feel the truth that we have nothing of our own and to cast ourselves on the mercy of God, freely, fully, unreservedly. Then we feel safe."

It was evidently this step that he took himself, a calm clear decision to stop worrying about himself and to trust himself entirely to God, believing that the God who created him would make the best possible use of his life.

But his mother seems to have been impervious to his arguments. It is hardly likely that she believed herself too great a sinner to be saved. She would then have been unhappy, and she was not only happy herself but had the faculty of making others equally so. She undoubtedly had her own religion which was very real and satisfactory; and to her all this doctrine and religious experience was interesting but apart from her real life. She always found some excuse for keeping to her own way. Mark continued to urge her; believing so implicitly that her salvation depended on this act of surrender he could not do otherwise. Two years later it was some doctrinal point that was her excuse and Mark writes: "I have long known that you found a difficulty in reconciling the two doctrines of which you speak and that whenever you turned your attention to the subject of religion you have been entangled in that difficulty. I do not believe it is right or safe to make the act which is essential to salvation depend on our capacity to solve a speculative point, and have long wished that you would cast yourself on the mercy of God in Christ as a little child." He goes on to show that even if her mind were satisfied the same act of surrender would be necessary. But she would not yield.

The old Hopkintonian system had blocked her progress just as in the case of Theodore Sedgwick and many others. She felt she could not honestly swallow it whole as Mark had done and trust God to explain it some day. She preferred to trust God to understand her attitude in refusing to become a nominal Christian, an attitude that must have cost her much in those days of strong prejudice, when few but infidels remained outside the Church.

But it was by no means in behalf of his mother alone that Mark labored. When he returned to Williams as tutor in 1826, the college was in bad way. Amherst had at length secured her charter, and there was a general belief that two colleges could not subsist in Western Massachusetts and that Williams was doomed. The number of students dropped from 120 to 80, in the middle of the year. They were demoralized, disorderly, openly irreligious and shockingly profane and drinking was general. They thought the college near to dissolution and seemingly did not care. An effort was made to arouse them in which the two young tutors, Hopkins and Hervey, took the lead. Hervey was a man of great ability whose devotion later carried him to India where he founded the station of Ahmednagar, at which thousands of Hindus have been educated. Albert, who had not yet graduated and who was still unregenerate, described a meeting held in the Senior Recitation room: "The hour arrived and immediately there began a flocking to the place. Many were bold sinners and came in whirling their hats as if in derision." The room became crowded. The two tutors directed the meeting. Then an extraordinary spirit came over the place. One student who had been notably profane, suddenly rose and cried "Will you trifle with your souls?" There was a most amazing response. The whole meeting was swept by this new spirit, and for several days all the college exercises were suspended and meetings were held in which man after man came out on the side of religion. The movement was pushed with the aid of two evangelists. Doctor Griffin threw himself into it with all his might. "Evening after evening, for several months, through darkness, snow, and mud, he went to a schoolhouse in the East part of the village, and poured out torrents of truth." The movement spread through the town and county. It drew the attention of all to Williams College, and roused a spirit there that, according to Doctor Griffin, saved the college from the shock and moral menace of the incorporation of Amherst.

It had another effect. Albert had been of those who took no interest in religion. Though he would have scorned to have a part in anything crooked or morally wrong, he had a part in all the drinking bouts and boyish pranks that were a part of student life, and scoffed at the pious with the rest. The serious-minded Mark, devoted as he was to his younger brother, thought him wild and in danger of falling under Divine condemnation. But this revival evidently took hold of him. Though he took no stand, the general excitement started the old doctrines long planted in his subconscious mind into a ferment from which he could not escape. It was not, however, until the next year, in April, 1827, that Mark writes to tell Harry of Albert's conversion. He seems to regard it as a great miracle in view of Albert's former careless attitude toward religion.

He says: "It is very affecting to think of it, considering his turn of mind, but God is merciful, exceeding merciful. He seems to have had a strong sense of being a sinner, a perfect conviction that the righteousness of Christ alone could avail in his Salvation and to have thrown himself entirely on the Mercy of God." Mark was evidently still worried that he had not been through this emotional cataclysm. "Something of this state of mind I hope I have been conscious of myself and I believe must be felt by those who are saved. Sin, as Albert says, is an exceeding evil and it is a great thing for God to pardon it; this He will do for us if we are humble, penitent, renounce ourselves and rely upon His mercy, and certainly there is no joy comparable to that which results from a sense of pardoned sin." Then for Harry's benefit he adds: "But if we choose to go on in our own way and rely on ourselves and the world for happiness and on our own righteousness for Salvation, then our doom is certain. I should sooner hope to put my hand in the fire and not be burned." Here is the mainspring of the New England attitude—the certainty of doom for those who trusted in themselves. Good deeds avail nothing to avert the doom. Nothing can make up for sin. And sin, as they saw it, is any act done with any other motive than a wholehearted devotion to God and to the advancement of His kingdom. Any selfish, vain or sensual thought was sin that required the deepest repentance—a standard that kept them in an agony of self-abasement.

To fully understand the psychological effect of this

terrible doctrine of the total depravity of man we must turn to Albert's journal. The journal begins in January, 1830, when he was made Professor of Mathematics and Natural Philosophy. It starts with a confession of sin and dedication of himself to God. He says: "I have in a most sinful and ungrateful manner refused obedience to those plain and equitable laws which in Thy condescension and goodness Thou wast pleased to give me for guidance. This conduct has made me a sinner. It has also made me miserable and odious. I have not loved to hear the offer of mercy which was made to me, and I have even esteemed the price which has been paid for it a common and unholy thing. Can mercy be extended to one so guilty—so awfully guilty?" And so on for pages in which he declares his vileness and unworthiness. To us, untrained in the old doctrine, it seems that he is working himself up artificially almost to a state of religious mania. The sin which he esteems so vile seems to be merely that he had not felt the need of being saved by the sacrifice of Christ.

Then follows the dedication—of his soul with every thought and feeling—of his body, promising to guard against every desire of the flesh—of his time, promising to give every hour to God—of his property, promising to spend it all for God's glory.

Such a terrible pledge was enough to torment him the rest of his life with fear that he had not completely kept it.

Subsequent entries lament the "awful wickedness"

of his heart as he tries to live up to this pledge. On July 17th he has come to feel that he must be holy as God is holy. Month after month the journal records his agonizing struggle—now overwhelmed with the sense of sin, now uplifted by the consciousness of forgiveness. When he had no sense of sin he prayed that he might see his sin, and so kept himself in a state that today would be considered religious mania, but it was merely the reaction of the old dogma on a highly emotional nature. He adopted the perfectionist theory, that it is the duty of every man to be perfect as God is perfect—enough to keep any man in agony. For six years, until February 11, 1836, these agonizing entries continue, and then as in the case of Luther and Augustine, the light broke at last. After a more terrible realization of his sinfulness than ever before he says: "I seemed to throw the responsibility over on to Christ and felt a relief I never experienced before." This seemed to be the end of the struggle. The old dogma had done its worst.

This of course is the inside view. Outwardly none would have imagined the tragedy within. He was full of humor and charm; his lectures were so popular that the students sent in a petition to have them two hours long instead of one hour. The inward struggle resulted in driving him to the most intense activity to save other souls. He took a leading part in all the revivals in college, and did even more by talking personally with the students, many of whom bear witness to his influence. He started a chapel in a forsaken corner of the township where conditions were as bad as possible, and was the chief influence in transforming the White Oaks village. There are many comments on the dramatic power and vividness of his sermons, which had a greater effect in rousing men to a decision than the sermons of his brother, whose chief gift was to solve doubt and make clear the problems of religion.

We have spoken of the effect of the old doctrine on Mark and Albert, but have said nothing of Harry. It is most unfortunate that we have no record of Harry's feelings on the subject. We only know that like his mother he remained impervious to its terrors.

The story of every age is told by its contemporaries —by men who were a part of it and who took its idiosyncrasies as a matter of course. One often feels the desire to drop back into some bygone age and see how it would appear to one unbiassed by the prejudices of the period, and also to discover what effect it would have upon the actors to come in contact with one who had the modern point of view and whose reactions were not conditioned by the old ideas as were theirs. Now the interesting feature in the story of these three brothers is that it seems as if Harry were precisely such a visitant. Through him his two brothers were brought in contact with another spirit and temper and through his letters we seem to view the period with modern eyes. For closely as he was bound to his two brothers Harry seems to belong to another age. In him there was something alien to the thought and manner of life that surrounded him—something distinctly modern in his temper and point of view. Mark could enter into the old thought and was thus able to harmonize it with the new ideas as they came upon the scene. But Harry seemed entirely impervious to the thought that surrounded him. It was not that he accepted the new revolutionary thought from France. That had no more effect upon him than the old thought. He went on his way, a gay and joyous spirit, taking in all of beauty and happiness that came his way, listening to all the stern old theology, attending all the revivals with their intense emotional experiences, and yet remaining an outsider who could criticize calmly and coolly all the ideas that so stirred the men about him. There was no cynical superiority about him. He was interested in everything. He had not adopted the modern thought, but he was a man of modern temper dropped into the midst of the old systems of thought which he instinctively rejected. He was a ceaseless perplexity to his brothers. One cannot but feel that much of Mark's tolerance for the new thought and the modern temper when it finally found expression, came from his long association with Harry, who must have made that temper familiar to him in a sympathetic way even when it distressed him. His brothers recognized that in many ways Harry's life was more blameless and unselfish than their own, and yet he steadfastly refused to take any stand as a Christian. This, of course, was a cause of great anxiety to both Mark and Albert.

During the revival in January, 1826, which caused Mark to take his stand, he writes Harry an account of the meetings, saying that "they are not like other revivals, there has been nothing of noise or ostentation or variety, it has been deep and solemn and still. It has led me to feel the importance of religion and to take a decided stand." He feels that his brother must share this experience with him. "My dear Brother," he says: "If you are without part or lot in the religion of Jesus Christ . . . you lack the essential ingredients of happiness and I hope you will let nothing prevent your acceptance of Him as your only Savior without delay. I do not wish to preach to you —I only wish your happiness."

He realizes that Harry has led a more unselfish life than any of them, and that he has some hidden spring of action, but he is still anxious lest his brother may miss the one essential. In January, 1830, he writes: "You have not spent your life basely, since you have not lived to vanity or passion, but to the comfort of your friends in the indulgence of kindly feeling to an extent that I suppose few have been possessed of." He goes on to speak of the relation of religion and morality and says: "I believe you have a quiet way of thinking on these subjects which does not altogether fall in with my feeling about them." He then urges Harry to make so sure of his salvation that death would mean to him merely passing from one apartment to another in the Father's house.

If Mark felt that he had taken a stand which set

him apart from his beloved brother and could not rest until Harry had joined him, Harry had an even deeper feeling of separation when he received the news of Albert's conversion and a bitter resentment which revealed his intense devotion to his brother. He writes: "If I am forgotten in consequence of his religion, then let all the world go, I care not if I die, for that fellow was more to me than all the world beside. My affection for him is so great that I never think of him without tears in my eyes. If he is so altered that he will never be Albert to me again, I declare to you now that I believe that religion to be false and desire never to know it, for, rob me of that affection for my friends which I now possess, and you rob me of the greatest and purest source of happiness which God has mercifully bestowed upon us in this world, as a forecast of that blessed state of society in Heaven where, through the Grace of God, I hope to meet you all beyond this world of trial, vexation, and disappointment."

It is rare that one finds such intense feeling between brothers, and rarer still to find it expressed. His statement shows that Heaven was as real to Harry as to the others and he felt as sure of arriving there. But he seems to have had the same obstinate streak that was in his mother. He would not have the old doctrine thrust upon him. Why it did not grip his subconscious mind as it did in the case of Albert and Mark is a mystery. It may be the artistic temperament that caused him to view it in a detached and critical way, without being himself a part of it.

When his brothers urged him to attend a revival meeting in Stockbridge in 1831, and there take a stand, he went indeed, but viewed it all much as a man from another age, interested in the psychological means by which the effects are produced.

"The ministers exhibited a good deal of knowledge of the human mind in keeping the congregation as compact as possible, having the singing done below, and by varying the form of service. There are many minds which would be affected by such novelties, sympathy acts more strongly in a small room than in a large, and in a compact body of persons than in a scattered. How far it is judicious to excite the imaginations of people by methods of that kind, I don't know. The imaginations of men are wrought upon in a variety of ways and it is a matter of no consequence whether the exciting cause is getting the people into a mass and whispering to them, or the groanings and hollowings of the Methodists. I believe there is no religion in either, and it strikes me there may be much danger to weak minds who have not the habits of self examination and reflection and never analyze the nature of an impression, mistaking these vague impressions for those which ought to be of a far different kind. Ministers should be possess't of a great knowledge of the human mind to impress rightly and direct properly."

This is an astonishing letter for a youth brought up on a farm without the opportunities of a liberal education. One would say that he and not Mark was the professor of philosophy and psychology. And through it all is the modern temper of investigating causes rather than yielding to effects. He saw the great danger of the revival, namely, that ministers should bring the same methods to bear on all types and thus risk doing serious damage. There are men of a sluggish type of mind that have become involved in bad habits and need some violent emotional stimulus to arouse them to a decision, and there are the sensitive souls, over-anxious about themselves, whom such treatment may easily unbalance and drive into melancholia. No one of that age save Harry seems to have seen this, and the path of the revivalists was strewn with wrecked nerves as a result.

Harry went on to criticize the methods of the various revivalists—one who pictured the beauties of Heaven, till "everyone was in love with the place without thinking whether he was fit for it," and one who pictured the terrors of the law. "He may drive sinners to Heaven but he will never draw them," says Harry. He objects to the methods used to get people on their feet to take a stand. A beginning was made by asking those to rise who desired prayers for their friends, and Harry objected to the pressure put on them by statements that without the prayers of Christians sinners could not be saved and he disliked "the unnecessary exposure of the feelings of tender minds."

It was the time of the great revival. Albert writes on April 10, 1831, "There never has been probably since the beginning of the world so general a revival as there is at present in this country. As many as twenty in College hope they have become different persons." It was a great emotional wave that swept the country under such leaders as President Finney. I can remember that it was said Finney had such power that when he entered a factory where he expected to hold some meetings and stood and looked at the girl operators, they all burst into tears. Harry's mind had been prepared in the same way as the others but while young men all over the country were being swept by the emotional tide, he stood aloof and viewed its progress as a scientific critic. It was certain that Harry would never be brought into the fold by methods such as these and his brothers should have appreciated the fact. But the next year, on the occasion of another revival, when one hundred inquirers in Williamstown had been swept into the fold, and among them Major B, one of the most prominent and "high spirited" men in town, Albert made a final effort. "Join yourself to the inquirers," he writes, "your example may do much. I want to have you come out decided in the cause of religion among the community in which you dwell. . . . I would not have you delay for all the worlds that God has made. Since before another call your soul might be buried in the very centre of Hell!"

Here we come again face to face with the terrific old doctrine. Albert, devoted to his brother, and knowing his fine unselfish character, was actually convinced that unless he followed the old formula his "soul would be buried in the centre of Hell." The whole system of thought and action of the age rested back on this motivation. It is hard for us to realize how stupendous a change a few years have brought about in the basis of life and reality, and in the motive power of human conduct. It is surprising that any virtue should be left when its foundation was thus suddenly knocked from under it.

There was, however, a certain process of adjustment in progress. Mark speaks of hearing Channing preach in New York. To quote: "Channing says that the end of all religion is moral purity or holiness and that Salvation is freedom from Sin," and to attain this and to gain forgiveness "he allows no other efficacy to what Christ has done but what results from example."

Here we have a complete reversal of the old doctrine. For the Calvinist the end of religion was submission to the will of God, good works and freedom from sin could not save, but only faith. The sacrifice of Christ alone could avail to satisfy the justice of God and counterbalance the vileness of man, and that only in the case of the few upon whom He had mercy.

In listening to Channing, Mark was getting the backfire of reaction from the steady cannonade of his uncle Doctor Samuel Hopkins under whom Channing had sat as a boy and received the full force of the Hopkinsonian system. Upon the sensitive high-strung youth it had a powerful effect. He saw before him the Creator erecting "a gallows in the centre of the Universe and publicly executing upon it, in view of the offenders, an Infinite Being, the partaker of His own Supreme Divinity, and then declaring that this execution was appointed as a most conspicuous and terrible manifestation of God's justice, and of the Infinite woe denounced by His law, and adding that all beings in Heaven and Earth are required to fix their eyes on this dreadful sight, as the most powerful enforcement of obedience and virtue." His soul was revolted by the picture which seemed to him to "calumniate his Maker." "The spirit of such a government whose very acts of pardon were written in such blood, was terror, not paternal love." This is quoted from a sermon preached in New York at the dedication of the Unitarian Church there—perhaps the very sermon which Mark heard, in which Channing gave expression to the feeling produced in him by the old theology. He had been influenced by French Liberalism, and man, to his mind, was not depraved and utterly wicked, but potentially noble. He felt the revolt of common-sense and of fine sensibility which was turning many like Harry and his mother from the old dogma, and he turned from the authority of the scholastic and even of scripture to the authority of the human soul. "The soul," he said, "is the spring of our knowledge of God." Thus before the scriptures had been seriously attacked by the critics, he shifted the basis of authority to the revelation of God in the soul of man. Man was God's child, made in His image. It was all a revolt not on doctrinal or metaphysical but on ethical grounds, against a God who was unjust and a conception of man that was degrading.

The old doctrine was on the defensive. When the new group gained control of Harvard, Andover Seminary was started in 1808 to combat them. The defenders of the old had a difficult task, to appeal to shrewd Yankee common-sense and demonstrate that man was predestinated and yet had free will, and it is not surprising that they failed to convince Mary Hopkins. Mark noted at once that Channing made little reference to the scripture. He agreed with Channing that salvation was not escape from damnation, but moral purity, and he puts his finger on the weak point in Unitarianism, in that Christ was presented merely as an example. This cut the nerve of that supreme devotion which the Christian felt toward one who had given his life to save him, and made of Unitarianism a rather cold ethical system in place of a religion of passionate devotion. Mark, however, does not defend the cruel judge of Calvinism. He fully accepts the idea of a God of love whose chief desire is "that we should be happy, and who only requires that we should love Him in order to our happiness." Channing had made a necessary protest against a cruel conception of God and a degraded conception of man, and his preaching was helpful to intelligent men of high standards. What would have been the effect on the ordinary ignorant man with sinful proclivities to suddenly take away the fear of punishment and also the moving appeal of the Christ who died for men and leave in its place only a noble example, is open to doubt. The world had not yet reached the point when men would follow virtue merely because they loved it. Some still needed the check of fear and most men needed a religion that stirred a deep feeling of devotion. For the mass of the people a leader was needed who would tide over this transition period by presenting all the strong emotional appeal of the old system, without its defects; revealing God as a God of love and not of cruel justice, and man as His child with noble potentialities that only needed to be awakened. One can see from Mark's letter that this was precisely the point of view to which he came while listening to Channing.

One would suppose that Channing would appeal to Harry, but even here he maintains the critical attitude of the outsider. He admires the eloquence of Channing and says "Channing's preaching is of the seducing kind. It would recommend almost any doctrine with success. If Unitarianism does not gain ground now when can they expect that it will?" He then proceeds to analyze the reason for its success. He notes that whenever there is any religion there is the belief in a future existence, and that men are anxious as to what their condition there will be. "Christianity, as it was given to the world by its author, requires a course of conduct throughout, to which the human heart with its natural propensities is very repugnant; this has been the cause of the innumerable systems, doctrines, and modifications proposed by man as a substitute. Among these there are few that come up to the original strictness, but there are few so far as I am acquainted, so congenial to the human mind in its natural state and that require the sacrifice of so little personal gratification as Unitarianism. Thus those on whom luxury, wealth, power, have fixed their seals are pleased to find Heaven and their desires upon the same road. This is one great secret of Unitarian proselytism." Here again was the great weakness of the movement. It did not demand a really great devotion, nor could it readily arouse such a feeling, and the danger was that it would lapse into a mere system of ethics and adjust itself to the standards of its wealthy adherents. Harry was trained in the old school of self-denial, and if he cannot accept the old doctrines, he certainly would scorn to try to enter Heaven by an easier road. In fact the passage seems to imply that he thought even the doctrine of the atonement to be a man-made device to get to Heaven by a mere act of faith without living up to the original precepts of Christ, and this may have been his reason for refusing to accept it. To suggest that the most sacred doctrines of Calvinism were a cleverly designed scheme to get to Heaven by a short cut was a most surprising performance for a youth of that age.

In Channing's sermons Mark came for the first time in contact with the new thought that was destined ultimately to undermine the old doctrines and the old religion, and it is undoubtedly due in large measure to Harry's clear headed criticisms that he was able to approach the new thought without prejudice and to see clearly the dangers and incongruities of the old system as well as the weak points of the new. Thus the groundwork was laid for his great work of interpreting Christianity in such a way as to retain all its great emotional appeal and free it from the dark shadow of the old Calvinist dogma—to avoid on the one hand the terrors of a religion of fear and on the other the barren outline of an ethical system, and dig through all the mass of accumulated doctrine to the heart of Christianity.

CHAPTER VI

NEW YORK IN 1825

As one pores over these letters of a hundred years ago, one cannot help feeling in a peculiar way the charm and attraction of Harry. While Albert's letters are full of queer crotchets and Mark's of sage reflections, Harry seems to have the artist's faculty of catching the vivid essentials of the scene. One can imagine the effect that a visit to New York would have upon a boy from a New England farm, and Harry's letters recall the scenes of that day and reveal the transformation effected in his own life.

The trouble with his eyes had prevented him from completing his education and he had given his time and energy to helping his father on the farm, but the family all felt that he should have his chance for self-development in whatever line he preferred. His chief interest was in painting and he wanted above all things to go to New York and study. Now the artist was commonly regarded as a futile and ungodly character and it is surprising that all the family should have seconded his plan with enthusiasm. Mark sent him the necessary funds from his savings, and Archibald arranged to get on without him, and on December 1, 1825, during Mark's last year at college, he started off on his great adventure, well equipped with a new suit and complete outfit, in which Mother had her share. Until 1831 the only regular transportation line from Stockbridge was the line of coaches from Springfield to Albany, and Harry reached the Hudson by stage.

The trip down the river was a revelation to him. With a mind unusually sensitive to beauty it is not surprising that the sight of the Palisades awakened "exquisite sensations," as he put it, but he was shy of expressing his enthusiasms. David Dudley Field, a son of the Stockbridge minister, had entered a law firm in New York, and was prospering to such an extent that Harry described him as "fat and flourishing." He was fond of Harry and devoted to Lucinda, Harry's adopted sister. He had a room in a pleasant house on suburban Broadway near Canal Street, out of the noise of the city, and he invited Harry to come there. He did what he could to help him gain a hold in New York. He started in with pleasant companionship, for William Cullen Bryant, whose oration in Stockbridge he had so admired and who was now editor of *The Evening Post*, lived in the same house. There was also an extremely vivacious French lady who helped Harry to keep his repartee in proper trim.

The New York which Harry visited in 1825 was somewhat different from the present metropolis. It was a city of some 150,000 inhabitants, a figure which we should have to multiply by twenty-five to equal the present population. There were still residences in

Wall Street, and in 1828 there were only nineteen banks in the whole city. The aristocracy were beginning to move uptown from Liberty and Pine Streets to Franklin and Leonard Streets, and some fine houses were building in the district around Market Street and East Broadway. Along Canal Street ran an open ditch canal and above it were only scattered houses, villas, and farms. Only two roads went the length of Manhattan Island through the open country to Harlem—the Boston Post Road and the Abington Road, passing through the villages of Yorkville and Bloomingdale, which was somewhere near 50th Street. The hamlet of Chelsea was near West 20th Street, and, southwest of it on the North River, was the village of Greenwich, noted for its healthful air and salubrious climate. Large numbers had migrated thither during severe epidemics in New York. A line of gorgeously painted coaches ran every hour from Wall Street to Greenwich, through open fields, across Lispenard's meadows and Minetta creek, along the foot of Richmond Hill, where Aaron Burr had built his country place, and south of the pauper cemetery on the present site of Washington Square. Near the cemetery stood the gallows where a few years before a murderess had been executed.

The shopping district was in Park Place. The city boasted four theatres, eight schools, two high schools, two hospitals, a dispensary, and ninety churches. Delmonico had started a little restaurant in William Street with six pine tables, where guests were supplied with excellent food served on earthenware dishes with two-tined forks. Until Niblo's was opened the great amusement place was Contoit's garden, where there were stalls under shady trees, lit at night by twinkling tapers. Gas was not introduced until some years later. There were no omnibuses until 1830. People drove in hacks or walked. The Harlem Railroad Company was building a line into the city from Harlem and ran the strange-looking train of coaches of which we see the model in the Grand Central Station. The water supply was derived chiefly from wells and a large reservoir had been built to store water in case of fires. The handsomest building in the city was the City Hall, which interested Harry especially since it was built of marble brought from Stockbridge. It was the only marble building in the city and was considered a marvellous work of art.

Such was the city to which young Harry Hopkins came to start his art studies.

Contoit's garden was frequented by a select clientele, but there were other places of amusement then as now, which were considered more entertaining by folk from out of town. One of these boasted the alluring name of the Seraglio. Harry's friends lost no time in introducing him to its excitements. He dined there the very first night. The music seems to have been an earlier edition of jazz, for he reports that he was "nearly assassinated" by it. He met the fate that overtakes a country lad when he attempts a secret venture into fast life. A fire broke out in the

Seraglio, and he was hemmed in in the midst of a terrified crowd, and thought that a blackened and disreputable corpse would be shipped to Stockbridge as a warning to the companions he had left behind.

On New Year's Eve he made his first appearance in high society. He and David Dudley Field were invited to dine with the Sedgwick cousins, "at the fashionable hour of a quarter past four." As a country cousin he was on his mettle and was greatly humiliated and much laughed at because he saluted his hosts by saying "Good Evening," instead of "Good Afternoon." He stuck to his guns, however, and insisted he had the correct salutation for a dinner engagement and defied them to prove him wrong. It was beyond him to "enumerate the courses," he says, and adds, "they did not sit as long as usual but rose from the table at half past nine o'clock—" a five-hour gastronomic tournament that would seem rather Gargantuan today. The cook-book of Abigail Williams published in London, is still in existence, and gives charts showing how the table was set in those days. For one course there were set out dishes of beef, pheasants, ducks, salmon, vegetables, savories, pastries, relishes, puddings, ices, and fruits. There followed other courses, similar in volume but different in detail, so we may imagine that some time was necessary to consume them all. "Coffee came earlier than usual," he says, "at the ungenteel hour of eleven, after which we sallied forth to make calls." Calls at midnight seem to have been "de rigueur" in those days. They found the streets swarming, as they would be today on New Year's Eve, with crowds seeking to excel one another in noise, "Blankshells, toothorns, drums, horse fiddles, and every kind of instrument for noise" were in full play, and on Broadway he met "a solid column of about five hundred" marching along, "completely equipped and in hot action——"

When they returned to the Sedgwicks' "as we drank only nine bumpers of wine apiece at dinner they had very kindly prepared a large quantity of hot whisky punch that we need not take cold, which must be disposed of." After this he suggests that there was some difficulty in getting home.

The Sedgwicks were fond of Harry and more than kind. The Henry Sedgwicks were going on a trip to Boston, and invited Harry to stay in their house during their absence, to protect Catherine Sedgwick and Miss Peakmoun who were left alone. He accepted with delight, but only stayed there at night. He delighted in the walk of a mile to and from his boarding place on Broadway; sights of the city enchanted and amused him. When the Henry Sedgwicks returned they asked him to remain and board with them, which he was only too glad to do. His funds were getting low and he moved his sleeping habitation from the elegant apartments of David Field and took a cheaper room on the Bowery, with Andrews, another Stockbridge boy. He kept hard at work at his painting and made portraits of all the

Sedgwick family which apparently pleased them greatly. The Sedgwicks' house was a center for the group of literary men and artists. Every Sunday night Henry Sedgwick invited in a dozen or so, both ladies and gentlemen, and provided a supper of oysters at ten o'clock. Harry thus made acquaintances which assured him of a future as a portrait painter, but he notes that most painters in New York seem to be extremely poor. He is anxious to get into the "higher branch of Historical painting." Portrait painting evidently was not highly esteemed. Although his board was provided, his little store of money dwindled rapidly and he wondered how many weeks he could keep going on the thirty dollars that remained.

One night in a reckless mood he and Andrews went off to the theatre and had a thrilling evening watching the great Kean act. There was a terrific jam, and a pickpocket got his fingers into Harry's pocket while he and Andrews were being "squshed" at the worst, so that he couldn't "stir his arms any more than if he had been in a vice." It sounds like a modern subway crush! But the press was so tight the robber couldn't get his hand in, so Harry escaped a loss. In his letter to Albert he tucked a charming sketch of himself and Andrews pledging each other in two "bumpers" on their return, with a spacious bottle on the table, Harry, with his tall silk hat and stock and stylishly cut coat, is quite the elegant young man about town, and might easily be mistaken for an eighteenth century beau. It

PENCIL SKETCH OF MARK HOPKINS BY HIS BROTHER

was quite a Bacchanalian scene, and Albert who was still unregenerate, hid it behind the looking-glass to be enjoyed in private.

Harry was beginning to feel some qualms at staying so long away from the old farm. His father, for all his New England exterior, was tenderly devoted to Harry and missed him cruelly. He actually penned a long letter, a most unusual feat, telling Harry how the apples he had gathered and the cider he had made are awaiting him and how his hunting dog is getting fat in idleness. Everything about the house reminds him of Harry for Harry has had his part in it all. He wants to accept Cousin Robert Sedgwick's invitation and come to New York to see Harry, "but you will recollect that when Spring comes there will be a great deal to do on our farm and I have no help but Mr. Brown, and I find old age is coming upon me and I cannot work as I have done. I have no doubt if I were in New York I should see many curiosities, but I would give more to see my dear son Harry than to see them all." One can see old Archibald scratching away with his pen in the lonely room whence all his brood have fled, conscious that the strength he had expended with such courage and devotion for those dear to him, was failing now, and wondering how many years he can keep up the fight all alone. And he sends a hard-earned ten dollar bill to enable his "dear son" to stay away a little longer. He has at least a man to help him and we note his democratic spirit in referring to his assistant as "Mr. Brown."

Harry nearly packed up and started home when he read this letter with its mention of the old swamp, of his dog and gun, the mountains, the old south room, the apples and cider, and the old love of home surged up powerfully in him. It was soon evident that he was not going to make a fortune by painting.

But Sedgwick who owned a mine of soft coal which he had not been able to put into marketable form, had started Harry on some experiments which he hoped would make him a rich man. It ended in his going up to the mine in Portsmouth, Rhode Island, to superintend the manufacture of the fine coal. It was quite a wild trip by sea in those days, waves "mountain high" and every one desperately seasick. He was promised a salary of $1000 a year, which seemed to him the acme of wealth, and he started in at once to manage the "wild Irish" miners, who were "brought up underground." The coal was too fine to burn, and his problem was to find some method of making it into bricks. He possessed a little of that somewhat mulish spirit that never turns back which characterized General Grant. He says: "At the mine about 70 feet below the surface there is a gutter dug for the purpose of carrying off the water to the valley below." He was asked if he would like to go through it "as far as a certain pit about 12 rods from that place." He was offered a guide, but said he would go alone and started off with a candle. "I went on bravely about a third of the way when it began to grow so narrow and low that I had to crawl on my hands and knees, and very soon so small that it was with difficulty I could crawl on my belly, being able to raise my back only about two inches, the soft mud being about three inches deep—but I was not the lad to turn back—too much pride had I to think of that! Thus I went like a fly in a Gluepot through a narrow crooked passage, until at length I saw the light from the Pit, which I at last reached. I made up my mind I should not go back the same road, if it is possible to get up the Pit, which is about 30 or 40 feet in diameter. So I blowed a little—stroked off some of the mud, and began to ascend, digging holes with my hands, for my feet. After infinite difficulty and hazard, and completely exhausting myself, I reached the top within about 6 feet, but by no contrivance could I get an inch farther. I could then have called and been helped out, but that I would not do, so down I went with much more difficulty than I had getting up, and to complete my misfortunes, found that in throwing down stones I had put out my light. Hurra! now! but I did not Hurra! then. My journey back I leave you to imagine, also the appearance I made when I delivered myself!"

It does not occur to us what a blessing matches are, but Harry would doubtless have given much to have possessed such an invention. His great achievement was not in refusing to give up when he found that the joke was on him, but in being able to laugh at the pride that got him into the scrape.

He was to need every bit of that spirit that he

possessed. Sedgwick invited him to join in a speculation from which he anticipated great riches. He was sent to study the Lehigh mines in Pennsylvania in order to find some method of using his fine coal. Mr. Sedgwick had purchased 11,000 tons of fine coal at a dollar a ton. Harry gave up his salary and instead was to share in what profit he could make applying the process he had discovered and selling the bricks for two dollars a ton.

He was already making plans to establish his father and mother in comfort if not in luxury, when calamity fell upon him. His fine plan went up in smoke; he even had to borrow five dollars to get home again, and on the way his trunk was stolen with all his earthly possessions. But his spirit remained undaunted. On his return in June, 1827, he writes Mark "Last Saturday the sight of the old poplars and the old towering maple made my wayworn world-worn heart leap and bound again as I jumped out of the stage at the corners and walked with a light step and a lighter heart toward the mansion of our childhood." He is "not one to cry over spilt milk," he says, as he takes up again the work on the farm.

Mark, though grieved enough at his loss, wrote him a cheery letter and offered to stake him again if he wished to return to New York and paint. For Mark had been teaching two years at Williams as tutor, and had lately been sent on a commission through New York State to start new branches of the American Tract Society. He spent some two months on this job, riding his horse first to Utica, and then on to Auburn, where he visited Uncle Jared Curtis his former instructor, now chaplain of the prison. On the way he lost his saddle bags, which gave Harry a chance to jeer at his absentmindedness, but he was paid enough for his work to enable him to give Harry a helping hand in his disaster.

In the meantime Albert had graduated (in 1826) and had been having adventures of his own in investigating for the legislature the possibility of a railroad from Boston to Albany, and surveying a line from Pittsfield to Westfield along nearly the same route over which his great-grandfather had built the first road, through Lee, Becket, Otis, and Blandford and down Westfield river. He writes: "As we were going along those steep hills for which Becket and Chester are so famous, the trace of the forward horse unloosed, this twitched the driver onto the neck of the rear leader. In the meantime the off wheels ran off from the bank and the stage pitched. I saw we were going somewhere, and knowing there was a steep bank below, squared myself accordingly. The stage struck first on the top and smashed the staves; it then rolled completely over and landed in Westfield river. All this was done in much less time than I have been telling it. We had just crossed a bridge and the stage was going very rapid; this in fact was all that saved us. For while our heads were down, had the whole weight of the wheels fallen upon us, it would have crushed not only the staves but us also. As it was the centrifugal force of the heavy part prevented half the weight striking at first. None were injured except Squire Blell of Springfield. We broke down again that night but no damage ensued."

Travelling by stage in those days had as many excitements as motoring today. It is perhaps not surprising that such an experience should have brought Albert to serious thought on the proximity of death. It was shortly after that his conversion occurred. He was undecided whether to go on with his engineering, or to enter a law office, or teach a girls' school, when in May, 1827, he received the offer of a tutorship at Williams. He accepted the offer and went to Williams just as Mark left to take up the study of medicine in New York.

CHAPTER VII

THE STRUGGLES OF A YOUNG DOCTOR

There are men who seem to know from birth what they wish to do in life, and who follow out their life purpose unswervingly, with no doubt as to the calling which they shall choose. Others stand uncertain at the crossroads or try the first path at hand, and it is only after a false start in some calling where they find themselves inefficient and unhappy, that they find at last the work for which nature has formed them and in which success and happiness await them. Mark had struggled so hard to attain his goal of a liberal education, that when he had once gained his degree and stood with his diploma in his hands he was at a loss to know which way to turn. Education had seemed to him the key which was certain to open the way to success and fame, but now there seemed many doors before him, and he knew not to which he should fit the key. The opportunity to serve as tutor in Williams College deferred the day of decision. With an eye out for every opportunity, while waiting for his position, he asked one of the doctors in Williamstown to give him some instruction in medicine; while he boarded with the Honorable Henry Hubbard, one of the trustees of the college.

His three years of tutoring seemed to take him nowhere. He still felt upon him the tremendous burden of responsibility to make good and justify the expectations of his friends and family, and here he was only marking time. He determined to make a plunge. He knew something of medicine at least, and decided to make that his profession and fit himself to become a physician.

It is strange that one with so marked a bent should have chosen a profession in which he felt so uncomfortable if not actually unhappy. It was perhaps the life of keen competition rather than the healing art to which he was unadapted. There were few positions open to a philosopher or he might have chosen that vocation. Few who knew Mark Hopkins in later years had any idea that he had put in three years of his life as a struggling young doctor in New York. That period of his life seemed to sink out of existence and disappear in the limbo of the forgotten. And yet one can see that there were impressions made there which had a vital bearing on his future, and connections were formed which were to stand him in good stead.

As one reads the letters of that period it is hard to realize that they were written by the same individual who was later known as Mark Hopkins. They prove that an unsuitable environment can greatly modify a man's outlook if not his character. In the struggle to gain a foothold in New York Mark put in three years of discouragement and disappointment, which he could not face with Harry's jaunty and dauntless spirit. Harry could write him in jocose vein that there was no news except that they were a little poorer than ever, but he could only feel the terrible responsibility upon him to make good and redeem the family fortunes. When Pa sold one of the oxen and sent forty dollars to Harry and Mark it was an added weight of obligation, and he had not yet thrown off the insidious melancholy that was undermining his health. To those who knew his cheery optimism in later years the letters of this period seem almost incredible.

In October, 1827, he took rooms with a professor of medicine in New York in the house of a Dutchman named Vosburg, who formerly navigated the North River, and who knew his uncle. He hoped to study medicine with the professor and to support himself by some outside job. The family had been troubled by his restless morbid spirit and Albert thought it would do him good to get into New York society and to have the stimulus of contact with able men. But when he found upon every other door a doctor's sign and noted that they were "coming up thicker than Pharaoh's locusts" he began to fear he had made a wrong choice. His father wrote to encourage him and suggest that he should start practice by trying to extract a tooth from some one. He also sent Mark a sovereign cure for rheumatism which he had tested out and felt sure Mark could use on his patients with advantage—"an eelskin bound round the limb affected."

In February, 1828, Harry joined Mark in New

York and wrote to ask his father if he should stay another year. The old gentleman replied: "I would say Yes quick if I could find the money, but it is a terrible thing to be in debt." At this period Albert alone of the family seemed to be secure in his position as tutor although, in May, 1828, he wrote: "The annals of the College this term have been tragic and boisterous. The sons of vice which formerly scarce dared to lurk in the kennels have come out into the broad day and scarce blushed to own their father. I owe it to myself to say that though I have been in the hottest of the battle I have not as yet heard of a dog's opening his mouth against me. As for my religious course, I find there is a cheating world, a tempting devil and a wicked heart."

Mark found that to acquire position as a physician he must graduate from some institution, and finally left New York and entered the medical school in Pittsfield in May, 1828. Here by dint of exhausting work he managed to support himself by teaching in a school started by Chester Dewey and known as the Berkshire gymnasium, while at the same time he continued his course in medicine. There were forty scholars in the school and five teachers, and to get through the necessary work he rose every morning at half-past four. He roomed with a son of Governor Clinton, an attractive lad of fifteen. Later he shared the room of Thomas Allan, an old friend. He found, however, that with this heavy load of work he was not progressing as he wished in medicine, and when, through the kindly offices of David Dudley Field, a chance came to him to teach in a young ladies' school in New York, where, for two and half hours a day, he would receive $500 a year, he gladly accepted. He knew he could study medicine in the afternoons, and he kept his connection with the Pittsfield School of Medicine and arranged to get his diploma when he should have completed his studies in New York and was ready to pass the examinations. He was to teach grammar, rhetoric, composition, general history, and arithmetic to a group of young ladies possessed of "a high tone of manners."

He reached New York, after being cheated out of two dollars, at 11 P.M. on December 16, 1828, and took a room in fashionable surroundings in Market Street with his college friends Field and Morgan. This proved beyond his income and he soon moved with David Field to a boarding house occupied by a group of young Frenchmen, where nothing but French was spoken, and where he paid but six dollars a week. Here he was pleasantly settled. A man came at 7 A.M. to make up his fire, and Field and he got up and read awhile before breakfast. At nine he was at Mrs. Smith's school, where he taught until 11:30. Then he went to Doctor Smith's office for instruction or to the hospital to assist in operations. He describes the case of a negro both of whose legs were frozen so that they had to be amputated—without anæsthetic of course, and with only a glass of wine to comfort him. At the first cut he cried: "You dog, you!" but as they carried him out he bowed to the students and, laughing, said: "Good afternoon Gentlemen, I have got my wine." Operations in those days without ether were somewhat gruesome.

At one he attended a lecture from Doctor Smith. At three was the dinner hour, and afterwards they drank coffee and talked with the six Frenchmen "who made as much noise as twenty Englishmen." At five he went to a lecture by Doctor Torrey, and in the evening he talked French again, or read. Harry joined him for a few months and took up his painting with the artist Inman, who treated him very kindly.

In May Mark moved away "from the City of New York to the Village of Greenwich," in order to get the practice among the poor from the Northern Dispensary, of which he was appointed one of the physicians, "to serve gratuitously." As explained above this was really a move to another town. He paid only four dollars a week for board and lodging, but evidently could not afford to take the coach across the meadows to his school in New York, and he found the walk to and fro so taxing that he doubted if it paid to remain in Greenwich. Harry returned to Stockbridge, and sent him some money to tide over his moving as he was running very close to the wind. With all his hard work he did not neglect the cultural side. He joined the National Academy of Design and was greatly interested in their exhibitions and in the progress of art in America. Harry's money came in very handily, for while he was calling at a mansion on

Liberty Street some one stole his hat and gloves, and it took five dollars to provide him with a new hat, and save him from the humiliation of walking the streets bareheaded.

In July he sent his final dissertation to Pittsfield and got his degree as M.D., upon payment of fifteen dollars. The next thing was to gain a practice and, with hope and good cheer, he engaged a pleasant well-furnished office in Greenwich Village at 53 Charlton Street in a fine new block with no doctors. He slept on a twenty-five dollar sofa bedstead, a "really genteel article of furniture," in the office. David Field made his first appearance in court at the same time. Mark felt himself now an established physician and took a seat in Cox's church.

We have already noted the salubrious climate of Greenwich Village, and it proved an unwise location for a doctor for no patients appeared, and finally, tired of waiting and with depleted treasury, Mark moved from his fine office back to New York. He took rooms in the sparsely settled suburbs north of Canal Street, at 79 Grand Street, and eked out his rent by taking the son of a bishop as lodger.

In the meantime his former roommate, David Dudley Field, had been prospering in the law sufficiently to venture upon matrimony, and there was another wedding at the old Cherry Cottage that stirred all Stockbridge. Mark's morbid conscience would not allow him to take the trip home even to see his adopted sister, Lucinda, married to his best friend.

Harry, as usual, was groomsman, and Mark remained in Grand Street, sadly awaiting patients that did not come.

Electa paid him a visit later, and he enjoyed showing her the great metropolis. Art in New York had not reached a very high peak, and visitors from London have even called the paintings exhibited at the academy mere daubs. They interested Mark and Electa, however, and Mark wrote that he spent an hour and a half before West's pictures of "Christ Rejected," and "Christ Healing the Sick," where it was undoubtedly the religious feeling rather than the technical excellence that appealed to him.

Grand Street seemed to bring Mark no nearer to prosperity. He was three months without a paying patient. The constant work at the dispensary proved wearisome and unprofitable. He decided it was "a plague" and gave it up. He was, however, making many friends who were destined to be of great value. Among these was Seth Hunt, whose wife invited him to a great party "in style" on Twelfth Night, with 200 guests. Even this failed to cheer him, and to add to his troubles Mrs. Smith informed him that she was closing down part of the school work, which would cut one hundred dollars from his meager salary. Among his friends was a Mr. Emerson, a brother of the famous author, who brought him in contact with the Unitarians. The newly organized Unitarian Church was arranging a series of lectures for the benefit of a library, and Emerson told him that if he would lecture, and there should be any surplus, he could share in it. This started him on his career as a lecturer in which he was to win such great fame. He delivered two lectures in the Unitarian hall, one on "Sensation" and one on "Vision." These proved quite popular, but did little to help his finances, and once more he had to move, this time to a poor section down town in Mott Street—"the meanest street in the city," in the hope of picking up a pittance from the ills of the poor.

Though he was discouraged himself his family all felt that he had done remarkably well, that he was making a place for himself and that he ought to remain and fight it out. His mother wrote him that she believed he "enjoyed New York more than any other place," that he "had good society, lived handsomely and enjoyed all the necessary comforts of life" which she thought "could be said of but few." There was however a danger in the offing which she had failed to envisage, and which was to cost her some anxious thought.

The danger was located in the dark eyes of a certain young lady. Whether it was one of the young ladies "with high tone of manners" in the school that he taught, or one of those whom he had met at Mrs. Hunt's ball he does not say. We only know that she was unknown to the family, save that his mother had once seen her and thought her extremely pretty. David Field's matrimonial move had evidently started Mark's thoughts, but before proceeding to tie himself up with further obligations, being doubtful concerning his judgment of young ladies, Mark wrote to his mother for advice. We can imagine the anxious hours which the old couple put in beside the fireplace at Cherry Cottage, discussing this new development in their philosophic son. From their discussions emerged a letter worthy to be preserved, wonderful in its combination of tact and good sense, a letter that he kept for future reference. "Could you with encouraging prospects enter the marriage state, it would be the joy of my heart to have it—I mean, should you unite with one who was worthy of you and who would make you happy—but," says Mother, "of such there are but few. I should be unwilling to name the many faults you might chance to meet in a wife, you can enumerate them as well as I, but one fault alone, you know, will sometimes overbalance all good qualifications, and make a man completely wretched through life." She went on to say that she knew that if he found himself unable to provide for the needs of his family "it would be a continual source of misery which your constitution was never made to endure, for I well know that you was particularly formed for peace and quiet, and that the cares and troubles and vexations and perplexities for a family with scant means would sink your spirits and 'vex your righteous soul to death.' " Here spoke the long and bitter experience of a lifetime. Her courageous undaunted spirit had been able to maintain in the home the atmosphere of peace and happiness where others would have sunk under the load of poverty and anxiety, but she did not think her son with his "highpo" could stand that strain.

"It is sometimes said that when hearts are united there is but little wanting, but take my word for it, it is a mere whim. Now to the point—or rather for leaving the matter to your better judgment. I do not know that I have seen or heard a syllable of the girl since I saw you last. You say she is thoroughly good natured; that, in itself, is truly desirable, but I have been in a habit of discerning that those who possess an uncommon share of it, are usually easy and careless to a fault, and beside have generally poor economy. Poor economy in a wife has brought many good men of affluence to poverty and want; but of that, generally speaking, it is hardly possible for a man to know what he ought until it is too late, but as you observed that you was not as well acquainted with her qualifications as you wished, it may be that by deferring the engagement a little longer, you may become better satisfied, and I should judge from your letter that your attachment was not such but you could yield to the sway of reason and your better judgement. I would not say too much but cannot help observing that I think any man who is not in independent circumstances, must be a great sufferer by marrying one who is and is to be wholly unacquainted with what we call household affairs, or manageing the business of a family, for should it not be necessary for her to perform a part herself, without that knowledge, she will ever be liable to impositions from those in her employment.

"I am very sorry that we have not had an opportunity of being somewhat acquainted with her; we all regret that you are not in a situation to be immediately settled in a manner most agreeable to your wishes. I have with the most earnest desire for your happiness, given you my thoughts as above, without wishing to dictate, believing you to be the only suitable person to determine matters of interest and importance to yourself—a sentiment, says your father, which entirely coincides with his feelings on the subject. I hope you will, as far as may be agreeable with yourself, acquaint us with whatever concerns you. Yours most affectionately. M. H."

One is inclined to surmise that in her brief inspection of the young lady, Mother had seen more than she allowed Mark to suspect. As an example of tactful negative suggestion the letter is unexcelled. It would have taken an impassioned and resolute soul to go forward in face of it.

A little later we hear of the young doctor at Niblo's Garden, a place of amusement that had just been opened at great expense by an acquaintance of Mark named Hull, who had spared no expense in making it the finest resort in the city. The gardens were considered very beautiful and there were also pictures on exhibition to interest the artistic element. It became quite the thing to go to Niblo's, and all New York society might be seen there. Mark went on a moonlit evening when it was at its best and says that he found nearly two thousand "well dressed people" there, evidently enjoying themselves greatly. For Mark such a venture was so unusual that one suspects that he was accompanied by a certain charming young lady.

No more is heard of her, however, and one wonders what would have happened had he married her and settled down as a fashionable New York physician. His mother's letter seemed to turn the tide, and influenced seriously his final choice.

In the meantime he writes Harry: "I am at present in that state of indecision in regard to several most important concerns (that is to me) which is most unpleasant. The whole tenor of my life may depend on the course I adopt in regard to what is best." He was at those crossroads which seem to come in the life of every man when his future and perhaps that of thousands depend on a single choice. Doctor Emmons of Williamstown had invited him to go into partnership with him, and Albert is eager to have him there. On the other hand it seemed foolish to leave New York. Then there were invitations to go into lecturing. His life hung in the balance, matrimony, medicine, New York—what should it be?

While he was sitting in despairing indecision Fate took a hand. A letter came from Albert to announce that he had been unanimously elected as Professor of Moral Philosophy and Rhetoric at Williams College.

CHAPTER VIII

MATRIMONY AND BEREAVEMENT

It seems a singular incongruity to turn to New York City for a professor of moral philosophy, and even more eccentric to look for him in the office of a struggling young doctor. Indeed when Mark's name was proposed President Griffin promptly declared that a young medico was not a suitable person to guide the feet of collegiate youth to those lofty heights scaled only by saints and men of genius. Moreover sundry remarks overheard led him to fear that young Doctor Hopkins was not sound on the great doctrine of total depravity and that through overconfidence in the mercy of God he might lead his pupils into the way of destruction. There was a certain Stockbridge bias in the Board of Trustees, several of whom came thence and knew Mark, and remembered his valedictory address in 1824, which had carried them almost beyond their depth in the ocean of philosophy. The ponderous opposition of the learned president would have put a quietus on Mark's candidacy, however, had not Colonel Henry Dwight, Mark's cousin, stood forth to defend him. He recalled Mark's master's oration delivered in 1827 at the close of his term as tutor, on the subject "Mystery." On this occasion young Hopkins had carried his hearers away to heights of which they had never dreamed and revealed the depths that yawned beneath the placid surface of commonplace thought. He had been proclaimed a genius both as speaker and thinker, and copies of "Mystery" had circulated widely through the state. Dwight's eloquent speech made plain to the trustees that they could not afford to lose the opportunity of securing to the college this budding genius and the fame he might acquire. Under the spell of his words the reverend president forgot Mark's doubtful theology and the trustees gave unanimous consent to his election. A brief speech thus determined Mark's career and the future of the college.

Professorships at Williams were somewhat erratic. Professor Kellogg then held the only permanent chair. The French department had disappeared as France became unpopular. The chair of science had been occupied by men of real ability and prominence. Professors Olds and Eaton had been followed by Chester Dewey who had been the mainstay and inspiration of the students. But the president as he grew older and more dictatorial seemed to resent any figure on the stage that drew the public eye from himself and had combated Dewey's influence to such an extent that in 1827, after holding the chair nineteen years, the professor resigned. Albert Hopkins then twenty-one had been called as tutor to fill the gap, and two years later, in 1829, though only twenty-three, he had taken his seat as full professor of the sciences.

The prominence given to science seemed to the president to distract attention from the true aim of the New England College, "to educate pious and promising youth for the gospel ministry," as it was phrased in sundry donations, and to counterbalance this materialistic tendency money had been raised to found in 1826 a chair of moral philosophy. This had been filled by Professor Porter, but was now vacant and awaiting the occupancy of the young city doctor.

Mark's training had been much more in science than in philosophy, but that was before our day of specialism when if a man teaches one subject it is assumed he can teach nothing else. Rather was it assumed that if he could teach one subject he could teach all, and he usually had to do so. If Mark had doubts of his philosophical ability he did not air them. He accepted promptly and just in time for Williams College. The intellectual powers of the president were failing rapidly while his oratorical power seemed only to increase with the result that he left the prosaic routine of teaching to Professor Kellogg and the tutors and devoted himself to turning the college into a mechanism for the conversion of youth. He threw all his energy into the revivals which were his main interest, and but for the timely arrival of the Hopkins brothers the students of Williams College would have received but little teaching in the knowledge of this world.

By his irresistible eloquence he roused the emotions of his hearers to fever heat so that each year—in

1830, 1831, and 1832, there was a period of "engagedness" when the students were cast down into anguished despair over their sins or uplifted to heights of ecstasy, and many conversions were made. We still have a picture of his sermons painted by a student who heard him:

> "He spoke of Hell! and with instinctive dread
> The affrighted heart recoiled. Despair's last
> Agonizing shriek ascending pierced the
> Soul and drank its spirits up—the never
> Dying worm with closer grasp embraced its
> Victim and deeper thrust its deadly fangs.—
> The lurid fires that quenchless burn, arose
> In forky flames and threw their painful light
> Upon the drear abode, where restless toss
> On raging seas of flame, the sinner lost,
> While on their heads the wrath of God in one
> Eternal storm descends."

Here also the president's dominating personality produced friction. He had strict ideas of the solemn atmosphere of dignity and awe that should be preserved in a church, but recent revivalists had introduced innovations to add to the emotional turmoil—shoutings and public confession of sins, and the mourners' bench. Mr. Gridley, the minister of the town church, had the modernistic outlook and attempted to introduce the "new measures" as they were termed. Doctor Griffin denounced him for irreverence, and the controversy split the church. The college had always worshipped with the village church, but in 1834, Doctor Griffin organized a separate college church to meet in the college chapel and withdraw from association with Mr. Gridley and the town. He seems to have had the endorsement of moral philosophy, for the first name on the roll of the college church is that of Mark Hopkins.

Never perhaps did Mark have a more difficult administrative problem. To teach all the president's classes and do all his work and to give all the credit and honor to Doctor Griffin, in order to avoid an outburst from his over-developed ego, was a problem worthy of a professor of psychology. With the president in this condition it was most difficult to keep alive any spirit of enthusiasm in the college. Albert, who felt that every true enthusiasm must rest back on religious devotion, started a noon meeting which became a most notable feature in the college, and became a fount of inspiration which had a most surprising effect on the life and character of the graduates of that period. Albert was a tremendous dynamo; his earnestness and sincerity radiated power which charged the young men about him with energy and devotion. He gained an even stronger hold through the excursions which they made with him into the mountains to study plants and animals and geological structure. We have already noted that the students were so interested in his lectures that they requested to have them doubled in length. His personal influence and Mark's teaching thus held the college together during this critical period with very little help from Professor Kellogg and some hindrance from the president. When he was ill and Mark took his place in the pulpit he seems to have resented the substitution, so that when Mark sought a licence to preach in order to help him out, he again accused Mark of heretical ideas, and for some time prevented him from securing the licence.

We have noted that on Mark's return to Williams he was criticized as lacking in "abdominal dignity" and on hearing of his appointment Harry wrote that he hoped Mark would soon "acquire such a rotundity of corporation as would enable him to wear as large a jacket as any of the Doctors of Divinity." When he made his famous oration on "Mystery" his success had been in spite of his personal appearance for his classmate Morgan exclaimed, "Mark, you are the awkwardest man I ever saw on the stage." At that time he seemed encumbered by his great height and large frame, but later he acquired a slow dignity of carriage and movement that made his bearing most impressive. Perhaps he felt that he had to live up to the title of professor of moral philosophy, for the young ladies of Stockbridge complained to Harry of the change in him, and said they were positively frightened by his manner.

He started in at once to read up on his subject. He even read Plato in French, a strange pursuit. The attitude of his mother and of Harry had caused him to question the old theology and Channing's sermons had added to his doubts, with the result that instead of instructing his classes in the Hopkintonian principles, he attempted to show their defects and to undermine the great system of Edwards that had so long been supreme—a course which must have horrified the president and renewed his suspicion of Mark's orthodoxy. He studied Butler's *Analogy* and Paley's *Evidences*, but found none of the systems of thought then in vogue satisfying. As the old theology went on developing the logical conclusions from its premises it grew further and further apart from reality—a perfect system of thought but apart from life. He felt that he must get back of this structure of thought to actual experience. He cast the old system aside and sought to arouse the young men in his charge to think out a philosophy of their own, which did not depend on books but on their own experience.

When Harry inquired as to his matrimonial prospects he replied: "To love and to be wise at the same time, says Burke, is not given to mortals, and as my station requires me constantly to be wise, I do not know when I can find time for the other." But apparently in some way he found time for a Bible class of young ladies, and this threw him into intimate relations with the young people of the town. It is a perilous endeavor to guide a group of pretty girls through the sacred groves of philosophy and religion. His class became popular and some young ladies even drove five miles to attend. We have already referred to the house built by Lyman Hubbell on the hill above the Rossiter Tavern in South Williamstown for his bride. He had now become a man of no small substance and fame, with a large family of his own. He had a wide estate and had prospered greatly by transporting his produce to Albany and sending it to New York by sloop. His family were well disciplined and trained to frugality and economy, and he had a reputation for allowing no spare pennies to slip through his fingers. The story was told that on one occasion when he failed to return from Albany on time, inquiry was made for him at the village store, and one of the men answered that the major, as he was called, saw a sixpence fall into the Hudson, dove after it, and hadn't come up yet.

Mary Hubbell, his daughter, was a very charming girl, small in stature, and delicate in build, unlike the rest of her family, for her brothers were of stalwart mould. She had a quick responsive mind, and had been trained from childhood in all the home arts and in the management of a household. She evidently felt the need of philosophy for she usually managed to drive the five miles to the Bible class, and it is not surprising that before long the young professor began to accompany her on her homeward trip. Few New Englanders were expansive about their love affairs and Mark was most reticent about his personal concerns. In August, 1831, he casually mentioned in the postscript of a letter to Harry that he was engaged to marry Mary Hubbell.

It was a bolt from the blue. They had thought of Mark as absorbed in philosophic problems, and impervious to the darts of Cupid. The announcement left the family gasping. At least he had remembered his mother's advice. His only comment is: "Tell mother she is a *good* housekeeper," the words heavily underlined. He had escaped the *hité tité* New York girl. The wedding was set for the Christmas season, and after the wedding the bride was invited to visit her "in laws" in Stockbridge. A wedding in the family was enough to upset all the normal routine of life. Cherry Cottage was all in commotion. November 20, Harry writes: "The old house begins to groan from pothole to garret with the din of the approaching wedding. There is no gimlet hole where you can for a moment feel yourself secure from mop water and sand. It is all clutter and spiders are squabbling for life among the mortar. Private counsels are held every ten minutes between Ma and myself—she says, 'Don't say a word to your Pa, but go and do it!' Pa comes in once in a while and says 'I won't! I will! you shan't.' Oh dear me what works! Ma's ambition is *up*." Mark sighs and says "If Ma's pride is up there is no use in saying a word," and, fearful that she will neglect herself in her thought of others, sends her money for a silk dress and a pair of spectacles that she may look her best in the eyes of his charming bride. And so they were married in the Hubbell house on the hill on Christmas Day, 1831, with Harry as groomsman, and Electa and Mary as bridesmaids.

Mary Hopkins, the youngest of Mark's adopted

sisters, had developed into a sprightly girl, surprisingly like her aunt in the quickness of her mind and the cleverness of her retorts. She treated her adopted brother with saucy impudence which cloaked the adoring hero worship which she really felt, but seldom allowed him to suspect. She was popular in Stockbridge and a natural leader in all the sports and amusements, now that her sisters were married. The bride, Mary Hubbell, was a favorite with all her relatives, and there was a great gathering of the clans at the wedding. Her sister had married a very bright, energetic young man, Daniel Dewey, by name, who was destined to achieve fame in jurisprudence, and he and Harry Hopkins with their jokes and high spirits, made the wedding party a most joyous affair, and taxed the dignity of the young professor of philosophy. Dewey teased his sister about the new name she was adopting, a ridiculous name beginning with a "hop." He continued to chaff her when the wedding was over and the bridal party started off for Stockbridge. The sleigh started off down the steep hill to the accompaniment of cheers and applause, but, being somewhat overweighted, it failed to negotiate the sharp turn on the abrupt descent and upset the whole wedding party into a huge drift to the intense joy of the spectators. The bride used to say of her husband in after years that this was their first falling out.

A letter from Daniel Dewey followed the bride to Stockbridge in which he chaffed her mercilessly concerning the accident:

Williamstown, Dec., 1831.

My Dear Mary Hop-Hop-Hopkins—dear me, two teeth gone in getting out that word—This change of name is a terrible puzzle to one's friends; and Mrs. Hop-Hopkins' stay with us was so short that we had no time to practice. To be sure, you made one desperate effort to go no farther than the foot of the hill near the old mansion, and clung to the ground with a determination worthy of the family—but you yielded again to an influence which has governed you in some other matters ere this, and flew away. O for graphic powers, to set before you the spectacle of new married *wife* (how does that word strike your ear) setting out in life and the first step, tumbling over—When I looked up, having just given Frank a parting bun, the old sleigh box lay upon its side, no human being appeared near it—shortly the black cap of Mr. Harry Hopkins began slowly rising from the hole in the snow, then his whiskered face was partly seen, he looked about him as if to see whether on top of the snow or under it, or perhaps to see whether any ill-timed laughter was ready with broad grin to greet the wedding party all in a heap—but the ladies who were impatiently looking on the hill declare that as the stage was being restored to its proper position the head of one Mark Hopkins appeared on the upper side while his walkers very imprudently obtruded themselves no inconsiderable distance through on the lower side—The ladies vouch for this, but among candid people it is doubted—I knew that morning wedding would wind me up and by 12 o clock at noon I was down, came home and went to bed. Wednesday at dinner our table was graced by the presence of your attendants, and now I have to ask what was done to these folks who had returned from Pittsfield—scarcely seated at table before the cry was made for champagne ho! and nothing would do—our old cider was gone, and the town was ransacked for this enlivening drink—it came once and again—I stood or sat mute, Temperance sighed—This was the Troy constitution, which every man carried in his pocket or some others to his liking—If my house is arraigned for this noisy dinner, I hold you responsible—I always said a morning wedding would lead to bad ends—I tell you these matters that you may know we have kept up the wedding like an Irish wake—without a bride too—but I think some of my friends are in danger of making one if not two—I wish my new (but I hope not always so) friend Mr. H. Hopkins could witness it all—It would either cure or confirm his singleness—But then there must remain some of the true politeness unmarried or what would single ladies do—My regards to him I hope you will make yourself sufficiently agreeable to him to induce him to come here to see you. We have talked of you and thought of you and now I have written to you—Wife says she will have a place for the baby on this letter—where O where—good night.

Yr Br D N Dewey.

They returned to Williamstown, February 24, in time for Mark to begin the term's work, and took temporary residence in the mansion house.

Colonel Sloane had the handsomest house in town. Its carving and ornamentation are unusually fine and were brought on mule back from Albany over the Taconic mountains. It has pilasters and fan windows and a carving appropriate to the residence of a bride —two hearts chained together. Sloane kept a boys' school, but fell on hard times and the sheriff turned him out of his house, sold his effects at auction and threatened him with imprisonment. The house, which is now the president's house, is opposite West College, and during Sloane's financial embarrassment Mark arranged to rent half the house for himself and Mary. Then came the excitement of furnishing, of which, indeed a philosopher was incapable. Not in vain had the bride been trained in housekeeping. She was trusted with the family funds and set off all alone to Troy, where she had a wonderful spree buying furniture and carpets without any stupid male interference. She soon had the house arranged to suit her ideas of interior decoration.

Matrimony combined with moral philosophy seems to have been too much for Mark. He came down with a bad fever. If he had been unimpressed by Mary's attempts at decoration, he was now convinced that she was the ideal wife, for she nursed him through the crisis with tender efficiency. The president had condescendingly agreed that if Mark would study theology with him for a year he would remove the heretical taint and withdraw his opposition to Mark's licence. So Mark at length was duly authorized to proclaim his ideas. He was anxious about his preaching, and tried out his first sermons in Stockbridge. His mother wrote that he had only written three sermons, all of them on the same text. She refused to hear the second and third. "Too much is too much" said she. The president's failing health made it necessary for Mark to take the evening service, where he spoke extempore, and sometimes both services.

In October, 1833, his first child was born and named Mary Louisa.

Albert boarded with them, at first in the Sloane house, and when that was redeemed by its owner, in a smaller house which they occupied for many years.

Albert was working hard in his department. In those days a professor had not only to teach but to create his own apparatus. Albert had no equipment for the sciences save what he constructed himself, and he was constantly at work building and inventing machines to show the students the action of electricity and the reactions of chemistry. He built a "shop" and furnace where he could work, and constructed a lathe. He made electrometers to measure the amount of electricity in the atmosphere. He constructed batteries and magnetos. He even made a clock, all by himself. His chief interest was in astronomy, but astronomy without a telescope was like describing a landscape to the blind. He wished Williams to remain at the head of American colleges in her scientific department and not to lose the prestige of earlier years. He finally decided to invest what money he had saved in seeking the latest information and the best instruments in Europe, and he prepared for the great adventure of crossing the Atlantic ocean —no small matter in 1830. He was just engaging his passage when a letter arrived from the South that upset all his plans and had a vast influence on the lives of both brothers.

After Mark's marriage Harry felt more than ever left out of it. He could not bear the thought of going on year after year with the grilling routine of the work at the farm with his brothers both away. He got a position as engineer, to survey a railroad in Pennsylvania from Phillipsburg to Petersburg, to carry soft coal across the summit of the Alleghanies. Mr. Phillips, with whom he stayed at first, was an English gentleman of culture, who had built a fine house in the midst of the wilderness. The surrounding cabins were primitive, "the inhabitants were hogs, dirty, shiftless, and saucy." All around was forest and wilderness, and the boys were soon out in the mountains camping in the forest in shacks and tents and living on bear meat, venison, and turkey, for game was plentiful. Some nights they were caught and slept out in the rain on the stones, stung by gnats and mosquitos. They carried their road through wild "gulphs" along the edge of precipices, not without serious danger. One man fell into the river below and barely escaped alive. Harry had a fall of some twenty feet and caught a bush just as he was going over a precipice. One of the men was bitten by a rattlesnake, and Harry saved his life by cutting his hand open with a razor and constructing a cup which drew out the poison, an achievement which got into the papers and made him famous. The men were careless in felling trees, and Harry was twice struck and injured by falling limbs. Another of the men was knocked headlong and his trousers torn completely off by the fall of a tree thrown down by another tree which the men were felling.

When the Pennsylvania job was done Harry went with his boss, Mr. Robinson, to build a road at Blakely, North Carolina. Here the work was all done by negro slaves, and Harry was given a heavy loaded whip and told to use it plentifully. He says the negroes were faithful and better laborers than were found in the North, and he was shocked at the cruelty with which they were beaten. He saw one cruelly flogged because he was frostbitten and "shirked his work." Even the Southern ladies laid on the whip in terrifying fashion. Harry pitied the wretched, ragged, half-clad negroes so that he gave away all his clothes to them and had barely enough left for himself. He was impressed by the brutalizing effect of slavery—that the men "thought no more of flogging a negro than of eating their breakfast." He was surrounded by men of the toughest, wildest type, "always fighting, clubbing, and drinking. I have made out to get away without being killed or killing any man." But it was also very unhealthful and Harry came down with a fever and was so ill and delirious that they found it necessary to transport him to Petersburg and thence to Richmond, where his cousin, John Henry Hopkins, then lived. John got a doctor and nurse for him and when he did not mend, wrote to Mark and Albert, asking them to come on if they could.

Albert had already gone to New York to take passage for Europe, but he joined Mark there and together they hurried on to Richmond where they arrived September 4, 1834. They found Harry desperately ill, but conscious. He threw his arms around them and murmured their names, with evident joy. He was well cared for by his landlady and a black nurse. He was delirious at times and Mark sat by him by the hour and fanned him. Albert was still greatly disturbed over his salvation, and kept inquiring if he would trust himself in the hands of the Lord, and would not rest until he had obtained a feeble assent. It seems strange that a mere verbal assent to the old doctrine should have been deemed so essential to salvation, and it seems doubtful if Mark so considered it, in view of his earlier statement that the important thing was to acquire a character adapted to Heaven.

On September 5, Harry passed away in the arms of his brothers. Albert was resigned, accepting it as part

HENRY HOPKINS

of the divine plan predestined for many months. Harry was buried in Richmond and Electa and the two brothers were present at the funeral.

It was surprising to find what a deep impression Harry's life had made on all who knew him. Catherine Sedgwick, who had acquired fame as the "lady novelist," wrote an obituary of her cousin which beautifully expressed the feeling about him.

"Mr. Hopkins' life was spent chiefly in the sequestered village of Stockbridge and in the occupation of agriculture. Mother earth was his friend and teacher as well as parent. His mind was as busy as his hand. He enquired into the mysteries of nature. He showed us how beauty and interest may be given to a rural home without expense or any artificial help. He set the flowers of the field in his garden. The economy of the Bee was a study to him. He tamed the shy squirrel and timid birds, and made them enjoy the social principle by which he linked them to him.

"Everything was so well proportioned and adjusted in his character that it did not, like the fabled statue, need the sun to elicit its music, but its harmonies were felt in all lights and in the deep shadows that too often fell upon his destinies.

"He was found of intellectual pursuits. He loved the arts. He had a gift for poetry and painting. He had the most refined and chivalric feeling for woman, manners that would have embellished any drawing room in our land.

"His gifts and graces were his own—they cannot

be obtained by imitation—but his industry, purity, disinterestedness, gentleness, his reverence for religion and his fulfilment of the law of love, are virtues that may be copied. It is a happy circumstance in the life of an individual to have known such a man. It may be a blessed one if those who grieve for him follow his example."

While the life of Harry seems somewhat apart from the progress of this narrative he was, nevertheless, a dominant influence in modifying Mark's view of the old doctrine and in creating his very modern and liberal ideas of education. Moreover in Harry himself we find the perfect flower that grew almost miraculously from the old stony farm lands of New England. From its hard toil and bitter economies and cruel struggle for existence sprang this character so full of charm and radiance, so alive and responsive to all the world's beauty. Just before he went South he wrote: "Do you know that Spring has come? Have you been out to inhale any of these soul-creating breezes? Another such a day and I shall be 'struck to death with mortal joy.' "

Those who sneer at New England Puritanism fail to see how its roots ran deep into the fundamentals of life from which spring strength and beauty and joy—the joy that none can take away.

CHAPTER IX

UNIQUE FEATURES AT WILLIAMS

It is certainly an indication of the adventurous spirit of these lads brought up on a farm in a remote New England valley, that one of them should have dreamed of crossing the high seas and visiting that world of history and romance which seemed so far removed from the Stockbridge farm. It was before the day of steamships. Only one, the *Royal William*, had crossed the Atlantic in passenger service. The first Cunarder sailed in 1840. Albert was in quest of knowledge as well as adventure and was determined that Williams should have the best and latest thing in the way of chemical and astronomical equipment.

On September 15, 1834, he set sail from New York in the sailing ship *Hibernia*, and was no sooner out of sight of land than a north-easterly storm swept them far south to the latitude of Washington. For three weeks the gallant ship fought the winds and waves, bounding and plunging through turbulent seas, while Albert struggled desperately against seasickness. He was only twenty-six, but his natural leadership asserted itself, and in spite of seasickness he organized religious services on board and got the passengers of all creeds to attend, including Quakers, Unitarians, and Catholics.

He was not sorry to land in Liverpool, and his letters show that he kept his eyes open for everything new and strange. Especially was he interested in all the late developments of science. Only recently, in 1830, had the Liverpool and Manchester Railway been constructed, and Stephenson had built a new high power engine for it. Albert's first ambition was to ride behind that engine. Ten miles an hour had been thought fast going, but this locomotive made forty-four miles an hour, and Albert had the joy of riding at this mad and desperate speed, and seeing this world wonder. He went on to London and was overwhelmed by its vastness. "Streets crossing streets—a rush of people and coaches, far more thick and furious than in Broadway." St. Paul's Cathedral, the first great work of architecture he had seen, moved him almost to tears. "I could hardly help crying. The impression comes from a soothing sense of fine just proportion combined with vastness and antiquity." He visited Covent Garden and Drury Lane, and other places of which he had read in *The Tatler*. The houses of Parliament burned down while he was there and he visited their smoking ruins. He even took a walking trip to Cardiff in Wales, the residence of Mr. William Coffin, the astronomer, whom he especially desired to meet. In London he found a fine transit instrument made especially for Mr. Coffin, but which the astronomer had given up on account of the failure of his eyes, and which Albert decided to purchase.

In Paris he got rooms and board in the Latin quarter at one hundred francs the month. He attended the lectures of famous scientists—Thernaud, Poisson, and Biot, and tried to see Cousin. He visited Cuvier's Natural History Museum and saw Lupine, Brogniart, Miobel, and others working in that line. When ill he was attended by a homeopathic doctor—a theory of medicine entirely new to him, but which seemed to work—rather to his surprise.

France was greatly disturbed by President Jackson's messages, and he feared that war was imminent. "The French are a Nation of Soldiers—war is their element. Paris is like a military arsenal. The whole country is filled with mercenaries who have little fear of death and nothing to live for, such butchers are not needed with us."

Mardi Gras was very upsetting to his New England principles, though he says "It is sometimes well to see the follies of men when it falls in one's way to do so." He gave most of his time to collecting a library of scientific books, both old and new, and also purchased various chemical products. Nor did he forget to provide his brother with tomes on moral philosophy. He had an interesting visit with the Irvingites who seem to have had some influence on his theology.

He returned to London by way of Brussels and Ghent, visiting the battlefield of Waterloo on the way. In England he visited the Isle of Wight and spent some time at Woolwich. On the first of April, 1835, after a six months' stay abroad, having completed his purchases of scientific instruments, he sailed for New York, full of a project to put Williams ahead of Harvard and Yale and all other American colleges in science by erecting an astronomical observatory—the first in America. (It transpired later that a similar attempt had been made in Carolina, but this was unknown in the North.)

Accordingly with the air of mystery he loved, he took a group of students up on to East Mountain a few weeks after his return and set them to work with crowbars, quarrying a ledge of quartzite and working himself twice as hard as any of them. Under his enthusiastic leadership the foundations soon were laid for that very striking and attractive observatory building which still stands—a landmark in the college quadrangle. Over the door he inscribed the text: "Lift up your eyes on High and behold Who hath created these." Most of the cost of construction he paid from his own savings.

No college had yet thought of sending out a scientific expedition, and that same year in the autumn, he organized an expedition to study the geology and flora and fauna of Nova Scotia, thus maintaining the lead of Williams in scientific investigation. His efforts differed from those of later scientists in that his chief aim was to interest the students in science, whereas in these days professors seem chiefly inter-

HOPKINS'S OBSERVATORY

ested in discoveries that will add to their fame, and the instruction of students is incidental. Albert had already noted that in Europe the professor, no matter how good a teacher, amounted to nothing, unless he had published a monograph that attracted attention.

Albert gathered a group of twenty, chiefly undergraduates with three teachers, and chartered the sloop *Flight* and sailed from Boston to Eastport, Maine, a forty-hour trip. Here they visited some extraordinary veins of lead, and then sailed across to Nova Scotia. They had a perilous moment when they thought the ship would be dashed on the rocks and the sailors in terror shouted "Say your prayers!" to Albert's amusement, who remarked that the time for prayer was earlier in the day. Now was the time for work.

They made a good collection of minerals and studied the tides of the Bay of Fundy. This, however, was incidental. He had wakened a deep interest in the minds of this group, and he had had an opportunity to gain a real and permanent hold upon them all.

He was accompanied on the trip by Doctor Emmons, who lectured in the college off and on from 1828 to 1863, on chemistry, geology, and mineralogy, and who added to the pre-eminence of the institution in the scientific field, and in experimental work. He was dull enough in his classes, but in his field work, as he explored the country around Williamstown he aroused the deepest interest in his scholars, and was another exponent of the Williams method of studying science from nature rather than from books. He surveyed the state of New York and made a geological discovery which he announced under the name of the "Taconic System." He was opposed and ridiculed by the authorities of the day but came out triumphant in the end, and Jules Marcou has called him the founder of American stratiography and the first discoverer of primordial fauna in any country. In 1851 he was appointed state geologist of North Carolina. Letters from him in 1857 show him in the midst of the fight with American geologists, while he has won over Marcou of Zurich and Sir Charles Lyall to his side. He announces the discovery of "a beautiful little jaw" in the Permian sandstone, and says "this mammal is the most ancient mammal of the globe."

Professor Emmons in his department acquired more fame than any other Williams professor.

In the meantime things were in bad way with the college. The president, ill and increasingly senile, ignored all hints that he should resign and made matters difficult for the Hopkins brothers who were exerting every energy to keep the college going. Finally, in 1836, when for a whole year the president had done no teaching, the suggestion became so imperative that he resigned. The trustees chose Absalom Peters of Bennington in his place, but he declined. The seniors then took a hand. For a whole year they had received all their instruction from Mark, and had come to admire and like him. They knew that any suggestion as to the presidency would be regarded by the trustees as unwarranted presumption and would defeat itself. Accordingly they drew up a most tactful letter stating their great satisfaction with the teaching of Professor Hopkins and expressing the hope that future senior classes might receive similar instruction and participate in similar satisfaction. As the seniors were always taught by the president the hint was sufficient. When the papers were read to the trustees, Doctor Shepherd of Lenox exclaimed: "If the boys want him, let them have him."

Without this suggestion from the student body Mark would hardly have been chosen president, and he entered on his work with the consciousness that the student body was behind him. He was a Berkshire man, and most of the trustees were from Berkshire. He was born in Stockbridge and Stockbridge influence had always been dominant since the first class graduated four Stockbridge men. He was the great-grandson of Abigail, the sister of the founder of the college, so that everything seemed to conspire to make his appointment fitting and successful.

His inaugural on September 16, 1836, on "A Wise System of Education" attracted wide attention, and drew an enthusiastic letter from Theodore Sedgwick. The college, which had already come into prominence through Albert's observatory and scientific expeditions, seemed to leap forward into prosperity. The classes which had averaged twenty-eight for the past nine years before 1836, increased to an average of forty-two for the next nine years and later to more than fifty.

In 1843, after Mark Hopkins had been president for seven years, was held the Semicentennial of Williams College, an event of real importance in the annals of Massachusetts. It was a hundred years since Ephraim Williams, Sr., was sent from Stockbridge to survey the valley of the Hoosick and lay out the town which was to be named Williamstown from his son. It was one hundred years since the first white child was born in Stockbridge, Electa, the daughter of John Sergeant and grandmother of Mark Hopkins. In that period a nation had been born, the wilderness had been settled with prosperous towns—the wigwam of the Indian had been replaced by churches, schools, and colleges, the smoke of his campfire by the smoke of a score of busy factories with their swarming workmen. The anniversary address of the president summed up in eloquent words the changes in the past fifty years since the college founded by Colonel Ephraim first opened its doors. Since then a thousand young men had been graduated and gone out to take their places in the world. He quoted President Griffin to the effect that the founding of the college had marked the beginning of a new era in the world. 1793! It was then that the French Revolution burst upon the world, and "the shock of that moral earthquake began to be felt among the nations."

Today we think ourselves in the midst of an upheaval in fundamentals, but it is really only an echo of that stupendous earthquake that shook the foundations of thought and religion and morals in 1793. Up to the French Revolution the dogmas of religion had been unquestioningly accepted by the mass of mankind, and along with them the divine authority of kings and rulers. The stability of the social order and of the moral order as well, was based on fear of that punishment in the flames of Hell which was certain for all who disobeyed the divine command.

These ideas of God and Heaven and Hell were the rock bottom on which the whole social and moral structure was reared. The authority of every father, of every judge, and ruler, as well as the virtue of every citizen rested back on these beliefs and the fear and awe which they engendered, and French Revolutionary thought had shaken this foundation rock until it threatened to crumble.

We, today, can hardly picture the amazement and horror of the defenders of law and morality as they witnessed this attack upon those great truths which had been as unquestioned as the solidity of the earth and as inviolable as the holy of holies. An echo of their feeling we find in the attitude of some toward Soviet Russia. Mark Hopkins says of that period when Williams was founded: "Infidelity, having gained the ascendancy in France, was then mustering and concentrating her forces, and was sending out her emissaries to convert the Nations, and Anarchy and Bloodshed were following in her train. Coming into being at such an era the first half century of Williams

College could not but be eventful in the history of the race. Perhaps no fifty years since the world began has been more so, and in connection with the great events that have taken place the human mind has been greatly agitated and aroused. Every institution has been scrutinized, every opinion has been tested." The most remarkable result was that out of all this welter the great principles of civil and religious liberty emerged—"so firmly established we trust, that they cannot be shaken."

And Williams had not been behind in the effort to establish those principles of liberty on a firm foundation and to resist the chaotic tide of atheism and license that was pouring forth upon the world from France and threatening to engulf the whole world as her victorious armies swept over Europe, until even across the seas men feared that they too would be subjected unless a firm and determined stand was taken. Even before Mark's time, in the infancy of the college, when President Adams was hesitating whether to resent the insults heaped upon his commissioners by the revolutionary government and to arm America to resist this gathering force of disorganization, the students of the little college in the Berkshire Hills, then five years old, gathered together and drew up a letter in somewhat magniloquent language to inform the President that Williams, as the youngest institution, wished also to be the first to assure him of their support against this anarchic attempt to undermine the whole structure of government and religion. The letter might have been written today in reference to Soviet Russia and I therefore quote it in full:

ADDRESS OF THE STUDENTS OF WILLIAMS COLLEGE TO THE PRESIDENT OF THE UNITED STATES

From *The Hampshire Gazette,* Northampton, Mass., July 25, 1798.

Sir—Though members of an infant Institution and of little comparative weight in the scale of the Union, we feel for the interest of our country. It becomes every patriotic youth in whose breast there yet remains a single principle of honour, to come forward calmly, boldly, and rationally to defend his country. When we behold, Sir, a great and powerful nation exerting all its energy to undermine the vast fabrics of Religion and Government, when we behold them inculcating the disbelief of a Deity, of future rewards and punishments; when we behold them discarding every moral principle and dissolving every tie which connects men together in Society, which sweetens life and renders it worthy enjoying; when we behold them brutalizing man that they may govern him—as friends to Humanity, as sharers in the happiness of our fellow-men, as Citizens of the world, our feelings are deeply affected. We commiserate the fate of our

European Brethren; we weep over the awful calamities of anarchy and atheism.

But when we behold this Nation, not contented with its vast European dominions, but endeavouring to extend its Colossean empire across the Atlantic, every passion is roused; our souls are fired with indignation. We see that their object is universal domination; we see that nothing less than the whole world, nothing less than the universal degradation of man, will satisfy these merciless destroyers. But be assured, Sir, we will oppose them with all our youthful energy and risk our lives in defence of our country.

Untaught in the school of adulation, or the courts of sycophants, we speak forth the pure sentiments of Independence. We give you our warmest approbation. We behold with true patriotic pride the dignified conduct of our Chief Magistrate at this alarming crisis. We are highly pleased with the moderation, candor, and firmness which have uniformly characterized your administration. Though measures decisive and energetic will ever meet with censure from the unprincipled, the disaffected, and the factious, yet virtue must eternally triumph. It is this alone that can stand the test of calumny; and you have this consolation, that the disapprobation of the wicked is solid praise.

At this eventful period our eyes are fixed upon you, Sir, as our political Father, and under Providence we rely on your wisdom and patriotism, with the cooperation of our national Council, to perpetuate our prosperity; and we solemnly engage, that, while our Government is thus purely and virtuously administered, we will give it our whole Support.

These, Sir, are the unanimous sentiments of the Members of Williams College, who, though convinced of the evils of War, yet despise peace when put into competition with National Freedom and Sovereignty.

Signed by a Committee in behalf of one hundred and thirty Students of Williams College——

DAVID L. PERRY.
SAMUEL COWLS.
SOLOMON STRONG.
SILAS HUBBELL.
Committee.

Williams College, June 19, 1798.

Another astounding feature of the period was the sudden awakening of science and invention. Mark Hopkins continues: "It had been the era of the application of Science to the Arts and of the extension of the dominion of man over physical nature. If man had been endowed with the strength of a giant and the wings of an eagle, the gifts would hardly have been greater." We have already noted that in its interest in the progress of science Williams was somewhat unique in that day. The early colleges existed chiefly for the training of men for the ministry, in order that each community might have as its leader a man of culture and one with a trained mind. The trustees of Harvard and Yale at first were all ministers and their influence dominated. Williams, however, started with a board of trustees in which the majority were laymen, and we have shown how they were able to vote the old theology out of the curriculum and to lay down a college course in which science bore a leading part.

In this memorable address in which Mark Hopkins summed up the special and unique achievements of Williams during the half century, he laid emphasis on what had been accomplished in science—an example of which was the building of the first astronomical observatory in the country. This was merely a part of a definite plan of scientific education which had its beginning as far back as 1818 when Professor Amos Eaton used to take groups of twelve students out into the hills to study minerals and plants, and which the Hopkins brothers had developed in a fashion strangely modern for that age. The fundamental principle adopted in "all education respecting sensible objects was that we are not so much to talk about a thing as to show it. You may tell me of the magnitude and motion of the planets, but let me see them hanging in space and passing rapidly through the field of a large telescope—or let me turn that same telescope upon one of the nebulæ, or into the depths of infinite space, and it is quite another thing to me. The idea is that the teacher is to make nature the principal, and, as far as possible, to let her do her own teaching. In pursuance of this idea the Magnetic

Observatory (a second building) has been built, very efficient Meteorological and Natural History Associations have been formed, and scientific expeditions and pedestrian tours have several times been undertaken." The direct object "was not so much the extension of Science as to convey a more accurate impression of the Universe as now known and to promote habits of observation. The student is led to direct communion with nature, and though you do not advance Science immediately, yet you kindle fires."

To us the laboratory and experimental method of education is such a matter of course, that we do not realize what a surprising and startling idea it was to those who listened to Mark Hopkins's exposition of the new Williams method, applied not only to Astronomy but to Chemistry, Physics, Geology, and Natural History. We have hardly yet learned the supreme importance in education of "kindling fires." An interest awakened is worth more than a thousand facts learned. As he says "You incorporate your course into the very being" of the student and of Nature too.

This is such an epochal address in the history of education that it is surprising it is not more generally known. Few thought of looking to the little college hidden in the Berkshire Hills as a leader in educational movements, and its achievements passed unnoticed.

A second unique achievement of Williams, which

Mark Hopkins placed first, was the kindling of the interest in world affairs, and the wakening of the sense of world responsibility due to the little group who started the great Foreign Missionary movement. It was this great wave of religious devotion and of sympathy with every race and tribe that he saw rolling out to meet and to conquer the advancing tide of Infidelity. For a time Williams College had been swept by this current of atheism and immorality. Then the counter wave, started by the earnest group of college boys beneath the Haystack, had rolled out not only through the college but through the whole world. The influence they have had upon the world may be judged from the fact that today the American Board, which sprang directly from their efforts, has in Africa, India, China, Japan and the Near East 10 colleges (in addition to those turned over to the Near East Relief) with 5000 students, 20 collegiate schools with more than 1000 pupils, 68 secondary schools with 12,000 pupils, 1000 primary schools with 75,000 pupils, 30 hospitals with 25,000 in patients and dispensaries where more than 600,000 were treated last year. Their influence in educating leaders and in relieving suffering is beyond calculation.

Another unique feature at Williams was the Society of the Alumni, organized by Governor Washburn in 1821, which had kept the Alumni in close association with the college and brought aid in troublous times. This was copied by both Harvard and Yale in 1842, but for twenty years Williams was the only college with such an organization to aid and advise in its government. It was the first instance of democratic government in a college, for a certain proportion of the trustees were chosen through this Society of Alumni, while other colleges were governed by self-perpetuating oligarchies. Yet another idea peculiar to Williams was the founding of a Horticultural and Landscape Gardening Association, the design of which was to interest the students in beautifying the college grounds, instead of attempting to deface them. The students did all the work in this landscape gardening "whose object was to promote health and a taste for the beautiful. It shows that students can make of college just what they choose. When standing in the midst of the beauty thus created my mind has had a vision of what a college might be." He emphasizes strongly the importance of this culture as a part of education.

It will be noticed that Williams sought as far as possible to interest the students in educating themselves, rather than to force knowledge upon them. Another instance in which Williams took the lead in this type of education initiated by the students is found in the two rival Literary and Debating Societies, the Philologian and Philotechnian, founded in 1796, and established in rooms in East College as soon as that edifice was finished. Many well-known orators, among them President James A. Garfield, were trained in the debates of these societies.

Williams had pre-eminence in yet another field,

in that the first Anti-Slavery Society in any college and probably the first in New England was founded there in 1823. In 1827 an oration against slavery was delivered on the Fourth of July and an ode written by one of the students was sung, which described the emotions of a liberated slave. William Lloyd Garrison did not begin his agitation until 1826, so that it would seem that the Williams organization was one of the first in that part of the world.

It was also claimed that Williams was the first college to build a gymnasium and to institute regular instruction in gymnastics. This was done in 1825. In 1886 Doctor A. P. Peabody wrote to Mark Hopkins attempting to prove that Harvard had not been far behind Williams in up-to-date ideas. He says:

> . . . There is in your exceedingly interesting historical sketch one item which I am disposed, not to dispute, but to call in question. I have not your *precise* date, & you may be right, yet barely so. I refer to the priority of Williams College as to gymnastic arrangements. Harvard must have been nearly coincident in time, perhaps a little before, perhaps a little after Williams College. Doctor Fallen came to Cambridge, as teacher of German, in 1825. I was of the first class under his tuition. I graduated in '26. Among his first enterprises was a gymnasium for Harvard College. Whether in '25 or '26 I cannot say, under his auspices the Delta, on which Memorial Hall now stands, & one of the large dining halls in

University Hall were completely fitted up with gymnastic apparatus, & the entire body of students exercised therein & thereon under Dr. Fallen's superintendence. The system had been in full operation, at least for several months, I think for more than a year before I graduated. A classmate of mine, George F. Haskins, afterward Father Haskins of the Romish Church, the year after we graduated, went to Providence, aided in the establishment of the first gymnasium in Brown University & was teacher of gymnastics there.

The subject is hardly worth the paper on which I have written about it; but it is among the infirmities of growing years to make much of little things. Ought it to be so, when we are drawing so very near the greatest of realities?

Excuse me, & believe me,
With sincerest reverence & affection,
Ever truly yours,
A. P. Peabody.

Having outlined the various lines in which Williams had taken an original, if not unique position, Mark Hopkins went on to explain the Williams plan of education, which was, instead of teaching a variety of incoherent facts and subjects, to present the student with a coherent system of knowledge. First came languages, as the basis of all communication, and mathematics as the basis of all scientific knowledge. Then came the natural sciences—man's knowledge of the external world, taught by the method of observation, and finally the study of man himself. This was chiefly the work of the president. He took up first the study of the physical man and every organ and tissue of the body. Then followed the intellectual man—his various faculties and the processes of the mind. Then ethics with a study of individual and political morality, constitutional history and the rights and duties of American citizens. Then æsthetics and the principles of the fine arts, and finally, theology and the reaction of the natural to the moral government of God. Thus when the course was finished the student had gained a comprehensive view of the body of human knowledge and the inter-relation of the various subjects, could talk intelligently of any of them, and had had his interest stimulated sufficiently to ensure that he would follow up some of them at least in his future reading. If it did not produce eminent specialists the system did turn out men of culture.

Mark Hopkins is not aiming to equip men for money-making or to secure them social prestige. He wishes to fit them to bear a useful part in the progress of the world. He looks forward to the Centennial of the College fifty years hence, and says: "The impressions which we choose to make in the yielding materials of time, will, before that, have been made, and have become set in the eternal adamant of the past. What then remains to us in this period of the birth throes of coming wonders but to meet our responsibilities as patriots, as scholars, as Christians, as the Alumni of an institution where the fire of a benevolence practically embracing the world was first kindled in this country and upon whose altars that fire has never gone out? Let us then throw ourselves upon the tide of this great movement—the advancing tide of Christian progress, which we trust is to rise and swell and flow over all the earth."

Considering the time and place the effect of this address was prodigious. For the first time the Governor of the State was present at commencement. The Lieutenant-Governor, Childs of Pittsfield, was a Williams 1802 man, and through his influence Governor Morton was induced to come. In the general reaction against the Whigs he had been elected governor against Edward Everett, who had held the chair for several years, by one vote. He was escorted from North Adams by a band of music, a cavalcade of gentlemen on horseback and a long train of carriages. Berkshire had never seen such a demonstration of enthusiasm as that which saluted him. Nearly half of the living Alumni were present to greet him, and the meeting of old friends and classmates after years of absence brought about an atmosphere of deepest emotion. Mark's uncle Jared, now Chaplain of Charlestown Prison, of the class of 1800, was present. He was introduced to the governor as "the only Alumnus who hails from States Prison" and recommended for an unconditional pardon. The Governor instantly rose and said "A pardon is impossible so long as he continues his present course of conduct!" Even the Whigs among the alumni were won by his quick wit and cheered as if he had not been a Democrat when he made his speech in the afternoon.

Mark Hopkins at this time was forty-one years old and in the prime of life. Even with his "scholarly stoop" there was something majestic and almost venerable in his appearance as he stepped forward, his tall frame spare yet massive, the wide dome of his forehead, the large high-bridged nose, and deep-set eyes with their bushy brows, his slow stately movement and clear solemn utterance all conspired to create a deep impression which grew as he continued his speech, until as it closed with a magnificent period, men were fairly lifted from their feet and stirred to the soul with enthusiasm for their Alma Mater.

It was needed. When Mark Hopkins accepted the presidency he stipulated that it should not be incumbent on him to raise money. He had none of Doctor Griffin's astonishing ability to conjure the dollars from men's pockets and such an effort was utterly distasteful to him. For the course on Anatomy and Physiology with which he began his teaching of the subject "Man," he felt it was necessary to have a model or manikin, which would cost $600—a huge sum in that day when his whole salary was $1100. He would not charge the college with it or solicit money for it. He gave his note for it and then started to earn thc money by giving lectures around in the neighboring towns. With the manikin packed in the back of his sleigh we see the young college president jogging along the weary thirty-five miles to Stockbridge through the snow to earn enough money to redeem his note. Many of his old friends attended and his lecture was received with the greatest enthusiasm. His adopted sister Mary Hopkins wrote him of the effect on the young ladies of Stockbridge. His earlier awkwardness was gone, and also the somewhat distant gravity of his manner when first inducted to the chair of Moral Philosophy. There remained great dignity indeed, but even greater charm, in the occasional twinkle of his deep-set eye, in the keen shafts of wit, in the play of expression when his firm lips broke into a smile, and most of all the sense of great power held in reserve, of a personality with vast depths of resource. Those who heard him were strangely and deeply moved as one would not suppose possible by a mere lecture on anatomy. Rather than to beg he endured the arduous toil of this lecture trip, in addition to his other heavy work.

It may then be imagined what a terrible blow it was when one Sunday afternoon, October 17, 1841, a man rushed into the church where the students were gathered at services and announced that the East College was on fire. In spite of heroic efforts of the students to save it it burned to the ground and they barely saved the observatory by hanging out wet blankets. There was no insurance. The building had cost $12,400 and was a total loss. Fifty students were homeless, and the junior and senior recitation rooms destroyed. Mark Hopkins was in despair. He had just succeeded as president in getting the college into good running order after the disorganization resulting from the illness of Doctor Griffin, and now came this blow in a fatal spot, where he felt himself utterly incapable. He could not raise money. Oh, for a Doctor Griffin who could gather up $15,000 in a few weeks. He expected that the seniors and juniors, having no place to stay, would all go home and the college come to an end. But their comrades in West College made room for them somehow and not a man left. But how to rebuild? He expressed his despair to a friend in town, a Mrs. Whitman, and she said: "Don't be discouraged, I'll give $1000." Her sister gave another thousand, and a paper was circulated through the town. When the alumni gathered, their dinner table was spread under the trees and, after an eloquent address by Nicholas Murray, a sum was raised among them also, one subscription coming from Morse the inventor of the telegraph. Mark Hopkins went to Boston and appealed to the Legislature. They inquired if Williams College wasn't somewhere near the North River and appointed a committee to investigate, but nothing was done.

The sting of this neglect was perhaps a stimulus to the superb Semi-Centennial address. In it, after telling the work that the little forgotten college in the hills has done, Mark Hopkins goes on to say that aside from three bequests, one for $5000 and two for $1000 each, the college had received nothing by legacy or private gift, no edifice erected or professorship endowed, that while other colleges were receiving large sums for superfluous extras, his appeal of dire emergency—a college burned—and homeless students—had not been able to elicit even $2000 from the city of Boston. He says that in this remote corner they do not ask for or expect wealth. They have health; not a student has sickened or died. They only ask the bare essentials of subsistence and they feel that they can give more priceless gifts than money can buy.

Although Mark Hopkins could not raise money, in some way enough came in to rebuild East College and to erect near it a third dormitory known as South College. These were both finished in time for the Semi-Centennial celebration, and the triumph of this achievement made an added point in the great address.

Although Mark Hopkins attempted no financial campaign the college gradually became better known as he was invited to lecture far and wide. Prominent men came there to speak and put the town on the map of that day. In fact Rufus Choate delivered an oration on Patriotism at Commencement in 1850 in which he dealt with the Fugitive Slave Law in such fashion that violent emotions were stirred all over the country.

In 1866 Governor Bullock came to Commencement and seems to have been deeply impressed with the superiority of Williams to Amherst and Harvard. In a letter from Cambridge on August 28, 1866, Emory Washburn says:

Cambridge Aug. 28, 66

Dear Sir

I had a conversation with Gov Bullock today which I think I ought to repeat for your satisfaction since every body likes to know how far he succeeds in his efforts to accomplish the great business of his life. He spoke in very strong terms of his visit at Commencement. He was delighted with the manner in which he was received & treated, with the place & all he said. He said he told one of his aids, Mr. Washburn, at the time, in reply to his remark "this is finer than any thing we have yet seen," that "he thought the exercises at Cambridge & Amherst about equal but that what he heard there was decidedly in advance of both those." Washburn had already expressed himself to me, in strong terms of surprise and approbation of the whole affair. And I understand Mr. Brigham was very much pleased. I quote once more from Gov B & I will pass on—"That old President" (the profane fellow) "I tell you is a trump—I never saw a man preside so well as he did. . . ."

CHAPTER X

THE TEACHER

So much has been said of the teaching of Mark Hopkins since President Garfield defined the true university as a log with Mark Hopkins on one end and himself on the other, that it is unfortunate that there are so few satisfactory accounts of his recitations. Among hundreds of letters from alumni testifying to the tremendous effect which his teaching produced upon them there is little that is definite and concrete.

First as to the substance of his teaching. We may say that although it covered also anatomy, psychology, and civics, his most important work was on the line of philosophy and ethics. Every system of thought acceptable to Christian men had to be based on the facts of the Bible as much as upon those of science. The Bible was as certain a source of information as the book of nature. It might be interpreted in a variety of ways, but its fundamental facts could no more be denied than the multiplication table. As we consider the various systems of philosophy today and the totally contradictory conclusions arrived at by idealist, realist, pragmatist, and behaviorist, and feel how far any of them are from the experience of the man on the street and how little help they seem to give to a true understanding of ourselves and of the real value of life, we turn back with a certain relief to the utter simplicity of the teaching of Mark Hopkins. He was not seeking to construct an elaborate philosophical system and thrust it upon his pupils. He sought to train them to think their way into the heart of things, and to think in such fashion that life would have a meaning and that they could use their powers to the best advantage. He turned away from all those sceptical systems that threw doubt on the validity of sensation and perception, holding that if one cannot trust the report of human consciousness there is then no basis for knowledge. It is easy to construct an idealistic system that ignores the material world, or a materialistic system that denies the reality of consciousness and of the soul, but in both of these paths one diverges from practical experience and is soon far away from the actual world of men. Although in those days most philosophers gave their chief attention to reason and the intellect, Mark Hopkins clung to sensation and feeling as the primary essentials of consciousness on which thought is based and from which life derives its value. While he did not accept the sceptical philosophy of the day, no more did he adopt Hamilton's method of upholding the reality of the spiritual world by asserting that faith was an organ of the mind whereby we apprehend with certainty the supra-sensual realities. Faith to Mark Hopkins was simply trust in a reliable person.

When it came to ethics he opposed the theories of

the day that there was an absolute right revealed by conscience, and held that nothing is right unless there is a reason for it, or unless it can be shown to bring ultimate happiness to all. The supreme good is the highest form of happiness and is found in right relationship to God and man. His recitations on the catechism were a special feature and were open to visitors, and I can remember attending them as a boy.

The first question "What is the chief end of man? To glorify God and enjoy Him forever," was one which few will forget who heard him discuss it. He would make it clear that to glorify God was really to enjoy Him forever, and also that to enjoy Him was to glorify Him, and he made very vivid that higher joy that came to those who found the glory of the Creator in all the beauty of nature, and in the marvel of its intricate laws and adaptations, as well as in the progress of man and in the powers of his mind and in the beauty of his achievements, and who in enjoying that glory added to it and carried it forward to new revelations of divine beauty.

There are few Williams graduates of the period who have not before them the picture of him as he sat at the desk in the old senior recitation room—his tall frame slightly stooped—above his great breadth of shoulder the massive head with sparse white locks brushed forward over its great dome, the long high-bridged aquiline nose, the piercing grey eyes beneath their bushy brows, the wide firm mouth, ready to break into a smile, a figure of superb majesty combined with ready geniality. On the desk was a little tin box containing pasteboard slips on each of which was inscribed the name of one of the class—his "pill box"—they called it. He would stoop forward and pick out one of these and read the name. This made the recitation as exciting as a game of roulette, for no man knew when or how often his name would come up. Some told me they had terrible luck with the pill box. The man who was called rose to his feet and the doctor then propounded a question. He cared little for textbooks or formal answers. He did not ask "What does the book say," but "What do you think about this?" He wanted to know what each man thought with his own brain, or if he did not think, to make him think. He showed no anxiety that the man should agree with him, but if he disagreed he had to defend his position under the fire of keen questions from the doctor. Whatever he taught were facts that he had thought out for himself. He read very little, but in all these years he had been thinking hard and had come a long way from those days when he had puzzled over the old theology.

Mark Hopkins made no effort to compel attendance and kept no list of absentees. Apparently he thought that if they did not want to come they might as well stay away. As a matter of fact they did come, partly because it was a college tradition to attend the doctor's classes, and partly because the recitation was nearly always interesting, and sometimes quite amusing and exciting. It was never the same and one never knew what might turn up. He was not trying to pump philosophy into men but to draw it out from them. His materials were not in textbooks but in their own minds, which made the course follow the most unexpected turns. He started some men thinking who had got little if anything from their other courses, and on the other hand the clever scholar who had all his lessons by heart, often got little from him. He admitted that there were eight or ten men in every class with whom he could do nothing, and he did not care whether they attended or not. Ordinarily they did attend, chiefly in the hope to see their classmates floored. He made little effort to compel attention or to discipline. Indeed it was seldom necessary. The interest of the quick fire of questions held them, and though his keen wit often provoked a laugh, there was a dignity and stateliness about him that preserved order. When he did speak in reproof, it came as a bolt, blasting, withering, scorching, and there was no danger that the offence would be repeated. I have been speaking of his later life, but he seems always to have carried that atmosphere of dignity. I can remember hearing of his annoyance when he was little beyond his fiftieth year, because a lady rose in a Boston horse-car and offered him her seat. This was by no means because he seemed feeble, quite the contrary —he gave the impression of massive strength, but there was a strange power about him that compelled reverence even from strangers. In 1855 he writes: "I seem to be getting more venerable, as a man I met today asked me if I was Prof. Hopkins' father." In spite of his venerable appearance he possessed great strength and endurance. On May 22, 1850, his old college friend John Morgan writes him from Oberlin to express his astonishment that Doctor and Mrs. Hopkins are contemplating a walk to Pittsfield, twenty miles away, a feat from which modern youths would shrink:

". . . You & your good wife must be stouter than we are, or the very thought of the walk to Pittsfield would appal you. When the walk is accomplished, it will be worth publishing in the Court Journal along with the exploits of Queen Victoria & Prince Albert. You must be a hale old couple. I don't know whether you have made much progress towards the normal rotundity of doctors of divinity—nor am I learned enough in such matters to know whether it behoves the wife to keep pace in dimensions with her rotund husband. The primitive leanness of simple Mark Hopkins would be more auspicious to a race with or towards a locomotive. . . ."

He was always amused at the comments of the press on his appearance and on October 17, 1877, he writes his wife:

". . . Louise has written the family news and so for the want of something better I will copy a paragraph from *The Republican* that has just come.——

" 'A fine steel engraving of Rev. Dr. Mark Hopkins ex-president, and now professor in W^ms^ College, is the most remarkable feature of the Eclectic magazine this month. It well represents the intense profound and eager face of this fine philosophical scholar and teacher, and does much to explain to those who do not know him the high place he holds among American educators and metaphysicians.' This probably will remind you of the description by the man who went through the tunnel and saw so much that was not there. . . ."

To Williams men he became the incarnation of all that they most revered, an unforgettable figure, as they saw him walking along the path over-arched by elms to the old recitation room, with his gold-headed cane, and long frock coat, and tall silk hat. Even with his slight stoop his massive head seemed to tower above other men. Or they see him as he stood in the pulpit, in the familiar pose with arms loosely folded, a position of complete ease, in which one felt vast energies in reserve that could readily be launched if his words with their clear solemn enunciation and steady gathering power, failed to reach the mark.

It is difficult to portray the power of a great teacher. To recount the words he spoke utterly fails to convey the impression. When Mark Hopkins spoke them they came with a new meaning. There was a power behind them that woke the intelligence. The sense of a great intellect, and more of a great personality behind them, invested them with an importance that seemed to make them penetrate to a deeper layer in the consciousness of the hearer.

Most words glance off from our intelligence and

fail to produce the impression they should. His words, though no more remarkable perhaps, seemed to penetrate and germinate, awaking thought and response in his hearers. He was always dignified, but in his recitations, his keen shafts of wit discharged at some youth who was intentionally obtuse, would waken prolonged laughter, which he enjoyed with the rest. Repeated, they make but little impression—it was the quickness of retort, and even more the sense of the man behind them that made them tell. He did not ask clever questions to answer them himself and develop his system. He asked them to make men think out problems for themselves, and he was sincerely interested in the answers. Sometimes he left them unanswered. I can remember when I was ten years old he called me to him and asked: "What do you think your conscience is?" I have been trying to think out the answer to that ever since. He never answered it. He would take any amount of pains to aid a man to work out whatever problem he was trying to teach. I remember when I was six years old sitting on his knee while he taught me to whistle, and I can see his face as he puckered up his lips time after time to show me how to make the required sound, keeping patiently at it until I succeeded.

When he undertook the management of the college matters were at loose ends and he was compelled to resort to some severe discipline. It created an atmosphere that he disliked, and he soon abandoned the method. His idea was that the discipline of a college should be like that of a family, where the children obey because they revere and love their parents. He thought it futile to compel students to attend recitations and to learn when they did not wish to do so, or to force them to behave respectfully when they did not feel respect. And so far as he himself was concerned discipline was seldom necessary. His whole aim was to provide instruction that would interest the men, and to have leaders that they would honor. As soon as it was possible he did away entirely with the system of tutors, and by 1853 all the teaching was done by full professors. If the teaching were what it should be he cared little for equipment and accessories. When he finally resigned he realized that he had done little to raise money to provide the college with buildings and apparatus, but he had seen to it that in place of the three professors there were then nine who gave the best instruction he could secure. "A college is like a lighthouse," he said. "If the light at the top be dim it is good for nothing. So the value of a college depends on its teaching and formative power, and these will depend more on right methods of instruction, including the arrangement of studies, and on having the right men, than on anything money can buy. Money *can* buy teaching power, which many, with knowledge enough, have not, but good common sense, and weight of character, and the power of inspiration and unselfish devotion to the higher interests of the young men, these money cannot buy." He goes on to say that what he had labored for was "to do for young men in giving them a liberal education and in forming them to a right character all that can be done in four years." "There is a false impression in regard to the benefit to undergraduates of the accumulation of materials and books and of a large number of teachers. It is not by the amount of food in the larder that might be eaten, or by tasting a little of a great variety of dishes that a strong constitution is built up. It is from these that dyspepsia comes. What is needed, and all that is needed, is enough of the best food so provided as to meet the changing wants of the system; and then appetite and digestion and assimilative power, and that is the best college, physically or mentally, where there is the most of these." This then had been his aim and the many Williams graduates of that period testify to his success. There were, of course, men impervious to his appeal, who were indifferent and on one occasion at least were even insulting, but he would not change his methods or ideals for them.

He preferred to have a college where men attended classes because they were interested and inspired by their leaders, and where they behaved courteously because they reverenced and trusted those at their head; and refused to submit all to a type of discipline necessary only for the few who refused to respond. The professors were free in their own departments but in the main they followed his lead. No record was kept of attendance and if students did not wish to come they could stay away.

This occasioned the one great difficulty that occurred during his administration. In 1868 there were certain young professors who came from Yale who felt that the discipline was shockingly lax, and wished to introduce the severe system of compelling attendance which was in use at Yale, and to approximate the discipline of the boys' school which Mark Hopkins had always regarded with aversion as unworthy of college men. As stated, he allowed a certain amount of conversation and laughter in recitations and relied on his tact to keep matters in hand, and in cases of misbehavior requiring discipline he preferred to treat these men by private conference, individually, as a father would talk with his sons, rather than to have a hard and fast rule; and he often moderated some of the sterner sentences of the junior professors after talking with the offender. This created some feeling as far back as 1860, and an appeal was made to the trustees to improve the discipline of the college, and put an end to the more liberal methods of Mark Hopkins.

In 1864 there was a case in point. A young man named Bishop delivered an oration at the "Freshman Wake" which the faculty regarded as an "outburst of depravity" and they promptly expelled the boy. After talking matters over with him the president decided that it was more a case of "lack of judgment," than inherent depravity, and promised to do what he could to mitigate the sentence. The faculty remained firm, and the father, greatly irritated, consulted authorities all over the country and appealed to the board of trustees. It was an indication of the difference in point of view between the president and faculty.

It became known that there were two or three professors whose zeal for discipline was great. Four years later a father whose son had been expelled writes as follows:

Pittsfield, September 10th, 1869.

Rev. Dr Hopkins
Dear Sir

. . . In the first place, I do not believe you, or some of your associates, would have put Tom in this position. If it could have been left to your judgment & feelings he would have had at least the little chance to redeem himself which he asked for. And I sincerely & confidently believe that both his conduct & attainments would have been such the present year as to have justified your indulgence—for if there was ever an honest purpose of reform he carried it back with him to Williamstown. He went back, hoping in time at least, with your consent, to regain the place in the class which he had lost. What he will do now God only knows. He has come home disheartened, mortified, soured.

Now as to the agencies & influences which have brot this about. It will not be denied that it was done at the persistent instigation of one person on the faculty. Now I have corresponded & conversed with this professor a good deal & I have for years been getting the impression that there is an element in the Faculty whose influence is not wholly nice nor happy. Certain members have brot in much zeal but not enough discretion—they have set up a high standard, but they fail in the adaptation of means to attain it. Their system is too ungenial, irritating, *pedagogical.* They do not win the good will or enlist the sympathy & enthusiasm of their pupils. And as a consequence I believe the college for years past has been losing not only the interest of the outside world, but the affection & sympathy of its own Alumni. They learn to look upon her not as an Alma Mater, but as a harsh step mother or crabbed mistress. They are glad to get away from her, & have little desire to return to her or speak a good word in her behalf. I know this is not true of all. Many young men go there "all right"—desirous of instruction & ready to avail themselves of it—Such get instruction in "book learning" abundant & good. But many go there in whom this character is not developed, & such need *educating* with influences other than simple instruction in books under pressure. *For such* I believe something can & ought to be done better than simply "sifting them out" as impracticable. And where will the system end which has "sifted" the present Senior class from between 60 & 70 to between 20 & 30? . . .

Yours very respectfully

DANL DAY.

In 1868 one of the young professors mentioned above protested so strongly that the discipline was inferior to Yale, that Mark Hopkins was somewhat troubled and afterwards remarked with a rueful smile, "Professor C. thinks we are in a bad way here!"

The agitation continued and the malcontents took advantage of Doctor Hopkins' absence while delivering an address in the West to pass a rule in the faculty meeting which introduced a stringent marking system, and provided that any student who was absent from recitation should be marked zero. If the absence was unavoidable, the professor, if he wished, could allow the student to make it up. If the professor did not care to take the trouble the zero mark remained. Although this was when the rule at Yale, it was totally foreign to the spirit of Williams, both in respect to marking and in compelling attendance. It was received by the students with intense indignation, and they at once sent in an appeal to the faculty to defer action until the president's return. When this was refused they drew up a protest which stated that

Whereas: they regard the imposition of this rule as a blow aimed at our personal honor and manhood, therefore

Resolved: that we protest against said rule and call upon the Faculty to annul it.

When this again was ignored by the faculty they took action as follows:

Whereas: our appeal has been disregarded, therefore

Resolved: that we declare our connection with said

college to cease from this date until the authorities repeal said rule.

Resolved: That we, as a body of young men, agree to remain in this neighborhood and abstain from all objectionable conduct until the final settlement of our difficulties.

This resolution was unanimously adopted by the student body.

They felt that after being treated as serious men and students they were now suddenly dealt with as a group of small boys who could not be trusted to behave. They said: "We are convinced that the system of marks and prizes defeats the end for which it was established; first, by calling the mind from the great aim of education to petty and selfish ambition, thus destroying the germ of manhood which it is the aim of education to develop; second, by leading the students to indulge in deceitful practices." The statement shows how completely the students had grasped the ideals of Mark Hopkins.

The president returned to find the college disbanded; perfect quiet, however, reigned in the town. The next day, Sunday, he preached in chapel and none but the faculty attended. It was a most difficult situation. He could not go back on his faculty though he entirely disapproved of their action. He could not countenance a rebellion of the students though he sympathized with them. The whole future of the college depended on him. One false step would wreck the work to whose patient construction he had given his life. All alone he faced this disastrous crisis sprung upon him in his absence and without his knowledge. He requested all the college to meet in the chapel Monday morning, and every man was present.

He took up first their action in resigning from college which he said was impossible. Matriculation was a formal contract which could not be broken by one party without the consent of the other. If a student was dissatisfied he could apply for an honorable dismissal which would surely be granted. It had not yet been granted so they were still members of the college, though they could have letters if they wished them.

He then said that the faculty governed the college and any rule made by them was law and must be obeyed until it was repealed. Any combination against the government of the college cannot be tolerated for a moment. If the rule objected to is not the best rule possible it can be rescinded and changed for such a rule. The faculty desires the best possible rule. They and they alone have authority to rescind the rule.

Such was the crude outline of an address that was listened to with breathless attention. It was clear and logical and left the students with no justification for the action they had taken. He emphasized the difficulties of the professors and the need of some rule, as there had been too many absences from recitation. He stated clearly that this might not be the best rule and admitted the right of the students to express their judgment. He showed plainly, however, that they had no right to take such action as they had attempted, and that the first necessary step was their recognition of the authority of the college and of the fact that they were still its members.

One of the alumni has described the impression made by this speech. For the first time the students saw their venerated president deeply moved. He stood erect in the pulpit with arms loosely folded as if seeking to control the emotions that were struggling within, seeming to tower above them in lonely solitude, opposed by his faculty, deserted by his students. His face seemed more deeply lined than ever beneath the broad dome of his brow with its scanty locks, and the firm lips trembled as he told of his struggles to make the college great, of his sacrifices for it, of his devotion to the institution which was in his charge and to the great body of young men to whose education he had given every energy of body and mind. Though he stood motionless, holding himself in rigid self control, one tear after another trickled slowly down his deeply furrowed cheek. And then he drew himself up and spoke with the majesty and force of one who though utterly alone does not fear to face the hostile opinion of his hearers and the ruin of his life work. "Much as I love this college I would rather see it razed to the ground than to see the discipline of its faculty defied. You all know me and you know that I shall see that no injustice is done to any student of this institution. But I shall not offer you any compromise now while you claim to be outside my jurisdiction. I shall conduct prayers tomorrow morning and every student not in his wonted place will be expelled from the college." The mingled tenderness and sternness of this masterly address had an amazing effect upon his hearers. Reserved in temperament and shy of revealing the slightest feeling to outsiders, never before had he allowed the world to see the intensity of emotion that was hid beneath the calm dignified exterior, and the revelation filled them with a new awe and reverence for the man who thus asserted his authority over them. At chapel next morning all but three of the students were present and they returned to their classes as usual.

There remained the obnoxious rule and the recalcitrant faculty. Here again his genius was shown in amending the rule so that it satisfied the malcontents and yet gave the students a loophole so they were not shut up to the iron-clad discipline of a boys' school. Neither then or afterwards did he speak one word of criticism of the action of the faculty which had involved him in such difficulty. Thus ended the only real difficulty during the administration of Mark Hopkins.

Some of the professors complained that Mark Hopkins was surprisingly lenient toward offences committed by wealthy and influential students, but we may be sure that whatever was the cause of his leniency it was certainly not the wealth of the offender.

Doctor G. R. Leavitt records an incident in this connection. Mark Hopkins had been greatly annoyed by the defacement of certain of the college buildings in a scurrilous manner, and when the offender was discovered and brought before him it proved to be a young man of known wealth. He stood before the president and jauntily pulled out his pocketbook and said: "Well, doctor, how much is the damage?" The doctor looked steadily at the boy until the grey eyes beneath their shaggy brows seemed to transfix him. "Young man," he said, "put up your pocketbook. Tomorrow at prayers you will make public acknowledgment of your offense or you will be expelled." When the confession had been duly made the doctor recounted the incident and said: "Rich young men come here and take that tone as if they could pay for what they get here. No student can pay for what he gets in Williams College. Can any student pay for the sacrifice of Col. Williams and our other benefactors? For the heroic sacrifice of half paid professors who have given their lives that young men might have at the smallest cost a liberal education? Every man here is a charity student. Reverence for those who have provided this venerable college should make the very thought of marring or defacing property, plain and homely though it seem, a desecration." He could remember years where the professors had each given $100 from their meager $800, and the president renounced $200 from his salary to supply the necessities of the college, and it was to him something sacred, built up by the sacrifices and suffering of noble men.

Such was the spirit that ruled in Williams and it made its effects felt not only on the campus but throughout the country. Doctor Llewellyn Pratt states that he met a distinguished teacher from the West on his way to Williamstown and asked the reason of his visit. "I meet many Williams men," he said, "and observe in them all the combination of qualities we call manliness, and I am going to see if I can find the reason." Questioned again on his return he said: "I have found the reason. The mountains and Doctor Hopkins." Seldom has the influence of any one man been so prolonged and wide upon any group. At the end of his sixty years' connection with the college he could say "Of the 1792 living graduates of the college I have taught all but thirty." And he had also taught a large proportion of the 531 who had then passed away.

I have at hand innumerable letters from graduates bearing witness to the impression he made upon them, and the influence he had upon their lives. As a sample I may quote from the letter of a boy named Nichols to his mother on February 9, 1877:

February 9—"I should be glad that I came to Williams, if for no other reason than to live in the vicinity of Dr. Hopkins—it is a perfect education to be under him—and a moral tonic to live within range of his example. His philosophy—the noblest of

Christian ethics—has been his guide—and in its grandness, its unswerving fidelity to right, & the precepts of Christ, mirrors his own career."

March 14—"Dr. Hopkins has just left my room, & in speaking of my examination, & my course with him, said 'you grasped your studies & did well in them.' I told him I would rather have him say that, than to have any honor the college could give—to have the Dr. my idol, & ideal, talk that way, it nearly upset me. . . ."

In spite of the atmosphere of dignity that surrounded him and the impression of awe that he created upon the students and that naturally would have held them at a distance, he nevertheless came into close and intimate relations with them. Coming from him any gesture of intimacy had a significance which seems to be lacking in the exuberant expressions of comradeship that one often witnesses. On December 11, 1860, C. F. Williams writes from Keokuk, Iowa:

". . . A reply to my inquiries, I will esteem a great favor, as it will furnish me *very material* aid in settling my plans, and it will somewhat serve to augment the debt of gratitude I already owe you, for the *fatherly kindness* which you were pleased to show me under circumstances when I most needed such kindness; and for the great and rich thoughts which, I feel, have expanded and strengthened my mind, and—what is far better—have, as I humbly trust, been—under God—the blessed means of spiritual nourishment and growth. And I cannot voluntarily give up my purpose to be once more under your influence. The friendly manner in which you put your arm around me as we walked together over to your lecture, the last Saturday evening I spent in Williamstown—though a 'little thing'—and though you may have forgotten it—has ever since drawn my heart towards you with a force *far stronger* than the arm which encircled me. And the encouragement you then gave me to return, transformed my *desire* to do so, into the glad *hope* that it would be *realised*. . . ."

He was always proud of the achievements of any Williams man and when Cyrus Field, the brother of his intimate friend David Dudley Field, returned after laying the Atlantic cable, he was tendered a great reception at Stockbridge, at which the Doctor said that in some ways he had transcended the achievement of Columbus, for while he had found the first pathway from the old world to the new, Cyrus Field had linked the two worlds permanently together, so that a word spoken in the one could be heard in the other.

CHAPTER XI

THE ARBITRATOR AND HARMONIZER

Men of predominant intellect are natural arbitrators. They see clearly both sides of a question and violent partisanship is impossible to them. They are fair to each and can show to each the point of view of the other. Such was Mark Hopkins. In an age of violent controversies, he remained always calm, unbiased, seeking to harmonize conflicting points of view and to find the truth in each.

His great-uncle, Doctor Samuel Hopkins, had died in 1803 two years after Mark was born, but the Hopkintonian system of thought still dominated the orthodox church of New England when Mark began his career. The Unitarians had revolted from it, but although their teaching appealed to men of intellect and high moral character it seemed more like a system of ethics than a religion. It lacked the powerful emotional appeal that has enabled Christianity to reach the most ignorant men and to transform men of base character; and with certain notable exceptions it did not seem to inspire men to lay down their lives in self-sacrificing service to their fellowmen. The great work of Mark Hopkins was to open the minds of the youth of his day to modern thought, to break down confining walls of the old narrow philosophic and theological system and give them a view of the glory and unity of the universe and its interrelating laws and correlations, as revealed by science, while preserving all the inspiration and power that Christianity had gathered during the ages. Nothing is so dangerous to mankind as sudden transitions of thought. There is an inherent tendency to throw out the baby with the bath, and when one point of a system of thought is proved false, to throw out all religion and morality along with it. If the earth is proved round instead of flat, or if it is proved to have been created a million years ago instead of six thousand, common folk conclude that there is therefore no God, no virtue and no sense in doing right. It is an appreciation of this tendency in human nature that has caused the Roman Catholic Church to insist so pertinaciously on all the details of its doctrine.

It was the genius of Mark Hopkins to show forth the eternal values in the universe and in life and to aid men to think through to the heart of things, so that no matter what changes came through new revelations of science, they had a grip on fundamental realities that enabled them to go forward in peace and happiness to aid the progress of the world. His training in science and medicine had given him a grasp of the laws of the universe and of human nature and he saw life and nature as a great whole in which each part had its significance, a realm of mystery and glory through which man could advance to power and happiness as he understood and obeyed its laws. It was the period when Darwin had launched his theory of evolution, which was at first regarded with such horror by the churches. No one had done more to prepare the minds of his pupils for such a theory than Mark Hopkins with his teaching of the unity of the universe and the correlating forces that brought the inert stone, the blooming rose, the mind of man into one great system in which all bore a part and each interpreted the other. All his teaching was an exposition of the progressive order in nature and in man. He taught the close relationship of man and the lower animals, and again of sentient life to the plant, but he set his face firmly against the first materialistic interpretations of the theory that excluded God and mind and spirit from the process of creation, and he put his finger on the great defect of the theory of natural selection which is causing it to be abandoned today as the chief cause in evolution.

He called attention to the definite steps in progress from inert matter to life, and from plant to animal, from sentient life to mind, and to the great difficulty in accounting for such forward steps. We know variation explains much, but not this. There are certain elements in the germ plasm of father and mother that can be combined in different ways to produce great variety of offspring, but how some new element can appear that was not in either parent and that had never before existed in the history of the race, this is something which the modern scientist and philosopher struggles to explain by a great variety of terms such as "élan vital," which really mean that the miracle is utterly beyond his comprehension; and yet upon these "sports" or forward leaps in variation all progress in evolution depends.

Mark Hopkins taught the survival of the fittest, but showed that if that which was fittest from the point of view of man was to survive, it required considerable assistance. Wheat did not survive in the midst of thorns and weeds without aid, and he spoke much of that superior selection by which those things that were fittest for man were enabled to survive.

One of his most eloquent addresses (Milwaukee, 1878) pictured Christianity as the least fit of all things to survive from the ordinary point of view. It began in a stable, it continued "in a disreputable town in a conquered province." It was carried forward by a "young carpenter, without letters, with a few peasant followers," who was "tried as a malefactor and disgracefully executed and laid in a tomb." "No one living fully understood his teaching." "The words he had spoken were dispersed in the air and no record of them had been left. I ask you if imagination can add a single circumstance to brighten the improbability that a world-wide religion would spring from such a source?"

"The substance of its teaching only adds to the improbability." "Its antagonism to all forms of iniquity was uncompromising. It had to overcome and displace those organized and deeply imbedded systems of religion and civil government which upheld the individual in his aversion to the holiness which Christianity demanded."

He then describes the various ways in which Christianity is the best fitted of all to meet the needs of man, giving "the assurance of peace, pardon, and eternal life." "It embosoms within itself the foundation of all reforms, individual and social. Beginning with the individual, not with organizations, it places him on the footing of his own moral responsibility and spiritual independence. It lays the foundation of purity in the Christian family. The foundation of peace it lays in the fatherhood of God and brotherhood of man. If peace is ever to be universal, it will not be from fear or interest, but from a recognition of these. The foundation of civil order it lays in its requirement of subjection to lawful authority. Its guard against tyranny it places in its command to obey God rather than man. Its provision for general enlightenment, at once for conservatism and progress, for reform without revolution, is found in its command 'to prove all things and hold fast that which is good.' It is the fittest of all things for man, but like wheat it needs constant care to enable it to survive."

Thus instead of teaching men in the old fashion to accept Christianity and obey its laws because it was commanded in the Bible and disobedience would result in eternal punishment, he showed Christianity to be the basis of all progress and happiness—the one path by which the individual and society could reach full development—worthy to survive because it was fittest.

All the divisions and violent disputes in religion seemed to him futile and due to emphasizing minor and unimportant points and forgetting the great essentials.

"Let the whole race fix their eyes upon the North Star and march forward with steady gaze upon that luminary and this march will bring them together in one vast multitude, over the center of which the object of their common regard burns in the firmament. They are brought together not because they planned to meet, but because they had a common object in view. Let the Christians of every name keep their eyes fixed upon Jesus Christ and the divisions of Christendom will be known no more" (Pittsfield, 1866). If all who are working so anxiously for church unity would follow this advice they might come at last to a real unity instead of the formal unity which they seek to achieve.

In the same way he makes it clear that men are to follow Christ not because He is Son of God and it is commanded, or because if they do not they will be everlastingly punished, but because that is the way in which humanity will reach its highest possibilities. "Let each individual be perfect and society will take on just those forms spontaneously which are requisite for the perfection of the whole. If, therefore, the possibilities of this race, individual and social, are ever to be reached, I know that the man Christ must be the model and leader of the race, and just in proportion as He is so, men will reach their highest possibilities."

This then is the meaning of Christianity. "We need to labor for the single end to make men like Christ." "It is the greatest blessing we can give to any man to make him like Jesus Christ" (Pittsburgh, 1869). "The higher life is in Him; in His matchless character, in His self-sacrificing love; in Him as the champion of humanity" (Lowell, 1880). It was for this that he supported foreign missions, because the greatest thing that can be done for any man is to make him like Christ, and because this is the one great road to world unity.

It is hard for us to appreciate the vast change here from the position of the old theology. His vision is as broad as that of Channing, but he has preserved the fire of devotion that is the essence of religion. Everything to him must be justified by reason. No arbitrary command avails. It is because Christianity is the path to progress and happiness that he upholds it. He always thinks through to the meaning and essence of everything. If it cannot justify itself in terms of some real good he will have none of it. "The religion of Christ works in man righteousness and self-sacrificing love. Unless these be produced in man the religion of Christ is a failure. So much of righteousness and self-sacrificing love as there is in this house, so much is there of Christianity—so much and no more" (Hartford, 1876).

It was on this point that he had his chief controversy with Doctor McCosh of Princeton, who upheld the old idea that man must do right because it is right and for no other reason, and called Mark Hopkins a utilitarian because he insisted that it was because an act tended to the good of all and their ultimate happiness, that it was right, and maintained that man should love God not alone because it was right, but because He was supremely worthy of love. "If God was as incapable of sensibility as a rock it would be impossible for us to love Him." His best-known book, *The Law of Love and Love as a Law*, expounded this idea, that back of duty was love as the supreme motive and law of life.

This and *The Outline Study of Man* were courses of lectures delivered in Boston before the Lowell Institute.

These books summed up his courses at Williams. *The Outline Study of Man*, as its title states, was a sort of primer on man's nature, covering physiology, psychology, and ethics, designed to stimulate thought and to act as a workable guide to life and conduct, rather than to solve the abstruse problems of the relation of mind to matter, or of brain centers to behavior, which vex the mind of the modern philosopher and psychologist, without greatly assisting the common man. In thus starting the study of the mind with the body he anticipated modern physiological psychology.

He was more interested in the phenomena of consciousness as they are ordinarily apprehended and understood, and in their effect on character, than in their ultimate causes—the problem over which the different schools dispute with such violence.

At that time there were few textbooks on psychology, and the Outline Study seemed to meet a general need. I have at hand innumerable letters from men all over the country who were using it in teaching classes, in school, and churches, and it became a regular textbook in many colleges. Many leading thinkers wrote to express their appreciation, but the real value of the book lay in the fact that it so simplified the problems of psychology that even untrained minds could understand it and were awakened to interest.

A letter written on January 20, 1883, from Ringoes, N. J., by Robert J. Kent reads as follows:

Dr. Mark Hopkins,

Dear Sir:

At the recent meeting of the alumni in New York I mentioned to you briefly the experiment I had tried in teaching your system of mental science to plain people. Thinking that you might be interested in knowing more fully about it, I have concluded to tell you how it came about and how it resulted. . . . It is a little agricultural village, declining rather than progressing. The old people think and talk about farming and politics; the young people regard a dancing party as the supreme good; Intellectual culture is at a very low mark.

Wanting to get the young people to look up a little higher, I at first tried a series of church sociables. . . .

They were too mild for the prevailing taste. I concluded the only feasible way was to get hold of individuals and try to get them on a higher level. . . . So I invited a few of the young people to study with me on Friday evenings the "Outline Study of Man——"

A young man who taught the district school, two other young men working on farms—four young ladies, all working for their living and none with more than the most elementary education, have comprised the class. We used no textbooks; but met around the fire in the parsonage, and, beginning at the bottom of the diagram appended to the Out-Line Study talked the different points over together, never leaving a point until each one could state it and illustrate it to the satisfaction of the rest. I regard the experiment as a complete success. Each member of the class became enthusiastic in the study. After finishing the Out-Line Study, they took a rest, and then began the "Law of Love."

The members of the class have all repeatedly told me that they never received such benefit from a course of study before. They had learned to think. They saw greater depths, loftier heights in Christianity. They had been studying themselves. A Baptist minister, about to leave for a field in the far west, spent an evening with us, and was so pleased himself that he bought both books and took them with him to help him in his work. Two members of my class were members of a neighboring church—They have, since their new pastor has come, got him to form a class in the "Law of Love."

Now all this would not be worth mentioning were it not an illustration and proof that it is possible for the plain people to become philosophers in the best sense of the word. . . . What we need in this age of physics is more metaphysics sharply defined and clearly presented in *plain language.*

It has been a great pleasure to me to feel myself once again in your presence while writing this letter. Each day I feel more deeply indebted to you for the instruction you gave me, and I suppose I am only one of the many.

Respectfully yours,

ROBERT J. KENT
of '77.

The first book of Mark Hopkins, his *Evidences of Christianity,* was also a course of lectures delivered at the Lowell Institute. The invitation to deliver these lectures in the winter of 1843 was a result of his Semicentennial address. They were written for a popular audience and they were popular. They became the talk of the town and were attended by all classes and all sects. Their breadth is shown by the fact that they appealed to the Unitarian element and won Mark Hopkins many friends among them. His delivery had great charm and his influence spread throughout the state and reacted advantageously to the college. He gave in all four courses of lectures at the Lowell Institute, "The Evidences" in 1843,

"Moral Science" 1861, "The Law of Love" 1868, and the "Outline Study of Man" in 1872, and two courses at Yale, the "Scriptural Idea of Man" and the "Scriptural Idea of God." Many of these are limited by the outlook of the age, but back of them all is the sweep of wide vision—the conception of a religion vast as the universe, leading man to the exploration of all its laws, to ever greater revelations of glory and beauty, a religion which is the stimulus to all progress and the basis of all enduring happiness. In reading Doctor Einstein's recent statement of the meaning of religion and the progress of man from the religion of fear, and the religion of Providence to the great cosmic conception of religion reached by a few great minds, I was reminded of the outlook of Mark Hopkins. To quote (Baccalaureate 1855): "The works of God are all expressions of His attributes and thoughts. He it is that through uniformities and resemblances and tendencies whispers into the ear of philosophy, not falsely so called, its sublime truths; and as we begin to feel and trace more and more those lines of relation that bind all things into one system, the touch of any one of which may vibrate to the fixed stars, this communion becomes high and thrilling. Science is no longer cold. It lives and breathes and glows and in the ear of love its voice is always a hymn to the Creator." This thrilling communion with great underlying realities suggests the cosmic religion which stirs the scientist to sacrifice time and wealth and life itself in his worship of truth.

Mark Hopkins was made president of the American Board of Commissioners for Foreign Missions in 1857 and retained that position for nearly thirty years. Some of his most significant addresses from which I have already quoted were delivered at the annual meetings of the Board, which were held in a different city every year. He only missed two of these meetings and travelled each year to the meeting-place sometimes far in the West at great sacrifice of time and energy. They relied upon him to set the keynote for the work of the year and to supply inspiration both to the missionaries on furlough, exhausted with the strain of their work, and to the workers at home, and they were seldom if ever disappointed. These addresses did as much to shape and enlarge the thought of the churches as any one thing. Unfortunately the committee in control of the Board were deeply dyed in the old theology and had little understanding of the meaning of Christianity as Doctor Hopkins saw it. To them the whole meaning and purpose of missions was to save the heathen from certain damnation which would overtake them if they did not accept the Christian creed. It was the old religion of fear that they taught, and they thought that if there was a chance that heathen without the knowledge of Christ could be saved there was then no adequate reason for missions. To Mark Hopkins this was a minor point. He believed in teaching Christianity as the only sure road to progress, happiness, and world unity. He did not care to discuss a point so difficult to demonstrate as the possibilities of salvation in the future life. But matters came to a crisis. The Board refused to commission certain young men graduated from Andover Seminary who believed in the "future probation" of the heathen, and even started a movement to prosecute the Andover professors who were responsible for such a belief. The liberal churches of Boston protested indignantly and threatened to withdraw their support, and a split was threatened which would wreck the work of the Board.

Mark Hopkins was then eighty-five. He had requested to resign the presidency, but all called on him in this great emergency.

I can well remember how disturbed he was when he set forth on the journey to the meeting of the Board at Des Moines which was to be his last. It looked as if that great organization to which he had given so much of his life, and on which he relied to carry the spirit of Christianity throughout the world, was to be wrecked by a wretched squabble over a point of theology. To him it was all so petty, so far from the main issue. In the great assembly at Des Moines all were on edge. The conservatives were determined to crush the liberals—the liberals were jockeying to obtain a majority vote by any possible means. There seemed little left of that spirit of love they were to carry throughout the world. And then he stepped forward and every eye was fixed upon him and a solemn hush fell upon the excited crowd. Four-score years and five had passed over his head. He had seen the first beginnings of the Board, had seen the first missionaries sent out to the Sandwich Islands, had rejoiced each year at the miraculous reports of progress that came from all over the world. The years had brought no sign of weakness in mind or body. He stood there, his massive frame and white head seeming to tower above the throng, calm, serene, the incarnation of the ancient spirit of wisdom and justice. His slow solemn utterance carried throughout the great hall as he sought to call their thoughts back to the great purpose that united them, to lift them above the petty squabbles that divided them. These questions of theology were not for them to decide. Let them be referred to the council of the churches. This contest was all aside from the mark. Their business was not to dispute over doctrines but to aid men to become like Christ. As he spoke on in calm even tones it was as if the sun little by little was breaking through the dark clouds of the storm. Light came and peace. His counsels prevailed. The doctrinal points were referred to the council and the great work of the Board went forward. Both wings held together, and little by little even the most conservative caught the vision he had held before them so many years. The old dogmas of fear and punishment sank out of sight and men went forth not to save men from a God who was seeking to torture them endlessly, but to bring healing and knowledge and joy to a world of ignorance and suffering. Once more his clear vision and wide outlook, his serenity and strength of purpose had brought men to harmony and saved a great institution from wreck.

In these great addresses before the American Board the teaching of Mark Hopkins was brought to bear upon the outside world, but perhaps even greater was the influence of his Baccalaureate sermons. In those days the Baccalaureate was the last lesson which the president taught the seniors who had been so long under his instruction, a final summing up of all the teaching that he wished them to carry with them through life, his last advice before they entered upon their work in the world. As such it was a peculiarly sacred and solemn occasion, one to which they looked forward with great anticipation and to which they looked back through all their years of active work. And they were seldom disappointed, for Mark Hopkins always had something of lasting value to give, and these addresses are among the most memorable that he uttered. It is a distinct loss that this custom has gone by, and that the Baccalaureate is now given by some visiting clergyman who knows nothing of these men and has none of the personal interest that they felt in a president who was speaking his farewell words. Until 1872 when he resigned the presidency, these addresses were delivered each year and marked the climax of the college course.

CHAPTER XII

"PROF AL."

For forty years the two Hopkins brothers worked side by side, pouring all the strength of body and mind and soul that they possessed into the work of the college that they loved. They supplemented one another in an extraordinary way—Albert teaching the wonders of the outer world, Mark those of the inner world of the mind. Albert was as deep in the intensity of his convictions as Mark was broad in his vision and sympathies. Albert seemed like an Old Testament prophet in the fiery vigor and power of his address, Mark was the serene expositor of the New Dispensation. With Albert feeling was dominant, in Mark one felt always the power of a balanced intellect. Every statement was fair and he saw the other side, which was more difficult for Albert.

Old graduates think of "Prof Al." as they called him, most often at the noontime meeting which he maintained for forty years. They dropped in one by one from the rush of the day into the quiet room and found the professor seated at his desk, dignified but courteous. There was a strange beauty about him in spite of the large features, a symmetry and sense of poise, but what they all felt was the radiation of power, as his eyes, piercing and brilliant, looked out at them from beneath their shaggy brows. He carried with him a consciousness of spiritual realities, and there alone with him in that quiet room, the world of sense faded away, and they seemed to feel the close presence of the eternal mystery. One by one each of them repeated some sentence of inspired words from the Bible, some phrase charged with peace and strength, and as each ceased the professor responded with another phrase that capped the meaning of the first. He was never at a loss and his knowledge of scripture was amazing. When the round was completed he would add a few words of his own, and then hold his auditors for a few moments in perfect silence by the power of those strange piercing eyes.

The influence of that little meeting was amazing. It seemed that more men were influenced by the intensity of Albert than by the wide vision of Mark, and transformed from idle careless fellows to strong men with a purpose in the world.

He was magnificently built, and his great physical strength appealed to the boys. The stories told of his feats became almost legendary. Many who were not moved by his moral qualities were in awe of his physical strength, and fled swiftly at his approach when engaged in some nocturnal prank. When forbidden revelry was in progress his knock at the door was enough to cause instant and unconditional surrender.

He was a somewhat warlike emissary of peace and never hesitated to step in to stop a fight. Two men,

ALBERT HOPKINS

fighting drunk, had started a violent row on the Pownal Road one night when a tall figure suddenly loomed out of the darkness and an authoritative voice ordered them to desist. Indignant that any one should stop a good fight, both turned upon the interloper. One was about to launch a blow at his face when he found himself looking into a pair of piercing, compelling eyes, facing a stalwart form that seemed to tower above him, and a voice said calmly, "You'd better not strike me, sir. If you do you won't strike another man in some time." Before the power of those eyes the man faded silently away, and Prof Al. continued his homeward walk from the service he had been conducting in Pownal. Once at night a student who was throwing a fireball felt an iron grasp on his shoulder and recognizing the grip of Prof Al. made a frantic leap to escape. He came free but left a large part of his coat in the professor's hand. Professor Hopkins never did the expected thing. While he was living in East College the students thought they would play a joke on him. They secured a cow and with infinite labor succeeded in hauling it up the stairs to the top floor. Then they sat in glee to await the professor's return and watch his struggles to get the cow down the stairs. The professor arrived, but although the presence of the cow was sufficiently evident he made no move. For a whole day the cow remained and made the life of the students miserable in a variety of ways that only a cow could achieve, and finally in desperation and with infinite difficulty they succeeded in hauling her downstairs and outdoors and spent a good afternoon cleaning up before they could breathe freely. They tried no more tricks on Prof Al.

He was devoted to nature and explored all the beautiful spots around Williamstown with groups of the students, and gave them names of his own which seemed to invest them with a romantic interest. Some thirty years after his death I climbed to the top of Mt. Williams, the northern summit of the Greylock range. It was densely wooded and we were regretting the lack of view when we discovered a rough-hewn ladder against the tallest tree. Climbing this we found "Albert Hopkins" carved on the topmost rung. This was characteristic. Wherever there was a fine view or a beautiful outlook he made the place a haunt of his own. In addition to building the first observatory and organizing the first scientific expedition, he started in 1863 the first Mountain Climbing Club of America known as the Alpine Club. Its members were students and professors and some of the young ladies in town, among them his nieces. After nineteen expeditions in which they climbed and explored the peaks in the neighborhood, they undertook a two days' camping trip to ascend Mt. Equinox at Manchester, and then made a final expedition in which they walked the whole length of the Presidential Range in the White Mountains, really quite a feat for girls encumbered with the voluminous skirts of the period.

You might have seen him with this group of students and young girls from the town, up on the camp ground under the shadow of the spruces on the shoulder of Greylock, with his coat off making the chips fly as he cut wood for the camp fire and then exclaiming: "Come, we must run to the Vista and watch the sunset." There through the forest he had cut a "Vista" through which one could look out to the valley below and to the distant western peaks, indigo blue, as the flaming sun marched westward surrounded with banners of scarlet and gold. Or he would cry "Come, we will all climb down to the Heart of Greylock," and off they would go, through the forest to the edge of the great gulf, and then scramble down precipice after precipice, the boys handing the girls from rock to rock, until they stood at the bottom of the deep canyon at a spot where three streams met, tumbling down in a series of cascades from cliffs far above, to form the "Jerusalem Brook." He was the life of it all—pointing out each rare plant and beautiful flower, or strange mineral, giving to each rock or peak or outlook some quaint original name.

Like Mark he believed in teaching from Nature rather than textbooks. As a boy of six he once strayed away from home and when found and asked what he had been doing, answered that he had been "looking at the big treeses." Then and always Nature had been the book he loved most to read and which inspired him most. He distrusted book learning, and thought it wrong to train ministers in theological seminaries. "They might as well teach Botany out of books," he said. He spoke of the "Lily fingered clergyman who never went into the Heart of Greylock or into the heart of anything." Instead of studying a commentary of critics and theologians, let them turn to the rocks and mountains and sea and sky.

He had his own ideas about missions also. Life was better than exhortation. Instead of sending ministers out to lecture the heathen he wished to send out colonies of young Christian craftsmen and tradesmen with their families, who by their example would show the ignorant people of foreign lands the Christian life in its entirety. Instead of talking about the teachings of Christ he wanted a community which lived them, and he trusted that their beauty and power would win more converts than many sermons.

He gave a large part of his time and energy to the church which he built, largely with his own hands, in the neglected community of the White Oaks. Strange folk and outcasts had settled in this secluded valley, and he sought them out and gathered them in, until before his death, he had a happy little community collected about his church. Here lived the old negro, Abe Parsons, the Bunter, with his Indian wife. He had a growth of horn on his head and could "bunt" so powerfully that they said he once cracked a millstone. Many other queer characters were hidden in these back valleys. Prof Al. sought not only to convert but to educate them, and bring light and happiness. He found an ancient tree some five hundred years old that had been cut down, and had a smooth section made. He then got the young people to inscribe on each ring the date of some great world event that happened in that year, from the nailing of Luther's Theses down to the Landing of the Pilgrims and the Declaration of Independence. That old tree section became their most cherished possession and men came from far to see it.

It was he who started the Landscape Gardening Society among the students and he did a large share of the work himself, rolling up his sleeves to dig and blast rocks and plant trees to the great admiration of passing farmers, who remarked that there was a good stout fellow who wasn't afraid of work. Much of the present beauty of Williamstown is due to the trees he planted and the parks he laid out with the aid of the students. In 1840 he built himself a house at the foot of the Fort Hill, and back of it and in the rocks on the hillside he made a fascinating garden which was the delight of my boyhood days, for in it he had many strange trees and plants and quaint nooks and corners, each with a mysterious and romantic name. We used to consider it a sort of enchanted land.

In 1841 he was married to Louisa Payson, a sister of the Mrs. Prentiss who won fame by her book, *Stepping Heavenward*, the diary of an unfortunate girl married to a conscientious and absent-minded young minister, who when thinking out some address or parish problem, at times seemed quite oblivious of her and of her housekeeping trials, through all of which she found a difficult path to Heaven in spite of her husband's shortcomings.

We have indicated something of the terrible inward struggle in the mind of Albert Hopkins as under the threat of the old theology he struggled toward perfection.

His later years were entirely free from the inner strain to acquire perfection himself, and all his energies seemed given to helping others. His wife entered enthusiastically into all his work for the poor and distressed, but she was very intense and high-strung and became a great sufferer herself, and a large part of his time was given to efforts to alleviate her pain. His son Edward grew up to be a young man of great charm and promise. His mother died in 1861 after cruel suffering and the father's love and hope seemed to center in the son. He entered the class of 1864 and showed much of his father's love of science and of nature, for he became president of the Lyceum of Natural History. When the Civil War came on he was anxious to bear a part, and in his senior year helped to organize the First Massachusetts Cavalry and entered the regiment January 6, 1864, as first lieutenant. It was a hard wrench for his father, but he did not forbid it. In May Edward was killed in a charge under Sheridan at Ashland, Va. The blow was a terrible one, but strange to say after the first shock was over, instead of driving him back to the darkness and harshness of his earlier struggle it seemed to create in Albert a new gentleness and geniality. Something of his boyish gaiety and sparkling mirth seemed to return, and those who knew him in his later years would never have suspected the terrible struggle and suffering through which he had fought his way to a new self, which was perhaps the self he would always have been but for the dark shadow of the old dogma.

Nothing is more extraordinary than the strange turns that character takes, sometimes from ideas within, sometimes from stress without. He was of those who, when outer circumstances were favorable, felt great unhappiness, and who, when disaster came, achieved happiness. Even in his dark days his keen humor kept bursting forth in strange quips and quaint phrases. When he was tutoring and disgusted with his inaction while his brothers were plunging forth into the world he wrote:

> "Some ride upon the rocking seas
> Some o'er the Eagle chew the cud
> Some live in Academic ease
> And teach the blossom how to bud."

And he is resentful that Morgan "sits there basking in the sunshine of munificence while I sit here roosting on the hen-roost of insignificance."

CHAPTER XIII

THE WORLD BEYOND THE BERKSHIRES

In those discouraging days when it seemed almost impossible to get the money that was essential to rebuild East College and when Albert was giving all his savings to buy equipment for his classes and to build his observatory, and Mark was driving about through storms and sleet to gain the funds necessary to his work by lecturing, and was denying himself and his family the comforts of life in order to give what he could spare to the college, he received many offers of work elsewhere.

In 1846 the Pilgrim Church in Brooklyn sent him a call to become their minister with a salary nearly three times what he was receiving. His old friend Seth Hunt urged his acceptance, saying that Brooklyn was now a city of 65,000 inhabitants and he hoped it might grow to 100,000. Mark Hopkins must have thought with some anxiety of his family of eight little ones before he turned it down. But he knew that the girl he had chosen as his companion had developed into a staunch and loyal ally, as well as a good housekeeper. He had in his pocket her letter telling how she had fitted the boys for the winter, having made seven pairs of trousers and made over two coats as good as new. She had made two dresses for Alice, and with the pattern sent from New York she had fitted the alpaca to herself and had put a lining to her bombazine. And could he buy her four and one-half yards of mourning ribbon to trim her basque? In addition there was all the housework, and she could only write letters in spare moments when she was rocking the cradle of a fretful baby with her foot, and overseeing the writing lesson of five-year-old Lawrence with one eye. Much as he longed to free her from this drudgery he did not hesitate. He had given himself to Williams College and he would stand by and finish his work.

Then in 1850 came a call to Union Seminary with a salary twice his own in amount, and later an offer of the chancellorship of the University of New York. When that was declined there came in 1851 a call from the Mercer Street Church, said to be the richest and most influential in New York. I have in hand this document signed by elders, trustees, and deacons, together with letters from many prominent men urging upon Mark Hopkins the importance of the call and the greatness of the opportunity to influence the life of the great metropolis. The salary was $3000, a huge sum to his eyes in those days. This was an offer difficult to refuse. Then in 1852 he received a call to become president of the University of Michigan at Ann Arbor. The salary was not so great, but this work was more in his line and he felt the appeal of the growing West. But this too was rejected after anxious consideration.

Invitations to lecture he accepted, and the courses he gave in Boston won him many friends and greatly enlarged his influence. His first invitation to Boston came at New Year's 1839. This was before his centennial address but his inaugural in 1836 had won him sufficient fame to open many doors to him and to give him access to many prominent men. Though he was only thirty-seven his influence was already felt.

On New Year's Day he wrote his wife describing his journey to Boston. The railroad from Pittsfield to Springfield was not completed in 1839 and he went part way by stage, stopping at Worcester to investigate the condition of a friend in the insane asylum. He writes that he was "highly gratified" with the institution and astonished to find it was heated by furnaces—a great asset, for on the trip he had been nearly frozen by the extreme cold. The inmates, to his surprise, seemed to be enjoying themselves in comparative freedom, and one who wore a lofty crown and declared himself the "Supreme Owner," had attained a state of happiness and self-satisfaction rare even in princes.

From Worcester he entrusted his life to the railroad, for trains were running thence to Boston. A violent snow storm was in progress and he started at 7 A.M. feeling sure that the train would be stuck in the snow. Hotels in Boston evidently looked after the morals of their guests. The Marlborough House, where he found a pleasant room and fire, allowed no one to smoke or drink, and the guests, some thirty or forty of them, were summoned for prayers morning and evening. His fame as an educator had been spreading widely and on Election Day he was invited to dine at the statehouse with the governor and council. He was more pleased by an invitation to dine with Mr. Emerson and meet the poet Mr. Dana. He also had a dinner with Mr. Webster, so he evidently made the most of his time between lectures.

The centennial address in 1843 brought Mark Hopkins at once into prominence. It was that winter of 1843–44 that he was invited to Boston to give the course of lectures on the "Evidences of Christianity" which proved surprisingly popular and were attended not only by scholars and church folk, but by the fashionable and wealthy, so that it became quite the thing to attend the course. As a result he won many lifelong friends among the influential people of Boston and chief among whom was Amos Lawrence. His wife went with him and remained until February when she returned home. His letters give a picture of an active social life which must have been a surprising change from the routine of Williamstown.

On February 7, 1844, he wrote his wife that he had found a warm room at 120 Tremont Street, where he was as well off as he could be without her. His dinner at Mr. Abbott Lawrence's was a violent contrast to the simple meals at Williamstown. The dinner began at four o'clock and was not over when he had to leave to go to his lecture. He notes that never in his life had he seen so much silver. The next day he dined with President Quincy of Harvard. He was driven out in state with Governor Briggs of Massachusetts, and Lieutenant-Governor Reed, by Josiah Quincy, Jr., in a carriage worthy of the occasion. The president showed them all the attractions of Harvard, the library, pictures, apparatus, etc., which must have made the equipment at Williams seem decidedly inadequate. Perhaps it discouraged him. He writes, "On the whole we had a pleasant time." The presidential mansion he says he will not describe for fear his wife will at once start altering her house in competition. For two nights he had terrible storms but he was cheered to find that his audience defied the weather and his lectures were well attended. He was invited to spend one evening with the Abbott Lawrences. He went at half-past eight which seemed late in the country, and was embarrassed to find the house dark and unlighted and not a soul there. He waited in uncomfortable loneliness and finally the guests began to arrive until there were 200 present. He dined at the Minots also but his chief friendship was with the Lawrences. They devoted themselves to him, took him to drive to see gardens where they raised flowers, and—rare indeed in those days—oranges and lemons. Mr. William Lawrence had him to tea and a crowd of friends drifted in to see him. He was growing really popular. Mr. A. Lawrence brought his minister, the famous Unitarian Mr. Lathrop, to call, and he was invited to preach in the Unitarian Church, in spite of the fact that he was also to preach in the

Park St. Church, Brimstone Corner, the bulwark of the orthodox—an astonishing proof that his theology satisfied both of the hostile wings of the church. The Lawrences took him quite into the family and introduced him to the grandchildren, who were about the age of his own boys.

On February 16, he writes again to his wife to tell of the success of his lectures. The eighth on the "Character of Christ," excited most interest, and strange to say pleased both the Unitarians and the Orthodox. Each lecture drew a larger crowd than the last, and he won more and more friends. He dined at the Stoddards, at Judge Hubbard's, and elsewhere, and every day Mr Lawrence called to take him for a walk. He writes: "Mr. Lawrence said he had the vanity to think you might like a vacant corner in some room of yours filled up by a bust of him and that he was going to send you one. I suspect he took a fancy to you."

The railroad had now reached Pittsfield but he says it will not be possible to go through in one day. Monday he will go to Springfield and arrive at Pittsfield Tuesday. He wants Parley, the stage man, to meet him there.

In the winter of 1867–68 Mark Hopkins delivered in Boston his course on "The Law of Love," which proved as successful as the earlier course, and brought him again into contact with the social life of Boston, whose contrasts with the simple life at Williams seemed to give him great amusement. He writes from Boston on December 3, 1867, to tell of the excitements of his journey. His son Lawrence had begun his career as a railroad man and met him at Pittsfield on his way to Springfield to look up some freight, and travelled with him as far as Westfield where the Doctor got off to visit his son Harry who was then minister of the Congregational Church there. Here he spent the night, and the next day was so absorbed by a visit to the Normal School, and dinner on an eighteen-pound turkey that he lost track of time and heard the train whistle when half a mile from the station. "Harry confiscated an old raw-boned horse and a crazy buggy that stood by a shop and we cut a figure, whipping and galloping, and made out to get there—the train standing across the track, and so I had just time to get my trunk and we were off." He does not say if Harry was arrested for horse stealing. This time in Boston he stayed at the United States Hotel, where he got a single room "which will do very well for one poor solitary man." He usually gave opportunity for questions after his lectures, but Governor Washburne called and advised against it, saying that he thought there were too many fools in the world. His popularity was still growing and his audience a third larger than any he had had in his previous course.

Again he was invited out for dinner every night. His account of one dinner is worth copying.

"I have just returned from my dinner at Judge

Wells and must give you some account of it so that you may be able to get up one like it. We had beside the Judge and his wife Mrs. Emerson, Dr. Peabody and a clergyman by the name of Foot. Gov. Washburne could not come—We had 1st four raw oyesters on the shells with 1/2 a lemon on each plate. I should say by the way that we were waited on by a man taller than I am with white gloves and a white cravat and black swallow-tailed coat such as it is necessary for people to have to attend weddings in. Then came two kinds of soup, white and dark. I took the dark because it was next me and the lady served it. Then came at one end salmon, and the other spiced oysters lying in the shells. I took the salmon—Then beef with olives, and partridges. I took the partridges. Then roast ducks—two kinds—very fine. With these potatoes, oyster plant and celery cooked in butter. What was next I am not sure, but think it was ice cream, chocolate. Then charlotte russe. Then splendid pears and black Hamburghs and several water grapes—no before that dry toast and butter and just where the lettuce came in I cannot say. Then lemon biscuit. Then nuts, and then sweetmeats. As to the wines, I can say nothing as I did not taste them. In the cooking everything was perfect. After we left the table coffee and tea were sent round in the parlor, so you see what you are losing by not coming down.

I find it costs me here four dollars a day for board and one for fire, making perhaps for small expenses and all $5.25 which is too much, and if you are not coming soon I may look about and make some change, though the freedom and vanity of a Hotel is pleasant. . . .

Your loving husband,
MARK HOPKINS.

A letter to his wife describes a visit to New York on May 20, 1847, to preside at the meetings of some of the societies to which he belonged. Apparently he did not think the religious lights of New York as illuminating as those of Massachusetts. He found the meeting of the Bible Society, of which he had been made an officer, somewhat lacking in fire and interest. In the evening Mrs. Field took him to the meeting of the Unitarian Association, where he had "a dull time enough." Miss Sedgwick sat near him and said she was watching him in trepidation, feeling sure he was going to "make wicked criticisms." At the meeting of the Foreign Board the next morning, however, he was thoroughly stirred by a speech from Henry Ward Beecher, who promised him to come to Williams and speak. He dined with Doctor Alexander and had some difficulty in escaping the clutches of an enthusiastic admirer who "nearly shook me to pieces." Saturday was devoted to "the laborious business of pleasure." He was walked around New York, covering some ten miles. He was much impressed by the water-works, and by the bath and shower Henry Sedgwick had just put in his house. He suggests that such an arrangement should be introduced in the Williamstown house. They had a stimulating dinner with Doctor Bushnell, whose new theology was making a great stir, Miss Sedgwick, who was always brilliant and stimulating, and Miss Kirkland who wrote "The New Home in the West." Sunday was given over to religious dissipation. He heard Doctor Bushnell in the morning, Doctor Knox in the afternoon, and preached himself in the evening to a very large congregation.

Monday he went down to the Narrows with the Fields and visited Fort Hamilton where he saw soldiers embarking for Mexico—"a most miserable looking set."

The next day he was greatly impressed by a visit to the iron works where he saw them working on "the new steamship *Washington* which is the best of anything yet seen." In the evening was the climax, for Judge Betts invited all the distinguished judges and lawyers of New York to meet him, and he had a most interesting and inspiring time. Trains started early in those days and he had to get up the next morning at half-past five to catch the train to Stockbridge on the Housatonic railroad. He says he was glad enough to find a quiet place at last after the rush of New York. The quiet did not last long. At Stockbridge he called on his mother and that energetic old lady tired him out completely by trotting him all over the place to show the apple trees she had been grafting. He ends with an exhortation to his wife to see that the garden beds are sown, and the beans and squash and cucumbers put in, for college presidents had to raise their own vegetables, when on a salary of $1200.

We have an interesting letter written on January 6, 1852, to his wife from Washington whither he had gone to deliver a course of lectures. There was then no bridge across the Susquehannah. The river was dangerous with floating ice and the ferry, with his train, barely got across before navigation was stopped, and all traffic blocked. He had brought his two daughters with him and like all American girls they were keen to see Kossuth, the great Hungarian patriot, who was to be received by the Senate. They were doomed to disappointment, for though they went an hour early the galleries were all jammed and they could not get in. They went to the Supreme Court and gazed in awe at the judges, and then heard a debate in the House as to a resolution to be sent to Kossuth—happy days when the energies of the House and Senate were absorbed by harmless legislation of this sort. His lecture was in the evening and by now his fame was so great that the house was packed and some hundreds turned away. His lecture was received with enthusiasm, but he was always doubtful about himself and writes "I have fears about the next" lecture.

Next day they had a snowstorm, heavier than any he had seen in Berkshire that winter, and they could hardly get through the streets. But the girls were determined to go out if they had to swim for it, for the clergy were to present an address to Kossuth and they meant to see their hero. But here was another disappointment. The clergy all assembled with a spokesman ready to spout forth his eloquent address, when Kossuth was called away by a summons from Daniel Webster. The girls waited impatiently in the room full of clergy, proud that they had got in when only eight other ladies were admitted. At last he came. The girls in their excitement climbed up on chairs and got quite close to their hero. Mark Hopkins thought Mr. Gurley spoke "with great propriety" and that once or twice he became eloquent but said he was much too long—probably the "great propriety"—part could have been skipped with advantage. He says "the whole scene was impressive," especially the girls on the chairs, one would suppose. They jumped down and were quite ecstatic when Kossuth came up and shook hands with them. Mark Hopkins was invited to go to the Great Congressional Dinner but had to lecture at the same time, and was trying to plan how to do both.

He comments on the expense of the hotel, two dollars a day for gentlemen, "but if they have ladies with them they and the ladies pay $2.50"—a most singular arrangement. "Fires were extra." This he calls "living fast." The girls are looking forward to a reception at the White House, he says, but we have no report as to their success in impressing the President.

Mark Hopkins was now in demand all over the country. In 1855 some Williams graduates arranged that he should lecture in Chicago. We have a letter written to his wife January 5, 1855, that describes how on his way out, when near Toledo he plunged into a terrible catastrophe caused by a collision between the engine and two horses, disastrous for both sides, for the horses were killed and the train was thrown off the track and the conductor pitched through a window. The result was that Mark Hopkins missed connections with his son Harry and had to ride all night. In Chicago all his old friends and graduates called on him "at the public house." Mr. Bross, editor of the leading paper, dined with him. He is dubious about his lecture. "It was not a failure but not very successful," he says. They were to take him out to see the prairies, and then he had to lecture in Kalamazoo and Detroit; quite a tour of the West for those days.

Ten years later, on October 4, 1865, he went again to Chicago, this time to the meeting of the American Board. His friend Mr. Bross had now become governor, and was awaiting him at the station. He stayed with the governor "in the finest block in the city facing the lake." "A magnificent situation," where he could "enjoy the sunrise over the lake" from his window. In the morning the governor drove him around the city "with one of his fine horses." The rest of his time was taken up with the meeting of the board where he presided.

He kept up his friendship with Governor Bross, who, as one of the wealthiest men in Chicago, had been very kind in contributing to the college and American

Board. By a strange quirk of fate six years later it was Mark Hopkins who was contributing to aid Governor Bross. For Williamstown was deeply stirred by news of the terrible Chicago fire, in which Governor Bross lost everything. Mark Hopkins and the professors contributed from their scanty salaries a surprising sum for those days. The women of Williamstown packed up boxes of clothing to be sent to the relief of the unfortunate victims, many of whom had nothing but their night clothes. Miss Bross wrote thanking him and her letter gives such a vivid description of the situation that it is worth quoting.

Chicago
6. 16th St., Oct. 24, 1871.

My dear Dr. Hopkins:

My father has gone East on business for *The Tribune*, and when he comes home his hands and head will be so full of anxious, though brave, cares that writing letters will be an impossibility, even in response to such tender and heartening writing as yours. Never in my life have I been so proud of having such a strong and noble father as in these days of trial, of trial more bitter than any one can conceive. Every source of income has been cut off in the four business blocks that were burnt, beside our beautiful home, with the larger part of our priceless treasures. Our best clothing was nearly all saved, but all our warm clothing, all our common clothing was burned. Poor

Father escaped with just the clothes he had on, and we had to take a clean shirt for him out of a charity box, for he had none, and there was no place in Chicago to buy one. It seems to me that all the horror and personal suffering of this fire cannot be conceived of by persons at a distance. I shall always love the Boston women for their prompt and wonderful benevolence. Their boxes were the first in Chicago, and from one sent to me I took a warm wrapping for my poor mother, a cloak for myself, and such needed and dainty things for the little ones of some of my mother's friends. One of them, the richest woman in her own right that I know, took with tears of gratitude an entire wardrobe for her little two-weeks old baby, which she carried for miles wrapped in a sheet from its crib on that terrible Monday Morning. That woman is today one of the poorest land owners in Chicago. The late rich! are the worst off, and you cannot believe too much in the stories of both actual suffering, and real inconvenience. Please tell Mrs. Hopkins that this very fastidious young lady didn't have a comb till many days after the fire. All these foolish little details I write just to give the ladies an idea of what it is when hundreds, yes thousands of delicately reared women are burned out of house and home, to say nothing of the increased wretchedness of the always wretched poor. I have engaged pleasant board in the hospitable home of one of my Father's most congenial friends. We saved all our pictures, part of our silver, our jewels, and our best clothing, beside a few of our many household treasures. But for our lives, and above all for the noble generosity of the world, and thc tender faithfulness of our loving friends we have so much to be unspeakably thankful for. There are so many gracious and providential mercies connected with our escape and savings from the fire which I shall rejoice to tell you if we shall all ever again have the pleasure of meeting. The money you of Williams have subscribed Father will delight to see suitably placed, for it is one of his severest trials that he cannot give to those whom he knows are suffering. So you see, dear Dr. Hopkins, you see the Williams' money will be a double blessing. Excuse haste and confusion of ideas, for I am writing in a room where many are talking. With loving greeting to all your family I am, with greatest respect,

Faithfully yours,

Jessie L. Bross.

We cannot follow Mark Hopkins in all of the trips that he took throughout the country as invitations came from all sides to speak. Some of his experiences were absurdly trying. On September 3, 1858, he writes to describe a trip to lay the cornerstone of the People's College at Havana, N. Y., an absurdly mismanaged enterprise in which he was pursued by misfortune. He took the train from Pittsfield to Albany—there being then no railroad in Williamstown—and went from Albany to Syracuse where he changed cars for Geneva, unfortunately leaving his overcoat in the train. He tried to telegraph for it, but the telegraph was a new instrument in those days and all the offices were closed "on account of the celebration." He nearly froze on the trip down the lake without any coat.

At Havana they were absolutely swamped by unexpected crowds. He estimates that there were 30,000! Why so many in those days before advertising is a mystery. There was no management. The procession was two hours late and the unhappy 30,000 stood in the sun, "a confused multitude" with innumerable complaining children, unable to see or hear a thing. The stand stood facing the wind and he saw he could not possibly be heard from thence, so he got an old wagon, had it hauled over to the other side of the crowd to get the wind with him and climbed up into it. He launched out on his speech, but soon saw that no one heard a word and gave it up and climbed down from his wagon.

Horace Greeley was the other speaker and he tried it from the stand. Mark Hopkins stood in the crowd and said he could see the gestures but could not hear a single word. Greeley might as well have done a pantomime. Then they served dinner to as many as could get into the tent. When they were seated Mark Hopkins was called upon for a speech. The wind had increased and just as he started the tent collapsed on his head. Fortunately he extricated himself without damage, but that finished his speech. It was all most annoying. He ends: "My dear wife if you had been here I should not have lost my coat or had to sleep here on a feather bed—hot—hot."

To the folk in the little New England village the great world across the seas seemed like a land of dreams and romance—unreal and far away, beyond the limits of time and space. Since his brother's return Mark had often thought of penetrating that land of mystery, but he had never had either the time or the money. His son Harry had made a flying trip in 1859 after graduation and his enthusiastic reports roused his father to action. For thirty years he had worked for the college without intermission, and his wife had worked loyally and patiently by his side, bringing up her family of eight, until now they were old enough to care for themselves. Mary deserved a vacation and they would have a honeymoon trip—deferred for thirty years, and see the world together. He had saved money from his lectures and the trustees in an excess of generosity voted him a thousand dollars for the trip—his first real vacation.

It was a glimpse into a different world and his letters are full of comments on the contrasts between the old world and the new. They landed at Liverpool, which seemed to him behind the times as compared with New York. They admired the walls of Chester, saw Kenilworth and Warwick and were especially interested in Oxford and its contrasts with Williams College.

He was greatly impressed with the age of everything as compared with the Hoosick valley, so recently reclaimed from wild forest land, and notes the tiled and thatched houses, mostly of brick and so different from the wooden New England farmhouses, and the fields divided by hedges instead of fences. The high cultivation of the land surprised him, and the wheat sown in rows or drills and hoed by hand. He thought there were very few people—no more than at home.

He liked Oxford, and commented on the advantage of the quadrangle where the students could be shut in at night, a plan that would have saved him many anxious nights. The buildings he thought must once have been magnificent, but are crumbling to decay, "and if antiquity did not cause deformity to become a beauty, would hardly be thought fit to be lived in." He went out to watch the rowing on the Isis, the boys simply in shirt and pantaloons, and he watched with amusement while the boats sought to gain the lead by "bumping" one another, a singular type of rowing race to his mind. He thinks "the times have outgrown the institutions" and "while there is something venerable about them there is also much that seems absurd and ridiculous."

His wife was much more enthusiastic and after describing the glories of the Bodleian Library says: "I must say I could but smile and sigh when I thought of our Alumni Hall at Williams." She was quite overwhelmed by London and describes how they went out with Miss Hoar from the Golden Cross to view the town, all five in one cab. She is lost in wonder at the Tower, with all its grim, historic associations and is dazzled by the crown jewels though she claims she has not a single desire to wear them.

Sunday they went to hear Spurgeon preach, and were astonished he could draw such a crowd—some 6000 persons. When it came to preaching she evidently thought her husband could do better, "simply a good sermon; I have heard many more eloquent and interesting." They sailed down the Thames to Greenwich and saw the observatory, carefully setting their watches by world time. She loved the park and the gayety of the people and children. "Merry Old England" she called it.

Mrs. Pilgrim in a white cap decoyed her in for tea, mutton chops, bread and butter, and tea for thrippence each.

The Crystal Palace she considered fairyland in truth, and wandered about until "head, eyes, and feet were aching."

And then she speaks of the terrible news from home of imminent war, and wonders if her sons will all be swept from their studies into the maelstrom of destruction. She ends with characteristic salutations to all the family including the housekeepers and cleaners, for she is evidently wondering if the house will be properly cleaned in her absence.

It is small wonder that they were disturbed on their trip. Letters from home became more and more ominous. Harry was then studying for the ministry in Union Seminary, New York. His letter gives such a vivid picture of the situation in New York that I shall quote it in full.

New York
April 23^d^ 1861

My dear father and mother:

. . . I scarcely know whether to think you fortunate or otherwise in being away at this critical juncture of our national affairs. We are in the very midst of revolutionary times. You will get some idea from the papers of the almost miraculous uprising of the North as one man but no description can convey any true impression of it. I dont believe that there was ever in any nation such a spirited and true outburst of patriotism. The reception of the Prince of Wales was nothing in comparison with the ovation to the 7th Regiment when they took departure and the scene at the mass-meeting on Saturday was more than sublime. Money flows like water and men are ready and anxious to go; thousands more than can be sent. The stories of true self sacrifice and devotion to country take one back to the war of the Revolution. The praises of Massachusetts are in the mouth of every one and emblasoned in the papers. You will read all the facts in the papers. That first Regiment that went through here were not half uniformed they had come away in such haste—and since the remarkable historical coincidence at Baltimore, the shedding of the first blood by her troops on the anniversary of the battle of Lexington, almost the whole population is ready to enlist.

I have had conversation with a good many of the troops on their way through and they all seem animated by one spirit. The Berkshire men were decidedly the finest looking company in their regiment. Their captain was a son of Gov. Briggs. Sunday was completely overridden & set aside. Armies were mustering in the streets all day and flags floated from many of the churches. The ministers almost without exception preached war sermons and prayed for our armies as engaged in a holy cause. The most violent democrats are the fiercest for war and all say that the capitol shall not be taken and that the union must and shall be preserved. This P. M. we hoist a flag over the Seminary and Dr. Hitchcock makes a speech. Dr. Adams has been down this morning to consult with Mr. Gallagher, who you know is a military man, about forming a body of exclusively Christian young men to be ready for any duty. Many from the Seminary have offered their services as chaplains and some have been accepted and are under marching orders. But the danger I imagine is past—Washington is safe, and immediate bloodshed need not be expected. Although I hope and believe that the war will be carried into Africa and every U S fort be repossessed.

Examinations are just at hand but study has been a secondary matter. I am getting somewhat composed now, yet the prospect of being out of the whirlpool in a quiet village where news comes but once a day is anything but pleasant.

Your aff son

HARRY.

It was not pleasant to learn that a former Williams student had been one of the chief agents in rousing South Carolina to secede. This man, Yancey, was one of those brilliant erratic fellows, who cannot be easily adjusted to any formal system of education, and after some violent clashes with the authorities, had left college without the benediction of the president, whose law of love he had entirely failed to absorb. He was a born orator and could hold his classmates enthralled, or rouse them to rebellion if he chose. Doctor Emmons, who was on a geological mission in Raleigh, North Carolina, wrote to Mark Hopkins early in 1860 to offer his unique collection of the fossils of North Carolina to the college. He adds: "North Carolina is not disposed to secede though every effort is being made to bring the people to the scratch. I cannot speak of the course of South Carolina with patience. I am tempted to swear at the course this state has pursued, and to think that the man Yancey has been able to exert such a powerful influence on the destinies of this nation is still more tempting to commit a sin." He evidently felt that he had already fallen into sin for he adds: "Correction: for 'swear,' read 'be indignant.' "

Their trip through France and Switzerland must

have been an anxious one, and they were glad indeed to find themselves back in the little village among the mountains. Their return was expected and the whole town was illuminated. A procession of students with torches met them at the station and escorted them triumphantly to their home.

The anxiety they had felt abroad was as nothing compared to that which they were to suffer during the next three years with three sons at the front. Archibald, as soon as he graduated in 1862, helped to organize a company in Williamstown, and with the title of captain, like his namesake, he went to the front, saw active service at Petersburg and elsewhere, winning quick promotion and finishing his career in the army with the title of colonel, at the age of twenty-three.

Lawrence, who was in the class of 1863, also secured a commission as lieutenant of cavalry when only seventeen, and showed himself an extraordinarily capable officer. He was wounded in a cavalry charge and his father went on in great anxiety to seek him, and found him at last in a hospital. Fortunately the wound was not severe and he was able to return to the service, finishing with the rank of major, though little more than twenty years old.

Henry served throughout the war as chaplain.

The war had its effect on the college. Many parents had to face the cruel decision as to whether their sons should give up their hope of an education and enter the war.

The following letter is a sample of many received by Mark Hopkins at this time, letters which added a heavy weight of anxiety to the burdens resting upon him.

New York, Sept. 5, 1863.

Pres Hopkins.

Dr Sir:

It is proper that I should explain the nonappearance of my son at Williams, to take his place in the Sophomore class. . . .

Ever since my first-born gave his life for our cause, I have had a yearning to make good his place and his purposes in the army;—but Joseph was too young to be drafted, or to go as a substitute in the ranks. When, however, I saw how the draft was evaded, and the government was likely to fail of men, at the most critical moment of the war, I said to him, will you go and link my name and your life with that despised race, whose destiny must be the key to ours? He deliberated upon it and assented. He began to rub up his tactics, with commendable diligence. I sent him to Washington for examination; the Board report that he "passed very creditably," and he is commissioned a First Lieutenant of the first class, in the 2^{d} Reg^{t} U. S. Colored Troops. Next week he will enter upon his duties, in the army of the South.

It is a great deal for me again to forego the hopes of education in a son. I have none left now but a boy of six years and two daughters. But the cause is infinitely greater than any individual plans or interests, and the path of sacrifice seems for me the path of duty. I keep back nothing.

With high regard,
Yrs truly
Jos. T. Thompson

It was natural that in the stress of the war the numbers of the college should have decreased. In the stringency of the post-war period fewer young men were able to afford a college education and the effect was felt especially in the farming communities of the Berkshires. The numbers fell off and from 1866 to 1872 the classes averaged only thirty-nine.

Doctor Hopkins had felt the strain of those terrible years of anxiety. He had borne the heavy responsibilities of the presidency for nearly forty years, and had built up the college from comparative insignificance to an institution known and respected throughout the country. He saw it now weakened and diminished in the general depression and felt that it would be wiser to turn over the task of rebuilding to another. Accordingly in 1872, being then in his seventy-first year, he resigned the presidency. He felt that he had done his bit and completed his work, and wished to give up all his work in the college, but such pressure was put upon him that he finally agreed to continue teaching his courses to the seniors.

For forty years the two Hopkins brothers had

worked side by side to realize in Williams College their ideals of an institution to form and develop the finest type of character. In May, 1872, just at the time when his brother resigned the presidency, Professor Albert Hopkins passed away, thus bringing to an end their long partnership. As one looks over the long list of those who came under their influence, as students at Williams, one finds many names that are familiar. The author E. P. Roe, whose books attained a sale of 1,400,000 copies; Stephen Field, for thirty-four years justice of the Supreme Court; Samuel G. W. Benjamin, author and diplomat; David Ames Wells, and Samuel W. Dike well known in sociology and economics; James H. Canfield, chancellor of the University of Nebraska; John Boyd Thacher, author and statesman; William K. Brooks, the famous zoologist; Frank H. Snow, chancellor of the University of Kansas; William Dwight Whitney, famed scholar; Samuel C. Armstrong, founder of Hampton Institute; Ronald S. MacKenzie, whom Grant called the most promising young officer in the army; John J. Ingalls, senator and statesman; these and many others spread the influence of Williams College far and wide.

The little school founed by the "gallant and generous" Colonel Ephraim Williams had become a real force in the great world beyond the Berkshires.

The climax came when a Williams graduate was elected President of the United States and made the name of Mark Hopkins familiar throughout the nation by his oft-quoted description of the ideal university. The following letter gives some idea of the impression created upon the country:

33 School St. Boston
Nov. 4, 1880

My dear Sir,

I think that you should be congratulated on having lived to see one of your pupils—one too who was trained by you to an eminent degree—elected to the Presidency. I do not know, but I doubt whether any college President has ever seen the same thing. There is hardly a station now in civil life from the highest down for which one of your pupils has not been selected: the Supreme Bench, the Senate, the House of Representatives, the Executive chair of a State, the State Supreme Courts—and I think you can feel that they have done well, and in their success you have received in your life time, a reward for your long and laborious services.

The tremendous majority are especially pleasing to Garfield's friends as the answer of the people to the dishonest and brutal attacks upon him, persisted in to the very last. When will party managers learn that abuse in the long run hurts the libeller far more than the man libelled; that, according to Bentley's fine saying, "No man was ever yet written down, except by himself."? I think the forged letter to Morey, is the worst thing of the kind in American politics during my recollection.

Ferry Jacobs of our class who is elected to Congress

from New York is a strong man, of great honesty and great independence and will be an efficient member of the House.

At the torchlight procession on Monday Evening I was pleased to see the Harvard students turn out five hundred strong to do honor to a Williams man. The reputation of Williams College here is steadily increasing notwithstanding the scarcity of graduates in this vicinity. Garfield's election, too, I think, will perceptibly help the College throughout the land.

I remain with great respect

J. H. Hill

The Rev. Mark Hopkins D. D.

CHAPTER XIV

FRIENDSHIP AND FAMILY RELATIONS

Mark Hopkins was well aware of his limitations when, on taking the presidency, he stipulated that he should not be held responsible for raising funds for the college. During the thirty-five years of his presidency almost the only gifts to the college were voluntary and unsolicited gifts from personal friends and admirers. On Professor Kellogg's death a small building was erected in his memory, containing recitation rooms and a few rooms for students and named Kellogg Hall.

We have spoken of the helplessness of the president at the tragedy of the burning of East College. Some funds were volunteered, but the college would have been deeply in debt but for an unexpected gift from Amos Lawrence, one of the friends whom Mark Hopkins prized most and who honored him in return. Amos Lawrence was a man of the widest interests and benevolences. As a member of the firm of A. & A. Lawrence he had been one of the leaders in developing the commerce and manufactures of Massachusetts, had been instrumental in the building of many cotton mills, and the city of Lawrence had been named for him. As his health declined he retired from business to his home in Groton and devoted himself to his various benevolences. He had been deeply interested in the first series of Lowell lectures delivered by Mark Hopkins, and had taken the pains to hunt up the lecturer and to invite him repeatedly to his house. Although he was a Unitarian the lectures appealed to him powerfully in their breadth of vision. The two men at once discovered a mutual liking which led to a friendship which was continued even after the death of Amos Lawrence through his son Amos A. Lawrence. The Lawrences insisted that Doctor Hopkins should stay with them when he came to Boston, and nearly every year he paid them a visit in which the two men would discuss together the deep things of life. When he heard of the East College disaster Amos Lawrence promptly sent a check for $5000 which cleared off the debt. This was but a beginning of his generosity and kindliness. He loved children and soon became acquainted with Doctor Hopkins' large family. The children all loved him and called him "Uncle Amos." Every once in a while a large box would arrive in Williamstown to be opened with shouts of joy by the children as they discovered present after present for them, of things they had longed for but never been able to afford. He did more than this. Learning the need of a library he presented the funds necessary for the erection of the charming and unusual building now used by the art department, which has in its vestibule a striking portrait of the donor in one of those flowered dressing gowns in which men of that period loved to be painted—per-

MARK HOPKINS AND AMOS LAWRENCE

haps because they thus avoided the harsh and inartistic outlines of coat and trousers.

Another to whom Mark Hopkins owed much was the little adopted sister who had adored him as a child. She became the chief influence in the transformation of her native town. Stockbridge had seen many changes. Gradually the valley had lost the wild picturesqueness of the days when Indian lodges flocked along the river-side and the chiefs gathered around their blazing campfires. The Indian wigwams gave place to the dignified houses of the first settlers, gathered about their white meeting house and the buildings of the Indian school. But again changes had come. As the richness of the valley became known settlers came pouring in to take the place of the Indians, many of them shiftless and ignorant. They herded together in the lower town, and little by little the town lost its trim New England neatness and simple beauty, and became sordid and dirty. Mary Hopkins, Mark's youngest adopted sister, had all the energy and zeal for cleanliness of her adoptive mother, and a real love of beauty. She married Mr. J. Z. Goodrich, one of the wealthy men of Stockbridge and, with his influence behind her, set to work to clean up the town and transform it. She had a way with her, and could charm or ridicule as the case demanded. Her keen sense of humor and spicy tongue kept people amused while she shamed them out of their shiftlessness. She organized the Village Improvement Society and her achievements were described in some eloquent verses, read by W. R. Palmer at the meeting of the Laurel Hill Association on August 12, 1857.

He speaks of the degeneration in the appearance of Stockbridge and says:

But, by and by, when things were grown almost beyond
enduring,
And Nature's wounds seemed past all hope of staunching
or of curing;
There came a Fairy to the vale, of most benignant presence,
And gently stole a genial spell upon its thoughtless peasants.

Her smile was like the softened sheen that plays on lake or
river,
When laughing ripples glance the shafts from Morning's
rosy quiver;
Her voice as musical as harps the summer wind just kisses,
And witching as the lays that charmed the comrades of
Ulysses.

He tells how as the result of her efforts the town was transformed.

The woodpile stole behind the house, behind the barn the
kine-yard;
The dooryard spurned its double use of milking-pen and
swine-yard;
And carts and kennels, sleds and sties, those old front court
adorners,
Slunk off and hid themselves away in proper holes and
corners.

At last the old house rubbed its eyes, and saw how sadly
shabby

It needs must look in gabardine so weather-stained and
drabby;
And thereupon it set to work, with earnest perseverance,
Like tattered wretch resolved to make a comelier appearance.

And vines were planted by the door—the woodbine or
clematis—
To curtain in the rustic porch and drape the breezy lattice;
And trees of graceful form and leaf soon waved along all
high-ways,
And sent their verdant kindred forth to farthest lanes and
by-ways.

And whereas, erst, no habitant, within those mountain
towers,
E'er deigned to spend one kindly thought upon the friendless
flowers;
There's not a cotter in the vale but will, by harder toiling,
Find time to cherish these dear waifs of Adam's garden-
spoiling.

Mary Goodrich still looked up to her adopted brother as her great hero and ideal and disguised her admiration by saucy and amusing challenges. She did all in her power to further his cause, and persuaded her husband to contribute largely to the college, and finally to erect the building which stood on the site of the present chapel and served as a laboratory and gymnasium under the name of Goodrich Hall.

Not content with transforming Stockbridge, she carried her influence to Williamstown, where the streets had become shabby and unkempt. Here also a Village Improvement Society was started. The old ramshackle fences in front of the houses were torn down, along with the old barns and sheds. Lawns were put in order and trees planted and the town began to take on its present aspect of neatness and beauty.

David Dudley Field, who married Mark's adopted sister Lucinda, was another life-long friend. He and his brothers were the sons of a minister in Stockbridge. His brother Cyrus became famous and wealthy by laying the transatlantic cable. His brother Stephen acquired fame as a lawyer in California, and was at last appointed to the Supreme Court of the United States. Henry was equally well known as a clergyman and editor of the *Evangelist.* We have noted that both Harry and Mark lived for a time with David in New York and with him belonged to that group of young men who frequented the Sedgwicks and passed many pleasant evenings at their house. It was the Sedgwicks who persuaded Bryant to come to New York and started him on his career in *The Evening Post* and he and James Fenimore Cooper and Irving and all that group of brilliant young writers were frequent guests at the Sedgwicks. Henry and Robert, who had taken Harry into their coal business, took David Field into their law firm, where he at once showed marked abilities. A friend had just begun to codify the laws of Louisiana, with the aid of the Code Napoleon, and David took the much more difficult task of codifying the laws of New York State. It was a life work, but was done with such genius that it was adopted not only in America but in England, where the old English law was in a state of great confusion. His success brought him fame and wealth, but he never forgot his college or his old friend Mark Hopkins, and made gifts which were of great value at critical moments.

It was through the Fields that the park at the head of the main street in Williamstown was constructed, and they also gave an astronomical observatory with an equatorial instrument, as well as aiding in many other enterprises.

Through his addresses at the American Board, Mark Hopkins made other lasting friends, among them Mr. William E. Dodge of New York. At the time of Mark Hopkins's resignation, Mr. Dodge presented to the college a fund, the income of which was to maintain a professorship to be occupied by Doctor Hopkins until his death. This was a most thoughtful provision, as it enabled him to live on in comfort and continue to give his services to the college.

As the college became better known a singular question arose. Men of prominence in England began to appeal to Mark Hopkins to give them degrees, apparently thinking that an American college would append to their names the coveted initials which were so difficult to attain from an English university.

I have in hand such an application for the degree of LL.D. from Mr. James Macnair, principal of the

Glasgow Modern Schools and Training College, endorsed by letters from prominent men, and another for the degree of D.D. from J. Cunningham Geikie, author of the well-known life of Christ. Mark Hopkins found some excuse for courteously declining such applications, which was as well, for soon after the English *Independent* burst forth in criticism of such degrees. To quote: "These Yankee degrees are a pest, and we devoutly wish the Americans would keep them at home and not let them loose upon us. They make the wearers ridiculous, destroy the value of distinctions fairly won and bring learning itself into contempt."

To succeed Mark Hopkins as president of Williams College the trustees chose Doctor Paul A. Chadbourne, who had formerly been professor at Williams, and who was then president of the University of Wisconsin. The reason for the choice seems to have been that the other two candidates who were strongly advocated were the men who had sought to introduce the system of marks and discipline that was so obnoxious to the spirit which Doctor Hopkins had sought to maintain at Williams. Both were stern disciplinarians of the autocratic type who had no sympathy with the foibles of youth, and one of them, though a man of pre-eminent ability and power, had a manner of announcing his ideas and beliefs that seemed to arouse the most surprising antagonism. Both left the college when their candidacy proved unacceptable. The trustees and faculty were glad to accept any suggestions from Doctor Hopkins, and Doctor Chadbourne was duly elected to the office. Unfortunately he was absorbed in so many business and political measures that it was difficult to make a success of any. The college ran down under his administration to an average of about thirty in each class.

We have noted that a democratic feature had early been introduced into the government of the college, and that the Society of the Alumni elected a third of the trustees and thus prevented the Board from becoming a close corporation. At Doctor Chadbourne's inauguration in 1872 the Society of the Alumni was represented by General James A. Garfield, one of the most eminent and devoted of Williams graduates. In his address to the new president General Garfield said:

"We cannot if we would transfer to any other the profound reverence and deep affection with which we cherish the name and fame of the retiring President. His title to these is inalienable and imperishable. He is and will continue to be *our* President of Williams College. In loving him we shall none the less love the College with the true loyalty of grateful children. . . . We do not expect you to bend the bow of Ulysses. Let it here remain unbent forever as the social symbol and trophy of victories achieved. But we do expect you to confront the future with its new and difficult problems in the spirit of fearlessness and truth—in a spirit conservative to preserve all the garnered wisdom which experience has purchased—

and courageous to adopt and lead all true reforms, and to work manfully by the light of each rising sun."

General Garfield was prepared for college in a Campbellite school at Hiram, Ohio, and intended to become a preacher. He had written to several colleges and had turned to Williams because of a personal note in the letter he received from Mark Hopkins, which appealed to him. Williams College made a very deep impression upon him. In the first place, coming from the plains of Ohio, the mountains around Williamstown had as overwhelming an effect upon him as the Himalayas would upon one more used to mountain heights, and his letters were full of descriptions of their magnificence and of the inspiration they gave him. He was a natural orator—at that time somewhat turgid and flamboyant in his use of adjectives, and he threw himself into the work of the debating societies—the Philologian and Philotechnian. He acquired fame in the college through his attack on the fraternity system, which was just beginning to take root. His oration on the subject was so moving that it brought about the organization of an Anti-Secret Society.

To support himself in college he taught in a school in North Pownal where Chester Arthur also taught later and which has the honor of being the only school taught by two Presidents of the United States. But to him the main thing in college and the predominant influence in his life had been the teaching of Mark Hopkins, who opened his mind to a wider view of life and freed him from the prejudices of the narrow theology in which he had been brought up, and gave him an inspiration to which he constantly referred in after life. He was turned by circumstances from the ministry to politics and his experiences in the war as General Rosecrans' chief of staff and chief adviser, and in Congress as the defender of sound money, had given him a deep understanding of life and freed him from the boyish extravagancies of vision and diction that had been manifested in his earlier speeches.

Mark Hopkins was one of the first to congratulate him on the unexpected nomination that made him instead of Sherman, Grant, or Blaine, the Republican candidate for the Presidency. In his letter he said: "How well I remember those early struggles and your manly bearing under them, the confidence you at once gave your instructors and received from them, and the combination, so apparently easy, and yet so rare among students, of a genial spirit with pure habits and high aims uniformly pursued. That was the beginning of a course in which you have not faltered, and the lesson therefore is that this hour is the result of no accident, but of achievement by steady work in scholarship and statesmanship, so that when the occasion called, the *man* was there."

To him it was a supreme honor to his teaching that the man who seemed most fully and deeply to appreciate it should be chosen as President of the United States. After his election Doctor Hopkins went to

Washington and on the afternoon of Inauguration Day, March 4, 1881, he presented the congratulations of the college and alumni of whom about a hundred assembled in the east room of the White House. It was an occasion that deeply stirred all who witnessed it, as the newly elected President of the United States, surrounded by the symbols and representatives of his high office, stepped forward to receive the benediction of the venerable teacher who had so influenced his life. In response to the address of Doctor Hopkins, the President, after acknowledging the greeting of the alumni, said: "It is especially grateful to me that your greetings have been delivered by that venerable and venerated man who was in our college days and always will be our President. For a quarter of a century Doctor Hopkins has seemed to me a man apart from other men—standing on a mountain peak —embodying in himself much of the majesty of earth and reflecting in his life something of the sunlight and glory of Heaven. His presence here is a benediction." He added that it seemed to him that Doctor Hopkins was more truly President than he himself.

In 1881 Doctor Chadbourne resigned the presidency and although General Garfield was then President of the United States he was asked to come again to Williams and represent the alumni in greeting the incoming president of Williams at his inauguration. He consented and it was in the railway station on his way to Williamstown that the bullet of the assassin struck him down. Instead of a joyous occasion that

Commencement became a tragedy during which, with distress manifest in his face and voice, the venerable Doctor read one telegram after another to audiences that sat in hushed suspense.

Mark Hopkins was to have delivered an address commemorative of President Garfield at the next Commencement, but was prevented by the death of his eldest daughter Louisa, which brought sadness to all who attended the Commencement and knew him.

He was deeply devoted to his family and they were bound to him by very close ties. He officiated as a patriarchal high priest at every marriage and christening as his grandchildren were born and added to the family circle. Every Thanksgiving the family gathered from far and near and sat together around the board with its regulation menu of oyster soup, a boiled turkey at one end of the table, a roast turkey at the other, and spare-rib in the middle, followed by the many pies—mince, pumpkin, cranberry, Washington, and Marlborough—a meal so extensive that to do justice to it the children had to run around the table between courses. In the evening there were certain family rites, hugely enjoyed by the children. "Lord Ullin's Daughter" had to be performed, with the big rug in the living-room as the lake, and a bench as the boat containing the run-away lovers; while Lord Ullin cried in distress from the shore "My daughter, oh, my daughter!" the sea, impelled by vigorous arms, rose and overwhelmed the two in the boat.

But most exciting was the battle of the Union and

Confederate ghosts over the body of the soldier. One of the uncles lay on the floor covered with a flag. The old war uniforms were brought down and one arm, holding a cross stick, was dressed in a Union coat and cap and the other in Confederate gray. The lights were dimmed and first one ghost rose from beside the dead, and then the other, and a fight ensued in which the gray ghost usually was knocked to pieces, to the joy of all. Mark Hopkins always sat in his big armchair looking on with a smile and twinkle in his eye at the excitement of the children, who would sometimes creep to his knee for protection when the ghost rose in the dark.

His ready sympathy with the children was sometimes rather disconcerting to parental discipline. One evening when we were nine years old we were having our supper of oatmeal at the table with the grown-ups while they ate their dinner. One of the two boys started to put sugar on his oatmeal and his father exclaimed: "Oh, don't put sugar on your oatmeal. I would as soon put sugar on my beefsteak." There was a large silver sugar-bowl, presented by Amos Lawrence, in front of Doctor Hopkins. Without a word, but with a sly twinkle in his eye, he reached over, took up a spoonful of sugar and sprinkled it on his steak. Every one looked up to him with such reverence that no one ventured a word. We boys nudged each other and sprinkled our sugar without further protest.

He had the patriarchal aspect that created the impression of great age and wisdom. One of his sons brought back from the war a darkey lad who said his name was Billy. He knew no further name, and when asked "Billy What?" always said "Billy Nuttin'," (meaning nothing). Billy Nuttin accordingly he became. Doctor Hopkins' daughters sought diligently to teach him his Bible lessons. When they reached Methuselah and explained elaborately how long a period he covered with his 900 years, Billy exclaimed, "Golly, he must be most as old as Doctor Hopkins!"

He was driving down to South Williamstown to preach one day, jogging along in his buggy, with Senator, his old black horse, splashing through the mud, which was deep in those days. It was raining hard, and he met a small boy who was trudging along barefoot, soaked through, and carrying a heavy bundle. He looked the picture of misery, and remembering his boyhood days Doctor Hopkins pulled up, and said: "Well, my boy, this is a pretty bad day, isn't it?" The boy looked up at him and with inimitable defiance called out, " 'Tain't, darn ye!" I can well remember how he chuckled over that incident for several days—the boy's determined optimism and resentment of patronage, and his surprising irreverence toward one whose presence commanded respect even from the President, created an incongruity infinitely humorous to him.

Like his brother Albert, he loved nature and the mountains. After Albert's death Mark Hopkins used often to go off with his family into the mountains as

Albert used to do. His favorite spot was the campground up on the shoulders of Greylock, a lovely grove of spruces, bounded on each side by a sparkling mountain brook, that came down in a series of cascades, and formed delightful bathing pools for those who enjoyed the stimulus of the icy water. To this spot Mark Hopkins retired each summer vacation with his family. Provisions were hauled up the steep road through the Hopper, tents were pitched, beds of fragrant balsam were laid, a fireplace was built of huge stones and a dining-table large enough for all was built. In the evening all would gather around a roaring campfire, and while the sparks leapt up to join the stars sparkling overhead, they would tell stories of the old days, of bears and wolves and wildcats, till the black forest around seemed alive with wild beasts. Across the brook was an open pasture and the ruins of an ancient house formed an elevation where all gathered each evening to watch the sunset, when the sky would be all aflame with scarlet and gold, a burst of color in strange contrast with the black spruces near at hand. One evening Mark Hopkins, then nearly eighty, had climbed up onto the ruin with the rest of us and stood admiring the gorgeous display of color, when a stone rolled under his foot and he fell backward into the deep cellar. I shall never forget the sudden horror of that moment. We expected the worst, but by some miracle he rose up unharmed and walked back to the camp.

Sometimes we would walk over to the Bluffs, a

mile away, and look down into the great chasm of the Hopper, its sides as precipitous as they could be and yet not be sheer cliffs, mountain walls, tapestried with the deep green of the beeches and maples and the delicate filmy green of the birches and patched with the black of the spruces. The great mountain shoulders swept down in smooth clean-cut curves like the sleek limbs of some mighty crouching leopard, expressive of the beauty of gigantic power in repose. Doctor Hopkins loved the place and never tired of gazing down into the depths a thousand feet below whence rose the ceaseless tinkling murmur of the Hopper brook, dimmed only by the whisper of the wind in the spruces.

We were all early initiated into the joys of the camp on Greylock. I was taken up before I was a year old. I have been told how during a storm my mother tried to prevent me from being soaked by rain trickling in through a leaky tent, by supporting a bathtub on her chest and holding a cup in each hand. It was thrilling when storms gathered and the thunder roared and reverberated through the mountain peaks and the jagged lightning flashed through the black pines. Mark Hopkins brought us all up to love it as he did in all its phases, in the clash and war of the storm and in the solemn quiet of the dawn when the clear sweet note of the hermit thrush was the only sound that broke the stillness; when the sun slanted down through the forest glades carpeted with moss and violets, or fragile anemone and hepatica, or when the full moon shone with eerie light through the black pines and spruces and the owls hooted solemnly in the distance.

If he shared thus in the life of the mountain and forest, he seemed even more an essential part of the New England village. Of a Sunday morning when the church bell broke the solemn quiet of the village and he walked down the street beneath the perfect Gothic arch of the great elms, there was a compelling majesty in his tall figure as he moved slowly on in the long black coat and silk hat, leaning slightly on his cane, stopping here and there to bow to the ladies of the village or to the students as they walked onward toward the chapel. Just as the college building—old Griffin Hall with its cupola and fan windows and the old houses with their delicate colonial carvings and pilasters—seemed to have gathered up the culture of the past and formed a nest for it here in this isolated valley, girt about by mountain ranges and trackless forest through which but a short time ago the only path was the trail of the savage Mohawks; so the man Mark Hopkins as he moved slowly forward through the elm-shadowed street seemed to incarnate in his stately massive form and wide domed brow all the finest traditions of the old school, preserving its reverence for God and man, its high sense of duty and justice, while he cast off all that was narrow and petty and looked out to the new vistas of knowledge opening before him with wide vision and deep understanding; holding fast to all that was best in the old and opening the way to that vast conception of the universe that was just beginning to dawn upon the mind of man.

This was the impression he seemed to make wherever he went. Although he had supported the orthodox belief, yet he had done it in so broad a way that in 1886 Harvard, the seat of Unitarianism, conferred on him the degree of Doctor of Laws. This came as a climax to his long life of service. He had received the degree of Doctor of Divinity from Dartmouth in 1837, from Harvard in 1841, and the degree of Doctor of Laws from the University of New York. And now Harvard was conferring upon him the highest honor in her power. He was not alone in the honor received. First Governor Robinson, head of the commonwealth, stepped forward to receive his degree with the customary applause. Then Secretary Lamar took his turn and received his share of handclapping. Senator Hoar followed and his stately figure was received with a greater round of applause. When President Dwight, head of Harvard's great rival, came forward, animosities were forgotten and a prolonged burst of applause filled the hall. As it died down, Mark Hopkins rose and stood forth as his name was called. Never, it seemed, had his form seemed so majestic, his bearing so venerable and impressive. As he stood there, the massive frame slightly bent with his eighty-five years, the stately head with its sparse locks seemed to tower above other men, and the great audience, moved and stirred as such an audience seldom is, rose spontaneously and cheered and applauded until it seemed they would never cease. It was a last great triumph. It meant that by defending the great truths of the past he had adjusted them to the needs of the present and laid a firm foundation from which men could advance fearlessly and undisturbed into the mystery of the future with all its astounding revelations.

He had lived through all the amazing changes that transformed the autocratic, superstitious medieval world into the modern world of today. In his lifetime he had seen greater changes than had occurred in the 2000 years preceding.

In his address before the American Board in Boston in 1885, he said: "Having entered upon life at the beginning of the second year of this marvellous century, I have seen all its wonders pass before me. I can remember when my lesson in geography told me there were 6,000,000 inhabitants in these United States. I remember the wars of Napoleon and can feel yet the throb of excitement caused by the tardy news of his great battles. I remember the War of 1812 and the Embargo, and the Battle of New Orleans. I remember the first steamboat and railroad and power press, the first photograph and spectroscope, the first telegraph and telephone, and heard the first whisper—and it was but a whisper—of the Atlantic cable. I remember the first spinning Jenny, the first sewing machine and mowing machine and reaper. All these I have seen so extended and applied as to increase the capabilities of the race many fold, and to make of the world that then was quite another world. I have witnessed the greatest Civil War ever known, have seen the dark cloud of slavery pass off, and a bow of hope brighter than ever before span our political heavens." If such were the changes in the outer world, the changes in the world of thought were no less great.

The old ideas of autocratic government on which society was based had been undermined by the example of a self-governing people. The existence of a divinely sanctioned authority—in king, aristocrats, father and husband and in the law, was no longer recognized. In the new world the only authority which A can hope to maintain over B was based on the superior wisdom of A and the affection of B. The flaming fires of Hell and the pearly gates of Heaven, which were only one short step away, had receded into the Infinite distance. Most astonishing of all, the fundamental motivation of man that had maintained law and preserved order and civilization was gone. The foundation on which morals and virtue and obedience were based, was knocked from under. The old fear of Hell fire, of the wrath of an angry God, had evaporated into thin air, and with it that reverence for all constituted authority. This had been due in large measure to the new conception of the universe given by science, and the new idea of the Bible resulting from critical study.

The great work of Mark Hopkins was that he had

seen in the old system the elements that were permanent and had thrown all his emphasis upon these. He had opened the minds of the young to the stupendous revelations of modern science and had taught them to adjust their thinking to them. He had cast aside the old motivation of fear, not so much because it was untrue as because it was ignoble, and had based all life and virtue on the law of love. Men were to serve God from love of Him, not from terror before His law. They were to serve their fellow-men from love and sympathy, and not because of future reward and punishment. They were to do right because it was the only path to happiness for all. He had not sought to found a new system of philosophy, and had refused to be led aside into those abstruse problems as to the nature of ultimate reality and the relation of mind and matter over which modern philosophers and psychologists dispute, and upon which each has founded an elaborate system which the others deny *in toto*. He wanted to make clear and plain the simple realities upon which a man could base his thought and his life and go forward undisturbed in the clash of opinion and the collapse of ancient systems of thought.

Thus when men were clamoring that science had proved the Bible was false since the world was not created in six days, and that therefore there was no God to punish, and man could safely "do anything that he could get away with," those who had been trained by him felt that all this was aside from the point. They had thought their way through to a firmer basis for right and duty. Although he, himself, did not abandon the old teaching, the narrow religion of terror seemed to him so unimportant as to be unworthy of mention. Just so a greater Teacher had accepted the old Jewish religion, and instead of attacking its many cruel and unjust commands, such as those that dealt with slavery and polygamy, had been content to select from its many hundred regulations, two upon which he threw the whole emphasis of his teaching and life, trusting that if men truly loved God and their neighbor other matters would adjust themselves. It was the same law of love upon which Mark Hopkins threw all the emphasis of his teaching, satisfied that the unworthy part of the old system would fall away of itself. And what he taught, he practised. He would have no stern system of discipline. He would have students attend his recitation because they wanted to come—for love of learning—not for fear of punishment. He would have them respectful, not because otherwise they would be disciplined but because they felt reverence for his wisdom and his character.

He kept to the old idea of the Bible and this handicapped him in his teaching. In his last course of lectures on "The Scriptural Idea of God," his idea of the God of love was necessarily limited by having to explain the acts of Yahveh in the Old Testament. And in the lectures on "The Scriptural Idea of Man," a similar limitation is present. His wide view of the universe and of the interrelation of its laws is continually obstructed by some ancient concept which he felt compelled to include. But if he had not retained this view of the Bible, his great work as a mediator between the old thought and the new would have come to naught, for he would have alienated just the group whom he was best fitted to help. Those beliefs would be dropped soon enough of themselves. The important matter was to give men something that would remain.

We find then that the life of Mark Hopkins covers a great period of transition in material and intellectual development. His great-uncle, Doctor Samuel Hopkins, had been the chief exponent of the old theology that once ruled New England and the Hopkintonian system was known throughout the country. He began his work when Stockbridge was first founded in 1736. He died in 1803, and his great-nephew Mark was born in Stockbridge in 1802, and died in 1887. The former expressed in his life and thought the old world that had existed for centuries and was passing away. Upon the latter fell the task of adjusting the thought of the old world to the new world that was dawning with all its marvellous transformations.

INDEX

INDEX

INDEX

INDEX

INDEX

INDEX

INDEX

INDEX

INDEX